History of
FLIGHT

History of
FLIGHT

Michael J. H. Taylor

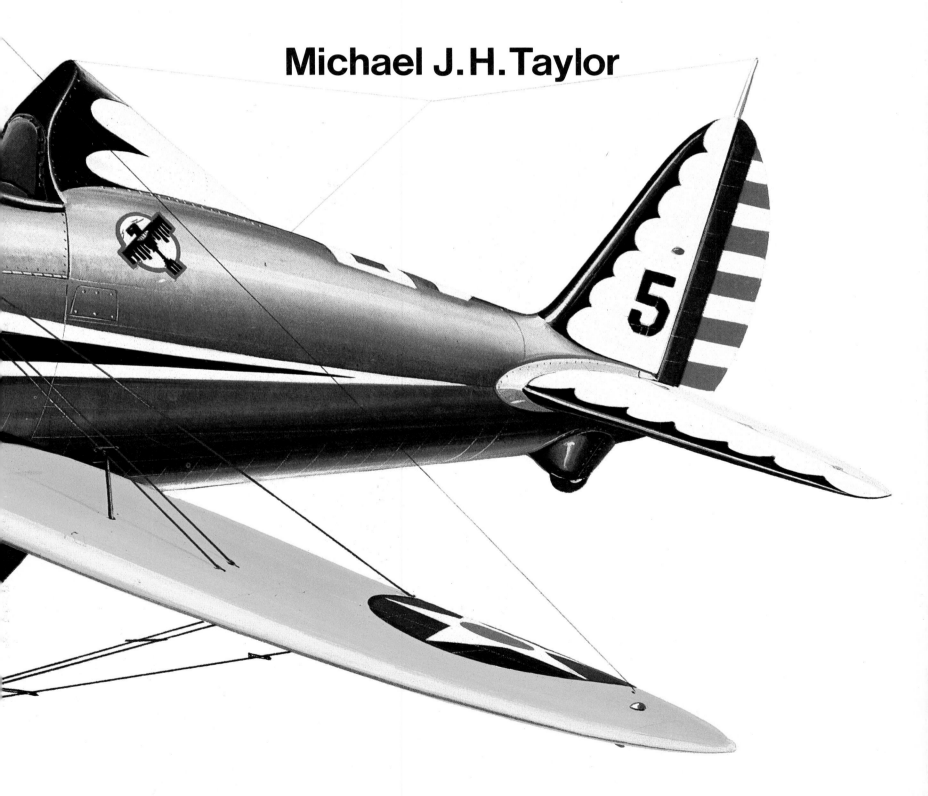

CRESCENT BOOKS
New York

Illustration Acknowledgements
All illustrations supplied by BTPH, except the following: John
Batchelor: Front cover, title page, 30/31, 55 top and bottom, 56/57,
58/59, 59, 60, 60/61, 62/63, 63, 64 bottom, 64/65, 66 top, 67 top,
68/69, 86/87, 87 top, 98/99, 100/101, 103 bottom, 106/107,
108/109, 110/111, 111, 113 top, 115 top, 120/121, 125 bottom,
128/129 bottom, 132/133 top and bottom, 134/135, 135, 136/137,
138, 138/139, 139, 140/141, 142 top, 142/143, 143, 148/149, 171
top.
Hugh W. Cowin: 42/43 top, 79 bottom.
Dornier: 94/95, 95 inset, 128/129.
Library of Congress: 15.
Mary Evans Picture Library: 16, 17, 39 top and bottom, 72, 73, 74
top and bottom, 75 bottom, 78 top and bottom, 80 bottom, 88 top.
NASA: 178/179, 182, 183, 184, 185 top.
National Air and Space Museum: 10 top and bottom, 20 bottom, 21
top left and right, 22 inset left and right, 22/23, 23 inset, 24, 25, 26,
28 inset, 28/29 inset, 35 top and bottom, 37, 38, 38/39, 41 top, 43,
47 inset, 52 bottom, 56 top, 58, 61, 64 top, 66 centre and bottom,
67 centre and bottom, 69 bottom, 92, 94 inset, 103 top, 104, 105
top and bottom, 107, 108, 112, 1115 bottom, 116 bottom, 117 top,
122, 123 bottom, 125 top, 126 inset, 126/127, 127 inset top and
bottom, 134.
Michael J. H. Taylor: 9, 14, 19/20, 36/37, 41 bottom, 45 bottom, 48,
48/49, 50 bottom, 51 top, 52 top, 81, 83 bottom, 84, 84/85, 86, 90,
91 bottom left and right, 93, 96/97, 97 top and centre, 99 left and
right, 100 left and right, 101 bottom, 113 bottom, 114, 117 bottom,
118/119 inset, 120 inset, 137, 142 centre, 145 top, 146 top and
bottom, 147 top, 149, 150, 151 top and bottom, 152, 153, 155 inset,
156 bottom, 157, 162/163, 168 inset, 173 bottom.
TRH Pictures: 10/11, 33 top left, right and bottom, 34 top and
bottom, 35 centre, 36 top, 42, 44, 45 top, 46 inset, 46/47, 49 top, 51
bottom, 75 top, 79 top, 80 top, 82 top and bottom, 83 top, 85, 87
bottom, 88 bottom, 89 top and bottom, 144 bottom, 147 bottom,
156, 186/187.
U.S. National Archives: 118/119 main pic, 140.

This 1990 edition is published by Crescent Books
Distributed by Outlet Book Company Inc.
A Random House Company
225 Park Avenue South
New York, New York 10003

Copyright © Brian Trodd Publishing House Limited 1990

ISBN 0-517-032058

h g f e d c b a

Printed in Spain

Contents

Introduction:
The Thousand Year Silence

At the very end of the 19th century, archaeologists working at Saqqara in Egypt discovered a curious toy, a wooden bird dating from around 300 B.C. At a time when aviation had not yet taken off, it was only of passing interest, and was soon boxed away in a storeroom at the Cairo Museum. Three quarters of a century later, it was rediscovered. By this time, man had set foot on the moon, and the little bird assumed a new significance. Carved from sycamore, it weighed less than 40g (1½ oz); its tapering wings, it was soon realized, had been carved to have a distinct aerofoil section. What was more, its tail 'feathers' were vertical, and a groove provided evidence that a horizontal tail surface had once been fitted. Was this strange artefact simply a child's toy, an elaborate weather vane – or was it a tantalizing piece of evidence of early aeronautical research?

Human beings have been obsessed by the idea of flight since the beginning of recorded history. The mythology of many cultures abounds with gods and kings borne through the air by winged horses and other fantastic creatures. Yet little evidence survives of any practical attempts to explore the possibility of flight in the ancient world, despite the technical sophistication in other fields of civilizations such as those of Greece and Rome. Perhaps the myth of Icarus explains why; flying too close to the sun, his wings of wax and feathers melted and he plunged to his death. Flying was for the gods; Icarus, a mortal, should not have tried, and was punished for his arrogance.

The long period between the age of mythology and the first practical attempts to fly may be termed the 'thousand year silence'. Yet here and there during this long interregnum we can catch a fleeting glimpse of experimentation, like the Saqqara bird. Archytas of Tarentum was a Greek-born mathematician, scientist and philosopher who resided in Italy. Born in about 400 B.C., his life was not especially long; he drowned in the Adriatic around 350–345 B.C. Among his well-documented scientific achievements was another, less well-attested, which is usually described in modern histories as a wooden dove attached to a whirling arm, driven round by non-mechanical means. But further research shows that there could have been much more to it. The dove, or pigeon, prepared by Archytas was indeed attached to an arm, but so well balanced by weights as to allow the bird to 'lift' in wavering flight by 'hidden and enclosed air'. In the second century A.D., Aulus Gellius wrote about the experiment in favourable terms in *Attic Nights* (not published until 1469), while Jerome Cardan (born 1501) went on to discuss the possibility of success with such a wooden bird if the body was of light construction, the wings large enough, and a favourable breeze employed. Both Gellius and Cardan mentioned 'lamps', and it is possible that the bird may have used compressed or hot air, steam or some other 'lifting' or propulsion force involving fire.

The Chinese connection

Probably the least understood aspect of aviation history is the huge but intermittent contribution made by ancient China over a period of 17 centuries from about 200 B.C. Indeed, China can claim to have made the first practical use of aircraft in the form of kites. In modern times we think of the kite only as a toy, forgetting that even in the 20th century the famed American Samuel Franklin Cody, who lived in Britain, devised man-lifting kites for observation duties with the British Army; that similar kites were deployed from German submarines during the First and Second World Wars; and that they also have a serious non-military application in meteorological work.

Who invented the kite, and when, is unclear, but indications point to the philosopher Mo Ti in China. Better known as Mo Tzu (470–391 B.C.), he believed in universal love as the foundation of a simple and sharing life, and is said to have constructed a wooden kite for pleasure. Better records exist of the use of kites in war: around 200 B.C., the Chinese General Han Hsin used them to help calculate the distance between his forces and an enemy fortification. The Chinese military appear to have used kites to pass semaphore messages from the 6th century A.D. Later still kites became the first 'bombers', releasing fire-bombs over an enemy.

Marco Polo was the first European to tell of man-carrying kites, while travelling in China (Cathay as it was then known) in the 14th century. These were used by sailors to foretell whether the pending journey would be one of prosperity or ill fortune, by the way the kite flew with its unfortunate (and probably involuntary) pilot on board.

The first illustration of kites in Europe appeared in 1326, in an illuminated manuscript by Walter de Milemete. It depicts a pennon (windsock type) kite carrying a fire bomb, held above a fortified city by three soldiers using a rope and pulley. Like many pennon kites, it had the shape of a long mythical creature.

Also from China came news of the first gunpowder rockets used in war, as described by Tseng Kung Liang in A.D. 1042, and in 1232 the defenders of Peiping successfully held back a Mongol army using artillery rockets.

Right: Roger Bacon (c.1214-94), the Franciscan monk who was also the first writer on the possibilities of flight.

Medieval Europe

Although only a quarter of a century was to pass before Europe became aware of the war rocket, it had little immediate impact since Europeans were still ignorant of the chemistry behind it. Marco Polo, for example, thought the 'arts of demons' enabled the Tartars to excite storms and fogs, although others knew that these effects were caused by 'the agency of certain minerals'.

One of the few Europeans to approach the question of flight in a scientific way had been the English Franciscan monk, Roger Bacon, born in Ilchester in 1214. His book *Secrets of Art and Nature*, completed in 1250 but not published until 1542, shows that he had an aeronautical mind several centuries ahead of his time. De Lana's idea for a lighter-than-air craft (see page 8) did not appear till 1670, more than four centuries after Bacon had suggested the use of large hollow globes of thin copper or other metal filled with ethereal (rarefied) air or liquid fire (some suggest he meant what is now known as hydrogen gas) to achieve flight. Bacon also considered seating a pilot in the midst of an instrument, where he could turn some mechanism to power artificial wings to beat the air.

The tower jumpers

Most would-be flyers, however, persisted with the simplest method of the lot: to strap on a pair of wings and jump. One of the most celebrated was another English monk, a Benedictine named Eilmer, better known as Oliver of Malmesbury or 'the flying monk'. In about 1020 he jumped from Malmesbury Abbey; his wings offered a measure of lift, and slowed his rate of descent enough to allow him to escape with only his legs broken. Some accounts suggest he may have flown a distance of a furlong. Some limited success may also have attended Saracen of Constantinople in the 11th century. He managed to 'fly' some distance until a rib snapped in his stretched cloak and he plunged to his death. And so it went on, century after century. Perhaps the most ambitious attempt was that by the Italian, John Damian, in 1507. Damian had visited Scotland, where he obtained the position of Abbot of Tungland in Galloway by royal favour after offering to use alchemy to create artificial riches for the treasury. Having failed in that, he contrived a greater scheme to astonish the courtiers: he would leap from the walls of Stirling Castle and fly to France!

Man enough to back his words with the deed, he constructed wings of feathers and jumped, crashing to the ground and breaking his thigh bone. Never short of an excuse, he declared he had been mistaken in using various feathers for the wings, since among them were the feathers of dunghill fowls which were by sympathy attracted to the dunghill. If he had used the feathers of eagles alone . . . But eventually success had to come, and one of the first flights – if not the very first – was performed by the Turk, Hezarfen Celebi, who in the 17th century leapt from a tower at Galata and flew some considerable distance before landing safely in the market place of Scutari.

Among the best recorded attempts to fly in the 17th century were those of a French locksmith named Besnier, although it is hard to attribute any competence to his apparatus. Contemporary woodcut illustrations of the flying apparatus he used at Sablé in 1678 vary in detail, but all show Besnier holding a pole over each shoulder, the ends of which were attached to his ankles by ropes. At both ends of each pole were hinged flaps, intended to fold during the upward motion but spread flat when pulled downward by hand or foot to gain lift. Details of Besnier's experiments were published on 12 September that year. Contemporary writings suggest that Besnier, after jumping from a roof, flew over neighbouring houses and could even span a river. He clearly made several 'flights', but could only have achieved the most marginal form of uncontrolled glide.

Yet it appears that the first set of apparatus was sold to a gentleman of Guibre, who is said to have attained similar success.

Going down!

Much has been written about the Italian Leonardo da Vinci, and his place in the annals of aviation history is secured. A man of extraordinary versatility, he was perhaps the greatest all-round artist and sculptor, philosopher, architect, engineer and inventor of all time. Yet in his ornithopter (flapping wings) and helicopter designs, he appears to have let his heart rule his head. His greatest misjudgments were to rely too much upon muscle-power, and to give insufficient thought to the lifting area, capability and weight of his machines. His thoroughgoing knowledge of anatomy, vividly expressed in art, led him to believe he could recreate the structure and movement of a bird or bat's wings in wood and fabric. Important, however, were his designs for an ornithopter with fixed as well as flapping wings, and his hand-held pyramid-type parachute of 1485, the first proper parachute design in history.

The parachute, although not an aircraft (relying on 'drag' to reduce falling velocity and not intended to sustain itself in the atmosphere), is nevertheless important in aeronautical history, not least as there is an inseparable connection between kites, parachutes and hang-gliders. Da Vinci's parachute was followed by the first published design, to be found in the Venetian work *Machinae Novae*, by Fausto Veranzio (*c.*1595). The Veranzio design had a cloth attached to a square frame, with the four shroud lines drawn into a body harness. The first documented quasi-parachute jump had, however, already been made in China in 1306 during the celebrations for the coronation of Emperor Fo-Kien. In September 1694, a missionary in Canton called Father Vassou wrote home to tell how he had discovered in official documents that a balloon ascent had been made at the same coronation.

Europe followed in 1783, when Frenchman Sebastièn le Normand made a controlled descent at Montpelier. But it was the descent of Frenchman Andre Jacques Garnerin on 22 October 1797 that gave real purpose to the parachute when he made a successful jump from a balloon at 680m (2,230 ft) over Parc Monçeau near Paris, making this the first descent from an aircraft.

As the 17th century drew to a close, real flight remained an impossible dream, the stuff of travellers' tales. The Italian Giovanni Borelli, in his *De Motu Animalium* (1680), explained exactly why the flappers and jumpers were doomed to failure; man simply did not possess the physiology to sustain his own weight in flight without mechanical help. Even in the high-tech 1980s, when composite materials offered the possibility of constructing wings of incredible strength combined with very light weight, humans still could not 'flap' into flight. But, with mechanical assistance, man can provide the muscle-power to fly; on 22 January 1989 the Massachusetts Institute of Technology human-powered aircraft *Michelob Light Eagle* covered a distance of 58.664km (36.452 miles) on the pedal power of pilot Glenn Tremml.

A leg-worked device used by a French locksmith, Besnier, in his jump from a tower at Sablé in 1678. The very fact that he is alleged to have landed without injury suggests that this, the popular impression of his device, is also another work of imagination!

Chapter 1: Balloons

Hand in hand with those who studied birds in the hope of learning the secret of flight were others – though no doubt fewer – who pondered methods of overcoming gravity for a similar purpose. The solution lay all around them in nature, but it would take unusual perception to notice it. When fire raged the smoke rose, lifting glowing embers skyward. Birds were capable of rising, with their wings perfectly still, on invisible columns of warm air.

The mastery of ascending flight can be said to have begun during the life of the Greek mathematician and scientist, Archimedes of Syracuse (born 287 B.C.), whose career was ended in 212 B.C. on the point of a Roman sword. Children still laugh at the story of how, at the public baths, Archimedes suddenly became aware of how his immersed body seemed to lose weight and that this was equal to the weight of the water it displaced, and leapt from the tub to run down the crowded street shouting '*Eureka, Eureka*', but the discovery of the principle behind the flotation of bodies in water and gas was fundamental to the understanding of the laws governing lighter-than-air flight.

To Archimedes, through ancient writings and poems, is linked a flying crystal sphere (*c.*250 B.C.) variously attributed with the theoretical power of flight by mechanical means or 'rarefied air'. Roger Bacon had similar thoughts in the 13th century. But it was not until 1670 that a Jesuit priest, Francesco de Lana-Terzi,

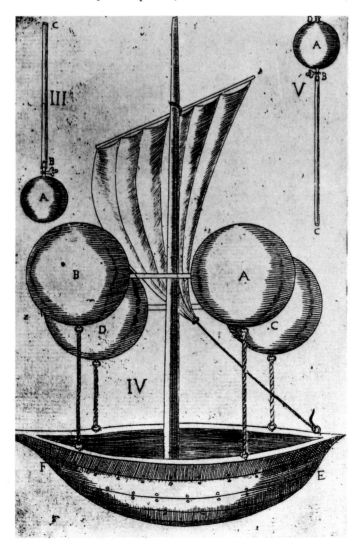

Over 300 years ago an Italian Jesuit priest proposed building this 'flying ship' lifted by four spheres of copper from which the air had been sucked out.

completed the first proper design for a lighter-than-air craft, comprising a boat hull with mast and sail borne up by four tethered copper spheres. The 17th century was a period of great learning and scientific accomplishment, and de Lana drew upon the findings of the newly invented barometer to back his proposition with verified mathematical data. He had calculated that a globe 'exhausted' of air to create a vacuum would weigh less than one with the air remaining. If that globe (a shape most likely to retain its structural integrity under outside air pressure) weighed less than the air needed to fill it, it was bound to rise. Equally importantly, de Lana calculated that a globe with twice the diameter of another had a cubic capacity many times larger, and would therefore rise many times more quickly.

The actual extraction of air posed no difficulty, as the air pump had been invented by Otto von Guericke and was demonstrated in public in 1654. But one seemingly insurmountable problem remained; it would have been impossible to make copper globes, 6.1m (20 ft) in diameter, sufficiently thin for lightness and yet strong enough to withstand the crushing effect of outside air pressure. Having reached this conclusion, de Lana stated that God would not suffer such an invention, prophesying how flying craft could be manoeuvred over buildings and ships to drop 'artificial fireworks and fireballs'.

Fire of flight

Such considerations did not deter others. On 10 February 1709, a letter from Lisbon was published in various scientific journals, together with a copy of a letter sent to the King of Portugal by a certain Father Bartolomeu de Gusmão. De Gusmão asserted that he had invented a flying machine capable of carrying passengers and of navigating swiftly through the air, and that he wished a prohibition to be granted against anyone else attempting to construct a similar machine. To this request, the King duly issued an order of 17 April stating that any transgressor would do so at the pain of death, and that not only would he offer de Gusmão a Professorship of mathematics and a place at the college at Barcelona but an annual pension for life so that he could improve the machine.

We know that de Gusmão's flying machine was the *Passarola*, comprising a large hull with wings intended to beat in ornithopter fashion, a vertical tail and a parachute-like sail. Engravings show the complete impracticability of the design and its fanciful nature, and if built it could not possibly have flown.

Far more importantly, de Gusmão is known to have demonstrated a model hot-air balloon to King John V, Queen Maria Ann and other dignitaries and courtiers in the Ambassador's drawing room at the Casa da India in Lisbon on 8 August 1709, and it is for this epic demonstration that his name is revered in aviation history.

De Gusmão's little demonstration balloon was a perfect miniature blueprint for the larger hot-air balloons that appeared later in the 18th century. Its rounded envelope of thick paper was inflated by heated air from burning materials carried in a suspended earthenware bowl. When released, the balloon drifted

to the window of the room, rising to a height of about 3.5m (12 ft). As the balloon brushed the curtains, two valets promptly beat it out before it set them ablaze.

The next major stepping stone was the isolation of 'inflammable air' or Phlogiston gas in 1766 by the English chemist, Henry Cavendish. He was thereby able to determine its weight compared with atmospheric air. This gas was later known as hydrogen. It is often misunderstood quite how simultaneous were the developments of hot-air and hydrogen balloons, although, until the development of present-day hot-air balloons made extra safe by the use of rip-stop envelope materials and easily-controlled gas burners, hydrogen balloons had the greater long-term impact. The first demonstration of the lifting properties of hydrogen gas was almost no demonstration at all; the Italian Tiberius Cavallo launched hydrogen filled soap bubbles in 1781. When trying to continue his experiments using hydrogen filled bladders, he failed to take account of the envelope weight, and these failed to fly.

The Montgolfier brothers

Hydrogen formed no part of Frenchman Joseph Montgolfier's thoughts as he watched smoke and embers rise from a fire and disappear up the chimney. Then, a shirt left drying too close to the fire billowed. Could the 'gas' that lifted the embers and inflated the shirt be harnessed, he wondered? In November 1782, to test his theory, he constructed a small bag of taffeta and held it over a fire. It filled out and rose to the ceiling of his lodging house in Avignon, witnessed by the landlady.

One of nine children, Joseph had, years before, left his father's paper mill at Vidalon-les-Annonay to start his own business. He had an inventive nature and introduced many innovations to his profession, as well as working on hydraulics and other mechanical systems. With his brother Jacques-Etienne, Joseph had long been interested in aeronautics. In 1779 he had constructed a 2m (6 ft 6 in) parachute on which a sheep was borne after release in Avignon. Parachute experiments culminated with Joseph himself jumping from the roof of a house in Annonay.

Joseph and Etienne followed the first silk bag experiment with others using paper envelopes, careful to maintain secrecy. With each test the balloon, or 'aerostatic machine' as the brothers referred to them, became larger. Finally, the brothers used all their experience in working paper to produce a balloon calculated to be large enough to lift 200kg (440 lbs). With a diameter of 12m (39 ft) and heated by the burning of paper, wood and straw, it was released at Annonay on 25 April 1783 and rapidly rose to a height of about 300m (1,000 ft) before cooling and alighting nearly 1km away.

At last the brothers were ready to tell of their work. On 4 June a balloon of linen and paper was inflated in the market place at Annonay in front of a huge crowd. As the balloon filled, the strength of eight men was needed to hold it down. Finally it was released, rising to above 1,800m (5,900 ft). They informed the Académie des Sciences in Paris, who invited a demonstration. While this was being prepared and news of the Montgolfiers reached all of the continent and across the Atlantic, the Académie (on the advice of Faujas de Saint Ford)

King John V, Queen Maria Ann and dignitaries look on with amazement as Father Bartolomeu de Gusmão releases his ingenious model hot air balloon. Drifting towards the window, it would soon have to be destroyed before it set the curtains ablaze. (Air BP).

9

started a public subscription to encourage further work on balloons. But, surprisingly, the Académie gave the money to the physicist, Professor Jacques Alexandre César Charles, for the development of a hydrogen balloon and to purchase the large amounts of iron filings and sulphuric acid to manufacture the gas.

Charles launched himself into experimentation by commissioning the construction of a small 3.5m (12 ft) balloon from the Robert brothers. To retain the gas, the balloon was made of silk coated with gum and was fitted with a valve of Charles' design. He also conceived the use of a net around the envelope and a hoop from which to suspend a basket, although the balloon had only a 9kg (20 lb) lifting capability. Inflation of the balloon at the Place des Victoires began on 23 August 1783 and public interest was intense. By the 26th the balloon was ready. Under cover of darkness to avoid being mobbed, it was taken to Champ-des-Mars in Paris under the escort of foot and mounted guards, the way lit by a cortège of torches.

With troops lining the avenues and in front of a huge crowd standing in light rain, the balloon was released at

5 a.m. on the morning of 27 August. It rose quickly to 1,000m (3,300 ft). Posters had been hung in the surrounding villages warning of the balloon, but clearly the simple folk of Gonesse were ill-informed. After a flight of three-quarters of an hour, the balloon descended here to the great alarm of the locals, some of whom believed it to be a strange and monstrous bird. Into its skin went pitchforks and flails; the monster passed a terrific stench as it 'died'. Finally, with the gas gone, the balloon was tied to a horse's tail and torn to pieces as it was dragged across the open countryside.

Meanwhile, Etienne Montgolfier had been constructing a hot-air balloon envelope worthy of showing to the Académie, highly decorated and nearly 23m (75 ft) in height. That August the Montgolfiers were given cash awards by the Académie for their outstanding contribution to the new art of flying. Louis XVI bestowed various honours, a cash prize and pension on the brothers and their father; Etienne received the Order of St. Michel, the first award for an aviation achievement.

Joseph and Etienne were requested to demonstrate their Académie balloon to King Louis XVI, Queen Marie Antoinette, dignitaries and a huge number of other people at Versailles. Unfortunately the envelope was ruined during a rainstorm and a new one was hastily fabricated in just four days. With the intention of making this an occasion to remember, the envelope was decorated with paintings in oil and a wicker cage was suspended beneath by a rope in which a sheep, cock and duck were to be placed.

On 19 September 1783 all was ready for the royal viewing. At about 1 p.m. that day the fire was ignited and in 11 minutes the 13m (41 ft) diameter envelope inflated from a convex shape to its full rounded form. Soon the balloon lifted; it reached an altitude of 520m (1,700 ft), and remained airborne for eight minutes before landing in the Forest of Vaucresson. The occupants of the cage, the first living creatures to fly in a balloon, were unharmed.

A new Montgolfier balloon, 15m (49 ft) in diameter, was prepared for what was intended to be the first ever manned ascent, offering sufficient lifting capability for two crew members. The King, concerned by the dangers of such a flight, offered two men under the

Left: *Before committing themselves to a voyage in a Montgolfier, the intrepid balloonists conducted trials with a tethered, or a captive, balloon in Paris on 15 October 1783. One of the occupants on this occasion was François Pilatre de Rozier. Maximum height gained on this occasion is supposed to have been about 84 feet, with the balloon straining at the retaining ropes.*

Far left, top: *Etienne Montgolfier.*

Far left, bottom: *Joseph Montgolfier.*

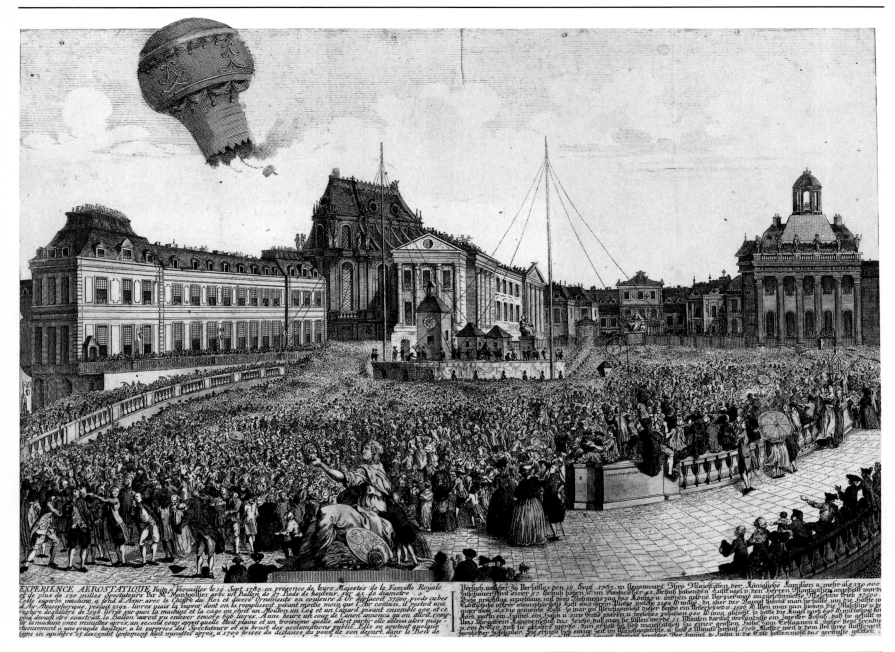

EXPERIENCE AEROSTATIQUE Faite à Versailles le 19 Sept.1783 en presence de leurs Majestés de la Famille Royale...

Above: *An accurate portrayal of the lift-off of the full-size Montgolfier balloon, carrying a sheep, a cock and duck in a wicker basket. The date was 1783.*

Right: *François Pilatre de Rozier and the Marquis d'Arlandes making the first untethered balloon flight on 21 November 1783.*

sentence of death as the crew. But Jean Francois Pilâtre de Rozier strongly objected to this honour going to criminals and, with the support of the Marquis d'Arlandes, and with the populace of the city behind him, he managed to change the King's mind. The Marquis offered himself as the second crew member but, on 15 October 1783, de Rozier alone took up the challenge.

The balloon, built more strongly than those before it, was heavily decorated and had a wicker gallery about 1m (3 ft) wide around the base, through which passed the neck of the envelope and a brazier suspended by chains. Small holes in the lower part of the envelope allowed the crew to throw extra fuel into the brazier to prolong the flight.

After a few tentative ascents close to the ground, de Rozier asked to be allowed to rise to the full height of the tethering ropes, some 26m (84 ft). By refuelling the brazier with straw and wool, he kept aloft for 4 minutes 25 seconds. Then, having descended gently, de Rozier left the balloon, only to see it immediately fly back up. Man had flown!

On 21 November, de Rozier (having since made further tethered flights) was finally joined by the Marquis in flight, ascending from the gardens of the Château La Muette in the Bois de Boulogne and alighting 25 minutes later on the Butte-aux-Cailles, having drifted across Paris one way and then the other. This was man's first free ascending flight and the first ever aerial journey.

Less than six months had passed since the Montgolfiers had first demonstrated an unmanned balloon in public and yet, on 1 December 1783, Professor Charles and one of the Robert brothers followed de Rozier and the Marquis into the air in free flight, for the first time

Far left: *J.A.C. Charles and Aine Robert making the first flight in a hydrogen balloon on 1 December 1783.*

Left: *Jean Pierre Blanchard and the American Dr Jeffries crossing the Channel, 1785.*

using a hydrogen balloon. Witness to the event, which began from the gardens of Les Tuileries, Paris, was a crowd of some 400,000. After flying 43km (27 miles) Charles and Robert alighted in Nesles.

By early 1784 balloon ascents had also taken place in several other countries, including Germany, Italy and the United Kingdom (both England and Ireland). The Marchioness de Montalembert, the Countess de Montalembert, the Countess de Podenas and Mademoiselle de Lagarde ascended in a Montgolfier balloon at Faubourg-Saint-Antoine, Paris, on 20 May 1784 to become the first women to fly in a tethered balloon. A free flight by a woman followed on 4 June, when Madame Thible flew from Lyon in the giant seven-person Montgolfier balloon named *Le Gustav*, watched by the King of Sweden. Also on board this largest of all Montgolfiers were Monsieur Fleurant, de Rozier, and Joseph Montgolfier who was making his first-ever flight.

Montgolfier type hot-air balloons were capable of staying aloft for considerable periods of time, but the hydrogen balloon offered greater possibilities and slowly took prominence. For the Montgolfiers, 1789 saw the demise of the balloon business. Joseph died in 1810, having outlived Etienne by 11 years.

Roll of honour

It is hard to take in the speed at which events happened in ballooning, given that this was still the late 18th century. Yet, on 7 January 1785, Frenchman Jean-Pierre Blanchard and American John Jeffries rose from Dover, England, in a hydrogen balloon to attempt the first-ever air crossing of the English Channel. Two and a half hours later and almost naked after throwing their clothes overboard to lighten the load and maintain height, they landed safely at Forêt de Felmores. It is sad to recall that an attempt to fly from France to England on 15 June 1785 in a composite hot-air/hydrogen balloon, ended early (near Boulogne) with the death of de Rozier and Jules Romain. They were the first aeronauts to be killed of many that followed. Madame Blanchard, already a widow by 1809 following Jean-Pierre's heart attack while ballooning, herself became a victim to conflagration, when her hydrogen balloon caught fire as she watched a firework display at

Tivoli Gardens, Paris, on 1 July 1819. A great aeronaut, she was the first woman to lose her life while flying.

Taking the high ground

The French Revolution at first brought balloon experimentation in France to a halt, then, quite as suddenly, threw the science into battle. Paris became a focus of world military attention.

In 1793 a military Aerostatic Corps was founded at Meudon, having 50 recruits under the command of Capitaine Coutelle. Its initial equipment was one 10m (33 ft) diameter hydrogen balloon. The gas was generated by equipment devised by the French chemist, Guyton de Morveau; the apparatus was bulky, but could produce enough gas to inflate the envelope in just four hours. Secrecy was the watchword, to ensure that none of France's enemies could gain the initiative.

The training balloon was kept constantly inflated and in the open, tied when not in use to the terrace of a house. But, whenever the weather was suitable, it was winched out to 150m (500 ft) or more with two persons on board to train the crews and observe movements around Paris. Eventually other balloons became available to Coutelle, including *Entreprenant* appropriated to the army of the north, *Hercule* to the army of the Rhine and Moselle, *Celeste* to the army of the Sambre and Meuse, and *Intrepide* to the army of Egypt.

Under the command of Jean-Baptiste Jourdan and Jean-Baptiste Kleber, a huge French Republican Army was engaged in fighting the Austrians and Dutch for the Southern Netherlands (Belgium). At the recommendation of de Morveau, the Committee of Public Safety accepted the benefit of sending balloons to the Army for observation use, but only if hydrogen gas could be generated without requiring sulphuric acid, sulphur being restricted for the preparation of gunpowder. Experiments and a demonstration of an alternative method of hydrogen production satisfied the Committee, and Coutelle was immediately dispatched to General Jourdan.

The Republican Army was then at Beaumont, some 11km (7 miles) from Maubeuge. Arriving after a hard journey through heavy mud, Coutelle reported to Duquesnez, the Commissioner of the Convention whose singular role was to ensure soldiers went into battle and that the generals won under pain of the guillotine. Arriving during dinner with a balloon did not sit well with Duquesnez, who threatened to have Coutelle shot as a spy. But reason prevailed and Coutelle was sent to Jourdan.

Under orders, Coutelle travelled to Maubeuge, where he observed the opposing army and returned to Paris to report to the Committee. Some months passed as he experimented with a balloon more suited to warfare, and with methods of tethering and signalling. Eventually Coutelle, now Brevet-Capitaine commanding the Aerostatic Corps in the Artillery Service attached to the General Staff, made his way back to Maubeuge and set up camp and the kiln for hydrogen manufacture while awaiting the balloon from Meudon. During the battle of Fleurus, on 26 June 1794, *Entreprenant* crewed by Coutelle and another officer flew two observation missions of four hours each from behind the front line, the second drawing rifle and cannon fire. It was the very first occasion a man-carrying balloon had been used in war.

In 1799 Napoleon Bonaparte disbanded the Republican Army's Aerostatic Corps, almost certainly after suffering immense problems with the immobility of the equipment during the Egyptian campaign, when *Intrepide* and its support equipment were lost overboard during the naval battle of Aboukir Bay.

Half a century later, on 22 August 1849, Austrian forces launched unmanned balloons against Venice, each carrying a 14kg (30 lb) bomb with time fuse. The Austrian balloons, like those launched by Japan nearly a century later in 1944 to cross the Pacific and strike at America, were intended to demoralize and cause extensive damage, but in both cases achieved neither aim. However, the 1849 attack was the first known

aerial bombing raid in history.

Although hydrogen balloons had been around for more than 70 years by the 1850s, it was not until the late Victorian and early Edwardian periods that ballooning became a popular sport, making this its Golden Age. The second half of the 19th century also brought new military accomplishments, punctuated by individual civilian events of historical interest. Among the latter were the very first aerial photographs, taken by Frenchman Félix Tournachon (better known as Nadar) in 1858 and depicting areas of Paris.

A showman who had a profound influence on military flying was flamboyant American Thaddeus Sobieski Constantine Lowe. With the fall of Fort Sumter in South Carolina on 13 April 1861, the American Civil War began, a conflict that required the rapid industrialization of both North and South. Incredibly costly in human lives, it also saw the birth of America's first air arm, the direct ancestor of today's US Air Force. Lowe entered the pages of history on 18 June 1861, when he flew the balloon *Enterprise* while an operator tapped out the first telegraph message transmitted from an aircraft to the ground, which was relayed to President Lincoln. Because of his work with the Army of the Union, on 1 October Lowe became Chief Aeronaut to General McClellan's Balloon Corps, attached to the Army of the Potomac. Between then and its premature disbanding in mid-1863, its seven balloons carried out extremely valuable observation and artillery direction work, using the converted coal barge *George Washington Parke Custis* from November 1861 as a mobile platform for transportation and towing. *G. W. Parke Custis* is thereby remembered as the world's first aircraft carrier. Unlike the French during their campaigns of the late 18th century, the Americans had the benefit of fully mobile and uncomplicated hydrogen manufacturing

Below: *Entreprenant flies at the rear of the French Republican Army, gathering intelligence vital to the outcome of the Battle of Fleurus. (Royal Aeronautical Society)*

Bataille de Fleurus gagnée par l'Armée Française, le 8 Messidor de l'An 2.
Commandée par les Généraux Jourdan Le Fevre, et batue Contre l'Armée Imperiale Commandée par Cobourg et Beaulieu

equipment brought about by a new chemical process involving dilute sulphuric acid reacting with iron to create a gas that was purified using lime.

In 1870 the Prussian Army founded two *Luftschiffer* (airship) detachments, which saw active service in the Franco-Prussian War of 1870–71. But once Paris had been surrounded and cut off from the outside world, it was the turn of the Parisians to make history. In a dangerous attempt to flee with despatches, Jules Durouf rose from the city in a balloon on 23 September 1870 and drifted over Prussian lines and on to Evreux, a flight of three hours. Five other balloons remained within the city, and Tissandier, Godard and Mangin also flew out, drawing gunfire as they went.

Of all European cities, Paris was probably the best equipped for the production of further balloons. A huge manufacturing programme began, using the large spaces within railway stations and other buildings for their assembly. By 28 January 1871 no fewer than 66 balloons, inflated at the Villette gasworks, had escaped; up to three million letters, carrier pigeons and over 100 people had been flown to freedom. The chemist Barreswil invented microfilm in October 1870 specifically to allow the pigeons to return with many messages. Of the 66 balloons, perhaps seven drifted off course, while two others may have been hit by Prussian groundfire.

In Britain, the War Office did not allocate funds for a military balloon until 1878, when it granted £150 partly for the construction of the coal-gas balloon *Pioneer*. Manoeuvres by the British Army using a manned balloon still had to wait until mid-1880, and in 1884 and 1885 balloon detachments were among the British forces sent to Mafeking in Bechuanaland and to the Sudan respectively.

Observation had always been the primary role of military balloons, but their round shape tended to affect their stability in windy conditions. As a mid-way

development between the balloon and the airship, August von Parseval and Bartsch von Sigsfeld conceived the tethered Drachen or kite-balloon. Its 'sausage' shape was intended to give stability and perhaps even lift in wind. It was first used in manoeuvres by the German Army in 1897 and was widely deployed during the First World War.

During the 1898 war between the US and Spain over Cuba, Sergeant Ivy Baldwin of the US Army Signal Corps managed to cajole his superiors into letting him use a balloon to observe the enemy. During the battle of Santiago, he became the very first American airman to be shot down on active service. He survived to live until 1955.

All for sport and science

'We climbed it because it was there': this attitude was no less strong for aeronauts than those remaining on *terra firma*. In 1785, the year of the first air crossing of the English Channel, the ostentatious Richard Crosbie tried on more than one occasion to raise his bulky figure across the Irish Sea. This feat was not achieved until 22 July 1817, however, when Windham Sadler, son of James (the first English aeronaut), finally made the crossing.

On 7–8 November 1836 the *Royal Vauxhall Balloon*, crewed by Charles Green, Monck Mason and Robert Holland, flew from the Vauxhall Gardens in London to Weilberg in the Duchy of Nassau, a journey of 770km (480 miles). This, the first very long flight from England and probably the longest contemporary air journey, achieved such fame that the balloon was renamed the *Great Nassau Balloon*. Some years after, on 7 October 1849, the Alps were crossed by a M. Farban, flying between Marseilles and Turin.

But not all such magnificent attempts ended happily. On 11 July 1897, Salomon August Andrée, Nils Strindberg and Knut Fraenkel set off in fine spirits from

The Civil War was the first of all modern wars and the observation balloon was one of its innovations. Balloons were used by Union observers at the Battle of Gettysburg, 1863. This photograph shows Professor Lowe's military balloon at a base near Gaines Mill, Virginia.

After becoming the first to reach the stratosphere, Professor Auguste Piccard ascends from Dübendorf, Switzerland, on 18 August 1932 to establish a new record of 16,201m (53,153 ft). He is accompanied by Max Cosyns.

Professor Piccard's August 1932 ascent becomes front-page news, the spherical capsule of his balloon drawn flying close to a Schneider Trophy seaplane.

Danes Island, Spitzbergen, on the very first exploration of the Arctic by balloon. Steering was to be attempted by use of a sail attached to drag ropes. Their bodies were not found until 33 years later, on White Island, Franz Josef Land, on 6 August 1930. The photographic records of the flight that were found with the bodies lent a particular poignancy to the tragedy.

In 1931 the Swiss physicist, Professor Auguste Piccard, managed to set a record altitude of 15,281m (50,135 ft), the first flight into the stratosphere. Today, the world altitude record for manned balloons stands at an almost unbelievable 34,668m (113,740 ft), reached by the Americans, Commander Malcolm Ross and Lt. Commander V. Prather, on 4 May 1961 in the Lee Lewis Memorial Winzen Research Balloon.

The first attempt to fly the Atlantic by balloon was a short-lived flight by John Wise in 1873; it was not until 1978 that the Americans Ben Abruzzo, Maxie Anderson and Larry Newman in *Double Eagle II* finally tamed this huge expanse of ocean by gas balloon. Their journey of 137 hours 5 minutes and 50 seconds covered a distance of over 5,001km (3,107 miles) from 12–17 August that year. The first balloon crossing of the Pacific followed in November 1981, by *Double Eagle V*, while from 2–3 July 1987 it was the turn of a hot-air balloon to conquer the Atlantic, Richard Branson and Per Lindstrand taking *Virgin Atlantic Flyer* from Maine, USA, to Limavady, Northern Ireland. This was the largest hot-air balloon ever constructed, with a volume of 60,314.8m³ (2,130,000 cu ft).

Finally, in any account of ballooning, the Gordon Bennett Trophy races should not be forgotten. These annual events (except for the period 1914–1919) between 1906 and 1938 became the most famous international balloon contests in the whole history of flight. Conceived and sponsored by the expatriate American newspaper magnate, James Gordon Bennett, the winners were those who flew the longest distance from the starting point. Contests were hosted in Belgium, France, Germany, Poland, Switzerland and the USA. The 1912 race, which was begun in Germany, saw the longest flight of all, with the French balloon *Picardi* drifting an unprecedented 2,191km (1,361 miles) to land near Moscow.

Below: *On 30 September 1906 the first international balloon race started at Les Tuileries, Paris, competing for the Gordon Bennett Trophy. Lt. Frank Lahm, US Army, won in* United States, *flying 647km (40 miles) to Fylingdales Moor, England.*

Right: *As recently as 1960 there were hardly any hot-air balloons in existence. Almost 200 years after its invention, it has staged a remarkable comeback.*

Chapter 2:
The Art becomes a Science

Whilst balloons had provided the means for ascending flight by the late 18th century, and airships were later to add directional control to lighter-than-air flying, many experimenters still believed the way forward lay with heavier-than-air machines. And in this there appeared three possibilities: the helicopter, ornithopter and aeroplane. As a later chapter relates, model rotary-wing craft had predated even balloons, but ornithopters and powered aeroplanes were still dreams. But a new age was dawning; the scientific spirit and technological resources of the Industrial Revolution was giving experimenters a new sense of purpose.

Foremost among these early pioneers of heavier-than-air was the English aristocrat Sir George Cayley. In 1796, at the age of 23, he demonstrated a model helicopter rotor made of eight feathers pushed into corks. But it is his subsequent work that has earned him the title 'Father of Aerial Navigation'. He established the mathematical principles of lift, drag and thrust; he pointed to the advantages of multi-plane wings and streamlining; and demonstrated how a curved wing in forward motion created lift by reducing pressure over the upper surface. Among the model aircraft he built for research purposes was the first ever aeroplane of what can be termed classic configuration. This, built at the end of 1804, was a model glider constructed on the basis of his wing loading calculations. It had a stick fuselage, with a kite-type monoplane wing forward and cruciform tail surfaces aft that could be adjusted for

Right: *Cayley's simple model helicopter, using eight trimmed feathers pushed into corks and a bowdrill.*

Below: *In 1804 Cayley produced a model glider of classic configuration, incorporating a kite-type monoplane wing and adjustable cruciform tail surfaces.*

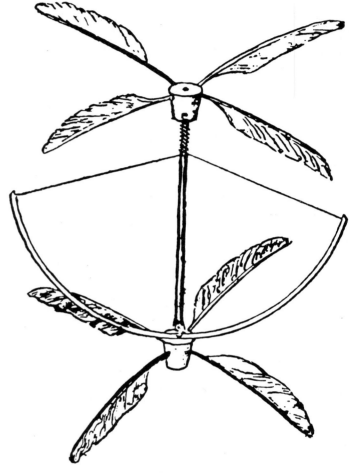

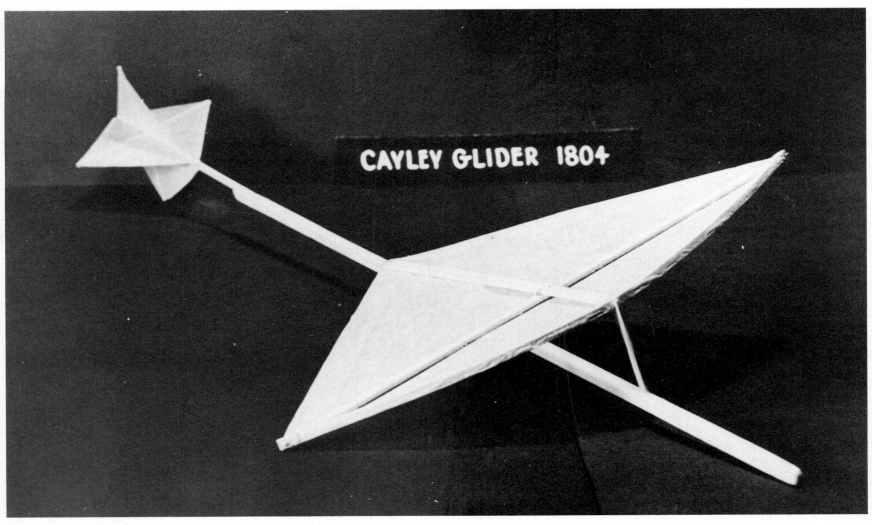

CAYLEY GLIDER 1804

angle. Indeed, the construction of this model followed experiments that same December into wing loading and angles of incidence, which had used a 'whirling arm' test rig.

Francis Wenham (1824–1908) took Cayley's research on wing aerofoils further by discovering the importance of a thick leading-edge and thin trailing-edge for lift distribution, thereby suggesting that the high aspect ratio wing (slender aerofoil-looking from above in relation to the span) would prove the most efficient.

The American Octave Chanute, though too old to fly, designed gliders of classic biplane form from 1896 which performed well, and it is no coincidence that he and Wenham exchanged views. Chanute, in turn, influenced the Wright brothers.

Cayley's own experiments had been punctuated by events of enormous historical importance. By 1809 he had constructed a full-sized aeroplane, intended to be flown as a glider, and then used for powered flying. When launched unmanned from a hilltop on several occasions that summer it attained stable and sustained flight. Unfortunately, the glider was destroyed in an accident that same year before powered experiments could begin. By then Cayley had dismissed the steam engine as being too heavy for aeronautical use. In 1807, he had invented the hot-air or caloric engine, and he also experimented with gunpowder engines. But he saw these only as temporary stop-gaps in the absence of low-flashpoint fuel oils to enable the construction of an internal combustion engine. However, had an engine been used on his 1809 glider it almost certainly would have been rigged to flap auxiliary surfaces in ornithopter fashion.

Then, in the spring of 1849, Cayley started testing his latest full-scale aeroplane. This combined many of his earlier innovations, including triplane wings with a kite-like tailplane and dorsal rudder attached to a rear strut at the height of the centre plane, and a wheeled boat-like fuselage with its own tail surfaces for steering. Between the wings and the fuselage were ornithopter-type flapping wings, intended for propulsion. The overall wing area was about 10 per cent greater than on the 1809 glider, but gross weight was reduced. On this a boy of about ten years old was carried aloft for 'several yards' during a downhill descent, so recording the first-ever recognized manned flight. Cayley's home of Brompton Hall, near Scarborough in Yorkshire, thus

became as hallowed to historians as Kitty Hawk 54 years later.

On a lighter note, it is worth recalling a later man-carrying experiment at Brompton Hall. In about the middle of 1853 – the date is unknown – Cayley's coachman was persuaded to mount a glider. Reluctantly he obeyed and became the first adult in history to make a sustained aeroplane flight, covering a distance of several hundred metres. For such an important event, it is incredible that the date, the name of the pilot and the type of machine used have all been lost to time. Fortunately the flight was witnessed and, according to one spectator, the coachman landed hard, capsized and shouted without due reverence for the historic occasion: 'Please, Sir George, I wish to give my notice. I was hired to drive, not to fly'!

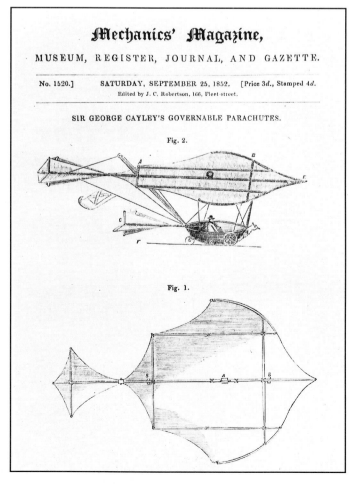

Right: *Otto Lilienthal, who constructed five monoplane and two biplane gliders during 1891–6 but was injured in an accident on 9 August 1896 and died the following day before he had a chance to fully experiment with a powered aeroplane using a carbonic acid gas engine to 'flap' movable surfaces.*

For want of power

The lack of suitably light yet powerful engines for aeronautical work plagued designers before the 20th century. Had the internal combustion engine been available decades earlier, history books would have recalled worthy manned and powered heavier-than-air flying in the Victorian era: Cayley, the German Otto Lilienthal who died in a flying accident on 10 August 1896 having made a huge number of successful flights at the Rhinower Hills from 1891 in gliders of his own design – up to 250m (820 ft) duration; the Englishman Percy S. Pilcher who flew his own gliders from 1895 until his death in an accident in 1899, the Australian Lawrence Hargrave (inventor of the box-kite structure in 1893 that was widely adopted for pioneering aircraft in Europe), the Wright brothers and others had all used gliders in the 19th and turn of the 20th centuries. These unpowered flights were stepping stones to intended powered flying, although only the Wrights achieved this long-term aim. It can only be speculated what Lilienthal in particular might have achieved had he lived on.

Right: *German Otto Lilienthal at the Rhinower Hills in about 1894.*

Far right: *Lawrence Hargrave, 1850-1915.*

Steam or bust!

The steam engine might have been the driving force of the Industrial Revolution but it was to flying as the pterodactyl was to birds, a huge cumbersome freak. To put it in context, it is interesting to recall some of the more eminent persons who gave steam a try. In 1894 the Briton, Charles Parsons, having designed the first practical steam-turbine engine, adopted steam for a model helicopter that achieved little or no historical significance. On 31 July that same year, Sir Hiram Maxim, inventor of the famous Maxim gun, tried his luck with steam on a full-sized (or outsized) aeroplane. This was a totally impractical 372m^2 (4,000 sq ft) giant biplane, weighing 3,630kg (8,000 lb). Carrying a crew of four and powered by two huge 180 hp engines driving 5.4m (17 ft 10 in) propellers, the monster lifted 0.6m (2 ft) off the ground during a test run on rails before being restricted in its flight by a guardrail. In flight, the aircraft would have been virtually uncontrollable. Maxim's biplane can, however, be regarded as a triumph of engineering if not of practical flight.

Various other 'hop' flights by aeroplanes using steam power are mentioned later, but these had less significance on the long-term prospects for flight than the invention by the German Nikolaus Otto of the four-stroke petrol internal combustion engine in 1877. This giant milestone in the annals of transportation was first translated to road vehicles and only later to flying machines. Director of the Otto factory was Gottlieb Daimler, whose 1884 single-cylinder engine found its way onto the first Benz motorcycle in 1885. But the petrol internal combustion engine was the very breakthrough aviation needed, although some years away from practical use; history records that the first piloted aeroplane to adopt a petrol internal combustion engine (30 hp Daimler) was a seaplane tested by Austrian Wilhelm Kress in October 1901.

Those magnificent men before the Wrights

What has come to be recognized as the first design in history for a modern aeroplane was the brainchild of William Samuel Henson, a civil engineer from Somerset, England with diverse interests. A devotee of Cayley's experiments, he set on paper plans to build a huge steam-powered airliner in the first half of the 19th century. It was a triumph of ingenuity. The cambered and constant-chord (i.e. with the same breadth along the whole span of the wing) monoplane had an impressive 45.72m (150 ft) wingspan, and was to be covered with canvas or oiled silk and heavily braced using kingposts and wires. Crew, passengers and freight were to be accommodated within the fully-enclosed fuselage pod, as was the 25–30 hp Henson steam engine expected to drive two 3m (10 ft) six-blade pusher propellers. Total weight was estimated at 1,361kg (3,000 lb). Recognizing that even with his

purpose-designed lightweight steam engine the gross weight would be beyond lifting into the air under normal take-off conditions, Henson planned to gain ground-roll speed using an incline, hoping that the engine would thereafter have enough power to maintain velocity once airborne. And, finally, to further help take-off, the machine 'advances with its front edge a little raised', according to Henson.

In early 1842 Henson ordered the steam engine from his colleague, John Stringfellow, who in return recommended to Henson that he should construct a scale model of the *Aerial Steam Carriage* (later known simply as *Ariel*) to test the design before committing himself to the expensive full-size version. In 1843 Henson duly patented the design and set about the task of finding a group of backers to finance the venture. Here, he made an unfortunate choice, and their over-willingness to promote the aeroplane in grandiose terms before it had even been built only served in the long term to exacerbate his later failure in Henson's mind. On the motion of a certain Mr. Roebuck, even an 'Aerial Transit Bill' was read before Parliament in March 1843, its purpose being to propose the formation of a public company to operate aeroplanes to the far corners of the world. Extravagant publicity by his agent was accompanied by marvellous engravings of *Ariels* flying majestically over English towns and even over the pyramids of Egypt. These were published all around the world, while souvenirs became abundant. It was the greatest aviation publicity campaign of the century. Even an Atlantic crossing was on the agenda.

Work on building the 6m (20 ft) span model began in 1844 and trials at Bala Down, Chard, in Somerset lasted from 1845 to 1847. The tests were as realistic as possible, and with the tiny steam engine at full power the model *Ariel* was launched from a ramp. Unfortunately it just couldn't sustain its own weight in level flight, but made very creditable powered glides. There seemed no point in continuing onto a large machine and Henson turned his attentions to other matters, married, and emigrated to the United States in 1848.

Stringfellow was not so willing to give up and he developed a new model of half the span, featuring tapered wings and a steam engine developed from the Henson. It was launched from a suspended wire at Chard (and elsewhere) in 1848 but managed no better than the model *Ariel*. Not daunted, he went on to construct other models with multi-wings that suffered similar fates, his triplane having prominence (suspended from the ceiling) at the first exhibition of the newly founded Aeronautical Society of Great Britain, at the Crystal Palace in 1868.

Steam and slopes

The excitement generated by *Ariel* outlasted the project itself, and tended to overshadow important but less dramatic achievements elsewhere. Yet, while Stringfellow temporarily abandoned his experiments, a model was devised in France that achieved all that its English contemporaries could not.

In 1857–58 a French naval officer by the name of Felix du Temple de la Croix constructed a clockwork model aeroplane configured as a tractor monoplane. This, it was found, had the skill to lift itself off the ground and fly a short distance before landing. Similar success attained the model when fitted with a small steam engine. Nearly two decades passed before du Temple progressed to build a full-sized version with a hot-air engine, and when he did a sailor made a genuine 'hop' flight after gaining speed downhill – the first by a manned and powered aeroplane in history. What happened when the same machine was refitted with a steam engine is unclear.

A businesslike aeroplane appeared in Russia in 1884, based on successful models flown over eight years. Designed by Alexander Fedorovich Mozhaiski and

Below: Henson's incredible Ariel, *the subject of the greatest aeronautical publicity campaign of the 19th century.*

crewed by I. N. Golubev, this had a unique rectangular wing with an area of 372m² (4,004 sq ft), measuring a huge 22.8m (74 ft 10 in) in span and 14.2m (46 ft 7 in) in chord. Two steam engines were provided, the 20 hp turning a tractor propeller at the nose of the fuselage and a 10 hp driving two pusher propellers inset in the wings. On one occasion at Krasnoye Selo it may have 'hopped' almost 30 m (98 ft) after gathering speed down a slope, but this assistance denies the 'flight' proper recognition.

Run up to the Wrights

In their quest for flight, the Wright brothers left nothing to chance: skills were learned and relearned before each new step was taken, and the resulting gliders and machines were soundly built and practical. The French flying machine that can be said to have begun the final run-up to 'proper' powered aeroplane flight was somewhat different, yet it too was a masterly piece of engineering, a product of the 'age of steam'.

Frenchman Clément Ader was an electrical engineer, and in non-aviation circles he is remembered for his pioneering work on telephones. In his late twenties or early thirties he began to show interest in flying and looked to bats and birds for their secret. A large model glider for tethered testing was constructed in 1873 and in the following year a model was exhibited to the public.

Construction of a full-sized powered aeroplane started in 1882 but progress was painfully slow. The resulting *Eole* was completed in 1890. The influence of bats was obvious in the distinctive shape of the wings, designed to fold for storage. The pilot sat inside a pod enclosure with no direct forward view. Power to drive the four-paddle propeller came from an ingenious lightweight steam engine offering an output of 18–20 hp. A ventral tailfin formed the rear of the pod. Mechanical means to adjust the wing profile and lateral position were incorporated, mainly for reasons of stability than control. Variation of engine power alone was believed adequate to gain or lose height.

On 9 October 1890 the *Eole* was set up in the grounds of Château Pereire at Armainvilliers and the engine started. The ground was level – an historically important point to note – and, with Ader occupying the seat, the aircraft took off for a 50m (164 ft) hop through the air. Man had now flown in a powered aeroplane without the need of a slope to gather velocity. Many believe this to have been the first powered aeroplane flight in history, and the French planned celebrations for the centenary in 1990. But even Ader admitted the *Eole* had insufficient stability.

Ader's second aeroplane, the *Avion*, was never completed. On 3 February 1892 Ader received a contract from the French Minister of War for the construction of a military aeroplane with accommodation for two and a 75kg bomb-load. The *Avion III* was taken to Satorg where a circular testing course had been constructed in advance. No track shape could have made flight more unlikely. The tests on 12 and 14 October produced only high-speed taxiing, the second almost inevitably ending in a minor off-track accident. That was that, and the *Avion III* became a museum piece.

A circular track was also used by Englishman Horatio Phillips to test his remarkable *Multiplane* at Harrow in May 1893. With no pilot on board but carrying a weight equal to that of a man (thereby forcing tethered trials), the *Multiplane* with its 41 long but narrow-chord wings lifted into the air. More than for the flight itself, Phillips is remembered for establishing the modern wing section. It was this development, along with the internal combustion engine, that was to pave the way for the remarkable and rapid advances that were to take place in the first years of the new century.

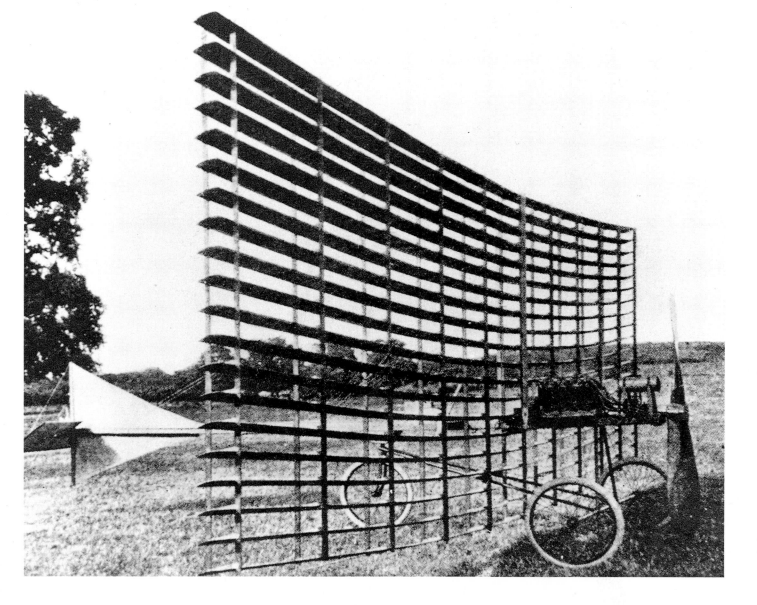

Left: *Horatio Phillips discovered the lifting properties of curved wings and applied his findings to a series of remarkable* Multiplanes *flown from 1893, each featuring high aspect ratio superimposed wings of extremely narrow chord. His 1907 example with 160 narrow-chord wings flew about 152m (500 ft) at Streatham but, while manned, was not officially recognized as the first powered aeroplane flight in Britain. The* Multiplane *illustrated had twenty sets of wings.*

Chapter 3:
Who was first?

Facing page, top:
Charles Manly plunges towards the Potomac river during the full-size Aerodrome's *first unsuccessful flight attempt on 7 October 1903.*

Facing page, bottom:
In his attempt to challenge an injunction filed against the Curtiss Company by the Wright Aeronautical Company regarding patents, Glenn Curtiss had the Langley Aerodrome *restored and flew it as a seaplane in 1914 at Hammondsport. Against popular belief, the restored* Aerodrome *was almost entirely original, proving it could have flown in 1903.*

Facing page, centre: *A near pilot's-eye view of the unfolding drama as* Aerodrome *arcs on its ill-fated transit from air to water.*

Below: *Langley's successful model of the* Aerodrome *which flew 1,280m (4,200 ft) in 1896.*

Among the pioneers of powered aeroplanes, it is the name Wright that immediately comes to mind. But Orville and Wilbur Wright were not the first to fly an aeroplane as so many think. Instead they are recognized as having made the first 'proper' flight.

It might seem strange that there is no clear-cut 'first'; after all, history is founded on facts and dates. But when deciding who did make the first powered aeroplane flight it is important to consider what constitutes a 'flight' – as opposed to a brief 'hop' or 'leap' into the air – one starting from level ground, using engine power, lasting a reasonable length of time, and with the pilot in control of the craft. It also has to be remembered that around the turn of the 20th century many attempts were being made in different countries unbeknown to each other. Many met with some measure of success, and even now new details relating to these are still emerging.

There were several pretenders to this historical crown, not least the German Karl Jatho, about whom many have remained blissfully uninformed. In 1903 Jatho produced an aeroplane that has come to be known as his 'semi-biplane'. Not as advanced as the contemporary Wright *Flyer*, it nevertheless had superimposed biplane wings, a pair of rudders, a tailplane and a power plant. On 18 August Jatho piloted this on an 18m (60 ft) 'hop flight', a distance he extended three-fold in the following month. Although these flights were little more than leaps, the latter was longer than Orville Wright's initial 36m (120 ft) flight of 17 December, which is judged by historians worldwide to be a proper flight (and the first). But history is swayed – perhaps correctly – by the subsequent achievements of the *Flyer* that same day, and that the Wrights quickly demonstrated flying machines that were far in advance of anyone else's, and remained the sole achievers of worthwhile aeroplane flight for the next four years.

Tandem wings

In retrospect, the greatest rival to the Wrights at the turn of the century was the elderly American mathematician and physicist, Professor Samuel Pierpont Langley, secretary to the Smithsonian Institution. Nobody came closer to producing an aeroplane capable of powered, sustained flight without actually achieving this aim, and he died, a greatly disappointed man, a little over two years after the Wrights flew. Restoration of Langley's *Aerodrome* by Glenn Curtiss in 1914 to challenge an injunction filed against his company by the Wright Aeronautical Company, showed it could have flown, as it did on 28 May that year. Today Langley's *Aerodrome* is acknowledged to have been the first man-carrying aeroplane capable of flight.

Langley's aviation experiments began in the last decades of the 19th century. In 1887 he first applied his considerable talents to aeronautics, beginning with fundamental tests aimed at calculating power-to-weight ratios (the amount of engine power required to carry a known weight in flight). Construction of free-flying models (known as *Aerodromes*) began in 1891, leading to the first test in the following year. All six models built by 1895 adopted small steam engines, but did not fly at all well. The main difficulties lay in designing wings sufficiently light, yet strong enough to resist distortion, survive the method of launching, and have stability in flight. As later events would prove, the launching problem would cost Langley his cherished aim.

Langley chose a floating houseboat as his launching platform, fitted with a catapult and anchored on the Potomac river. In 1895 he rebuilt his last two model aeroplanes, giving each new tandem wings in addition to the cruciform tail surfaces. The gamble paid off. On 6 May 1896 one 4.25m (14 ft) span model flew 1,000m (3,280 ft), bettered by the other in November with a flight of 1,280m (4,200 ft) on just 1 hp!

It is not always appreciated that Langley was satisfied with these flights and had decided not to continue towards a manned machine. So what changed his mind? President McKinley had studied the experiments with great interest through the reports of a special commission, with the result that Langley was offered a $50,000 subsidy to build and test a full-size machine. It was all the coaxing he required.

Langley considered his airframe design proven but the power for a larger machine could not possibly come from even a well-designed steam engine. His attention turned to Stephen Balzer, who had already produced a petrol motorcar engine. Unfortunately, Balzer's subsequent *Aerodrome* engine proved to have a very low output. To remedy this, Charles Manly was assigned the task of developing a higher-rated engine based on Balzer's. Incredibly, by his skill he produced a 52 hp radial engine from the basic design of the Balzer 8 hp rotary, though more than two years had passed by.

As an interim step to the full-sized *Aerodrome*, Langley built a 3.2 hp quarter-scale model, which was not very good. Continued work on it over the next two years was finally rewarded (in 1903) by a good flight, making this the first aeroplane with a petrol engine to make a sustained flight. But by then the far more significant full-sized *Aerodrome* was being completed, along with a new launching mechanism on the houseboat. With Manly at the controls, the 14.6m (48 ft) span *Aerodrome* was first tested on 7 October 1903. It caught the launcher and plunged into the water below. Manly was unhurt, except for his pride. A second attempt was planned for 8 December, success depending as much as anything on the houseboat launcher. Again the worst happened and the aircraft fouled, broke and fell into the Potomac.

The US War Department viewed the failures with some disappointment, commenting that years of work lay ahead before a practical machine would be developed. Wilbur Wright, just before making his bid for the sky, wrote that 'I see that Langley has had his fling and failed. It seems to be our turn to throw now, and I wonder what our luck will be.' The success of the Wright brothers only a short time later was the final straw, and support for Langley ended.

Meanwhile, across the Atlantic, in October 1901, the Austrian Wilhelm Kress had 'hopped' from the Tullnerbach reservoir on a tandem-winged aircraft powered by a 30 hp Daimler. To this machine goes the historical distinctions of making the first flight by a manned petrol-driven aeroplane and also the first 'hop' from water.

Success

The sons of a bishop, Orville and Wilbur Wright had a successful bicycle business in Dayton, Ohio. Wilbur, the elder, had followed with interest reports on the marvellous gliding flights by Otto Lilienthal, and in due course persuaded Orville to take up the pursuit of flying as a scientific challenge. Wilbur saw it as an absorbing hobby, albeit one which if successful could possibly be turned to profit.

Although the long term goal was to achieve powered flight, it was necessary first to gain some experience of heavier-than-air flying in its most simple form – gliding. This also offered another benefit, allowing the brothers early opportunity to test the theory of wing warping control, as conceived by Wilbur after many hours of watching birds in flight. Thus they immediately tackled a fundamental necessity for purposeful flight, laying aside the primitive 'weight shift' method of control used by Lilienthal and other hang-glider pioneers.

Their first glider, with a 5.18m (17 ft) span, was ready in 1900. On the advice of the Weather Bureau, the Wrights chose Kitty Hawk in North Carolina as the testing ground.

Glider *No 1* was flown in three modes, as a kite, as a

Above left: *Wright Glider No 2 with Wilbur on board at Kill Devil Hills in 1901. Although not very successful, more than 40 flights were made with it.*

Above centre: *The Wright brothers' camp at Kill Devil Hills.*

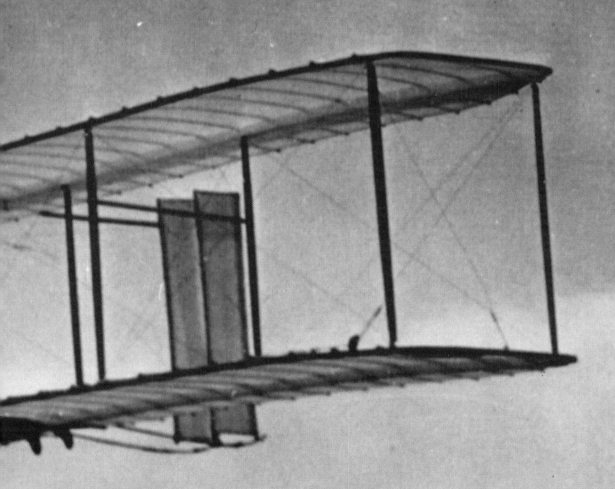

Above right: *Glider* No 3 *after modification to have a single rudder in place of the twin fins, which meant that the rudder (the control cables of which were attached to the wing-warping cradle) could compensate for warp-drag.*

Left: *Wright Glider* No 3 *in original twin-fin form, which tended to want to spin when the wings were warped to achieve level flight.*

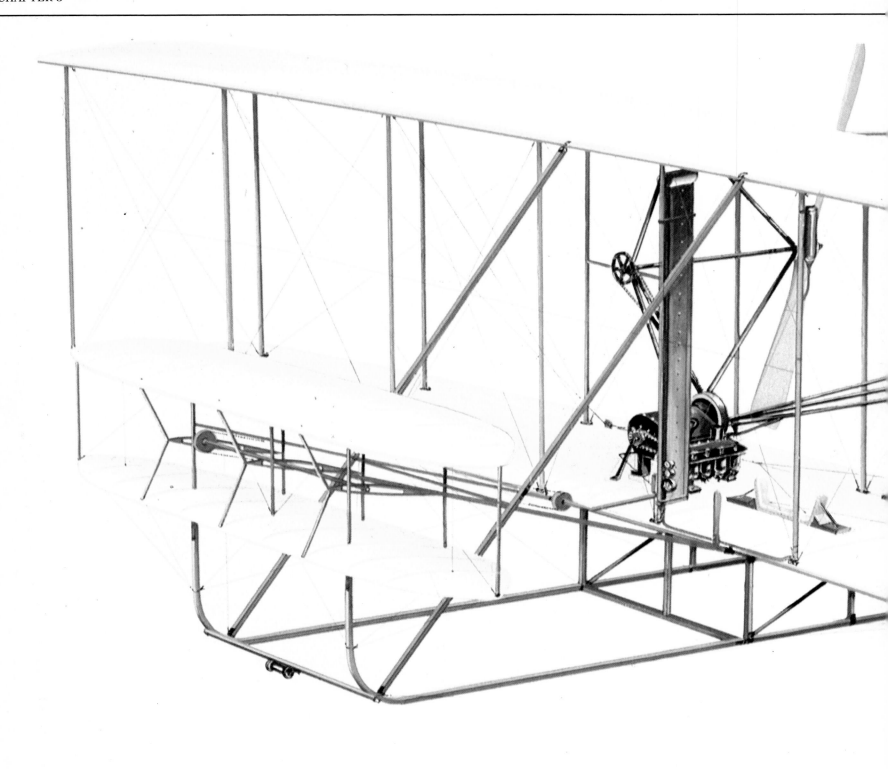

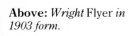**Above:** *Wright* Flyer *in 1903 form.*

Right: *Wilbur Wright hangs back as the* Flyer, *piloted by Orville, leaves its launching trolley on the first recognized flight by a piloted, powered and controllable aeroplane.*

manned kite and as a free-flying manned glider, meeting all expectations. But it was small, and the Wrights set about designing a larger glider with an 80 per cent increase in wing area. Glider *No 2* was taken to Kitty Hawk in the summer of 1901. It also featured wing camber and anhedral, and a new foot-activated method of warping. Unexpectedly, it did not perform well.

Now came a realization that was to keep them in good stead for years to come. It became clear that the calculations on 'lift' published up to then were not entirely accurate, something they had not even considered. Obtaining new figures was going to require a research programme going back to fundamentals. Eventually a handy starch box was modified into a crude wind tunnel, with a fan producing air flow to excite suspended aerofoils. This worked very well. Over two months, 200 or more aerofoils were tested in the tunnel. The results were designed into Glider *No 3*.

No 3 was the largest glider yet, with a span of 9.75m (32 ft). Other changes included the adoption of twin aft fins. Testing began in September 1902. It flew well except for one aspect. When warping was applied, the aeroplane tried to spin. The problem was overcome by replacing the fins with a single steerable rudder, controlled from the same hip cradle as the warping. Now hundreds of fully controlled glides were made. The time was right for the big push to power.

Knowing the kind of engine they needed but couldn't locate, the Wrights again put their engineering skills to the test and, with their mechanic Charles Taylor, produced their own 12 hp petrol internal combustion engine weighing just 77kg (170 lb). This, based in part on a Pope-Toledo motorcar engine, was fitted to the bottom wing of the new 12.2m (40 ft) span *Flyer* biplane, driving two efficient pusher propellers via bicycle chains.

Wilbur and Orville returned once again to the Kill Devil Hills at Kitty Hawk in September 1903, their first intention being to reacquaint themselves with the air on Glider *No 3* before testing *Flyer*. When they arrived they found the old camp in a mess and the glider non-airworthy. Hurriedly, they set about the business of re-establishing order and repairing the glider, and during October made many gliding flights. Then, finally, the time came for the *Flyer* to do its stuff.

Flyer was rigged and readied. The engine was started. Suddenly it backfired, causing a propeller shaft to distort. Replacement parts did not arrive until late November, and these too were damaged. Orville rushed home to construct new stronger shafts. As he returned he learned of Langley's second failure with the *Aerodrome*. How easily the Wrights might have lost the race!

Flyer was again ready for flight trials on 14 December. Wilbur won the flick of a coin and mounted. The engine was started. It ran well. Slowly the machine gathered speed down the launch rail, then off the end, the trolley falling away. Wilbur immediately tried to gain height. He stalled. *Flyer* plunged to the sand. Just three and a half seconds. No good at all.

In the cold morning air of 17 December 1903 the *Flyer* was yet again made ready. At last the weather was suitable for another attempt. It would be Orville's turn. The engine started pounding sweetly. The crew of the local life-saving station stood by. A 23-knot headwind blew. *Flyer* moved off, held steady for a moment by Wilbur. Then it lifted. For 12 seconds Orville battled to control the machine as it covered 36m (120 ft), finally over-controlling it back into the sand. It suffered slight damage, but the experiment was a triumph. There was more to come. Repaired, *Flyer* was remounted on the trolley again, then again, and once more that day, the final time covering 260m (852 ft) in nearly a minute of powered flight. This was also the machine's last flight; back at camp it turned over in high winds and was wrecked.

The Wrights never looked back. Using the much improved *Flyer II*, a flight of 4.5km (2¾ miles) and over five minutes duration was made on 9 November 1904,

Below: *The Wright Model A on its launching rail at Fort Myer prior to the crash that injured Orville and killed his passenger.*

and *Flyer III* covered 39km (24.2 miles) on 5 October 1905, with Wilbur at the controls for 38 minutes. Then, incredibly, at the height of their fame, the brothers gave up flying altogether, concentrating on the business side.

Just a few days after their first powered flights, the brothers received a letter from businessman Godfrey Lowell Cabot, who enquired whether their aeroplane was able to carry mineral cargo over a 26 km (16 mile) route in West Virginia, at a rate of $10 per ton. Of course, even if the *Flyer* survived it could neither fly that far nor carry much of a load. Notwithstanding the reply, Cabot promoted the idea of the US military using a Wright machine. This probably fell on deaf ears, but talks between the Wright brothers and the US Army did take place on 18 January 1905. Nothing much came of this. However, on 23 December 1907 the Army issued the first specification for a military aeroplane, the terms of which included the need for two seats, a speed of 64km/h (40 mph), and capable of holding sufficient fuel for a flight of 200km (125 miles). On 10 February 1908 the Army signed a contract for the construction of a Wright Model A, encouraging the brothers to resume flying on 6 May. Trials began at Fort Myer on 3 September with Orville at the controls; meanwhile Wilbur thrilled enthusiasts in France with demonstrations and passenger flights (see page 40).

Military flights with the biplane went well until 17 September 1908, when a propeller failed, causing the machine to plunge to the ground from a height of 23m (75 ft). Orville was seriously injured and his passenger, Lt. Thomas Etholen Selfridge of the Signal Corps, was killed – the first powered aeroplane fatality. Orville never really got over the accident. A long delay followed, but on 27 July 1909 Orville flew a Model A for 1 hour 12 minutes 20 seconds to pass the first official test. On board was Lt. Frank Lahm. On 2 August the Model A *Miss Columbia* was accepted (the first aeroplane bought for military service in the world), and the Wrights received $25,000 plus a further $5,000 for exceeding the speed requirement. Commercial success also followed from licenced production, notably in Britain and France. Wilbur died of typhoid in May 1912 but Orville survived until 1948.

Above: *Wright Model A being transported by wagon at Fort Myer, Virginia, during the military aeroplane trials.*

Above left: *Lt. Thomas Etholen Selfridge of the US Army Signal Corps (left), talking to Alexander Graham Bell, 1908. On 17 September that year Selfridge was passenger on the Wright Model A when it plunged to the ground from 23m (75 ft) altitude.*

Left: *Lt. Thomas E. Selfridge (left) and Orville Wright, prior to the test flight on 17 September 1908 at Fort Myer, Virginia in which Selfridge suffered fatal injuries.*

Above: *A sad day for aviation – the wrecked Wright Model A immediately after crashing on 17 September 1908. Although he survived with injuries, Orville never really got over the experience. Unfortunately Selfridge did not survive.*

Right: *The diminutive Brazilian-born Alberto Santos-Dumont, famed for his lighter-than-air and aeroplane exploits in France. His later Demoiselle monoplane that appeared in several forms from 1907 is regarded as the first low-cost 'homebuilt' aeroplane for the enthusiast.*

Runners up

Europe, which had dominated the development of flight in the two previous centuries, had to bow to the Americans when it came to early powered heavier-than-air flying. Notwithstanding Jatho's attempts, Europe wasn't even close. It took until 12 September 1906 for even a sustained *tethered* flight to be recorded, accomplished by the Danish engineer Jacob Ellehammer in a primitive 20 hp biplane. And the distance was only 43m (140 ft) – while Wilbur Wright had covered 24 miles 11 months earlier!

Hopes for better things probably rested on the ability of the Brazilian-born aviator, Alberto Santos-Dumont, whose ballooning exploits in France had already excited admiration (see page 77). In 1906 he came up with a peculiar machine in which he seemed to be piloting backwards. The *14-bis* was, actually, a tail-first boxkite, powered by an excellent 50 hp Antoinette engine. On 13 September it hopped 7m (23 ft). Well, it was a start. On 23 October it did a little better, covering nearly 60m (197 ft). Incredibly, for this he won the Archdeacon Prize of 3,000 francs, for the first sustained free flight in Europe of over 25m – no good setting the goals too high! Finally, on 12 November *14-bis* flew 220m (722 ft), a worthy effort that took 21 seconds. This gained the accolade of being the first accredited sustained flight by a manned and powered aeroplane in Europe. It also set the first internationally ratified world distance record for powered aeroplanes – the Wrights hadn't been witnessed by the official FAI governing body.

Below: *Frenchman Henry Farman, who flew Voisins alongside countryman Delagrange in 1908, tests the wind prior to making a flight.*

An industry develops

The ball was now rolling and Europe very quickly progressed. During the initial pioneering years would-be aviators had to possess particular attributes: money was certainly one, a cool nerve another, with more than a sprinkling of skills in design, engineering, aerodynamics and construction. It was not until at least 1909 that factory machines became available in numbers.

A man with all the attributes, plus a body seemingly able to take the strain of frequent accidents – pioneers had to be their own flying instructors and test pilots – was Frenchman Louis Blériot. He also pioneered new shapes, and on 11 July 1907 flew the first aeroplane with cantilever wings (not supported by wires or struts), the type VI *Libellule*. Another innovation on this was wingtip ailerons (flaps), although ailerons had first appeared on fellow Frenchman Robert Esnault-Pelterie's 1904 biplane.

On 14 May 1908 Charles W. Furnas became the world's first aeroplane passenger, flying with Wilbur Wright, while Europe showed it was closing the technology gap just 15 days later when Ernest Archdeacon flew alongside Henry Farman. Another Frenchman, Léon Delagrange, reinforced this point by making a stunning 24.4km (15¼ mile) flight at Issy-les-Moulineaux in a Voisin (taking 29 minutes 53 seconds), although Wilbur Wright (who was, by now, in France) almost immediately eclipsed this when he made a 66.5km (41 mile) journey.

Left: *One of France's greatest aeroplane pioneers was sculptor turned aviator, Léon Delagrange, who recorded several 'firsts' including the first aeroplane flights in Italy and Denmark. He is seen here in the cockpit of his Voisin biplane. Like so many others, Delagrange finally paid the ultimate price for his pioneering spirit, losing his life on 4 January 1910 while piloting a Blériot monoplane.*

Above: *Second only to the Wrights as America's greatest pioneer aviator, Glenn Curtiss flew the Aerial Experimental Association's* June Bug *in 1908 to win the Scientific American trophy for the first official public flight in the USA of over 1km.*

Right: *Having won a £75 Daily Mail prize in a model aeroplane competition on 6 April 1907, Alliott Verdon Roe spent the money constructing an unsuccessful biplane. With little finance, he then constructed a triplane, using the same 9 hp JAP engine found in the biplane and having to cover the wings with treated paper. With this he made the first recognized flight by a Briton in an all-British aeroplane, on 13 July 1909 at Lea Marshes, Essex, covering 30m (100 ft).*

By now Glenn H. Curtiss had established his place as America's foremost aviator after the Wrights, having won the *Scientific American* trophy on 4 July 1908 in his biplane *June Bug* for making the first official public flight in the USA of more than 1 km. Also in 1909 Yakov Gakkel flew a successful aeroplane in Russia, Hans Grade became the first German to fly in Germany, J.A.D. McCurdy flew the Aerial Experiment Association's *Silver Dart* in Canada, Austrian Igo Etrich flew his bird-like *Taube* in that country, Harry Ferguson flew a monoplane in Ireland, and Alliott Verdon Roe became the first Englishman to fly in Britain on an all-British aeroplane. Although flights also took place in other countries, the significance of those mentioned is that all were by nationals of each country, in aeroplanes of their own design.

The Austrian *Taube* later became the most important aircraft of the Imperial German Military Air Service at the beginning of the First World War, built by most German aircraft companies. Similarly, Roe's paper-covered 9 hp triplane that first flew just 30m (100 ft) on 13 July – stretching this to 274m (900 ft) ten days later – helped him on the road to establishing the Avro manufacturing company.

Women, who were not newcomers to balloon flight, also made their mark on aeroplane history quite early on. Madame Thérèse Peltier became the first-ever woman passenger (with Delagrange) in Italy on 8 July 1908. She later became the first woman to fly solo, but never officially qualified as a pilot. That honour went to Mme. la Baronne de Laroche, who gained the French Pilot's Certificate No 36 on 8 March 1910.

Left: *Henri Fabre, whose* Hydravion *seaplane made the first officially recognized flight from water in March 1910.*

Firsts, firsts, firsts

There was a sure way of becoming one of the immortal names of aviation – to be first at something. By 1910, with so many good aeroplanes flying and so many skilled and daring pilots, being first was becoming hard. Frenchman Emil Aubrun managed on 10 March by making the first night flights in an aeroplane (in Argentina). Frenchman Henri Fabre also managed by lifting off from La Mède harbour at Martigues in his *Hydravion* on 28 March, recording the first officially recognized flight from water. Taking more risk and paying the ultimate price with his death on landing, Peruvian Jorges Chevez made the first aeroplane flight over the Alps on 23 September.

The year 1910 also saw the first carriage of freight (7 November), when a Wright Model B flown by Philip Parmalee carried an assignment of 542 yards of silk as a promotional gimmick for the Morehouse-Martens Company of Columbus, Ohio.

1911 witnessed the first air mail flights. After an experimental (but official) mail flight between Allahabad and Naini Junction in India on behalf of the British Government on 18 February, Frenchman Henri Pequet was joined by Captain W.G. Windham for the start of a regular service four days later as part of the Universal Postal Exhibition. Each letter carried was franked *First Aerial Post, U.P. Exhibition, Allahabad, 1911*. The first air mail service in Britain began on 9 September 1911 and ended on the 26th, having been organized only to commemorate the coronation of H.M. King George V. By then official mail carrying had started in the USA (on the 23rd), with Earl L. Ovington gaining the prized title of Air Mail Pilot No 1.

Conquest of the Channel

The aviation meetings held at Reims in France and then in other countries from 1909 did much to promote flying, as did the offer of cash prizes and generous sponsorships. But even before the famous Reims meeting took place, Louis Blériot – that accident-prone and overweight Frenchman – had flown the English Channel. This was undoubtedly the most important flight since 17 December 1903, and its ramifications were incalculable. For a start, it was the first long-distance aeroplane flight with real purpose.

As it happened there were two main contenders for the *Daily Mail* £1,000 prize for the first Channel crossing, both French and both mounting French monoplanes. The most likely to succeed seemed to be Hubert Latham, English educated and still in his twenties. His mount was the graceful Antoinette IV with an engine from the same company, both the work of Léon Levavasseur. At 04.30 hours on the morning of 19 July 1909 wireless telegraphy was used to transmit a weather report to the Lord Warden Hotel in Dover, the first transmission of the day. At 06.42 Latham took off to pass over the cliffs of Sangatte near Calais, his engine purring and the wind in his face.

Then, at about 13km (8 miles) out, the Antoinette's engine began to play up. Then it stopped completely with Latham at a height of 300m (1,000 ft). The substantial wing span of the Antoinette helped him make a shallow descent, alighting perfectly on the water. Frustrated, he lit a cigarette and waited to be rescued by the *Harpon*.

Wanting a second try, Latham hurriedly ordered a new machine from Paris. While he waited for the Antoinette VII, Louis Blériot began his own preparations at nearby Les Baraques. In the early morning of the 25th the 25 hp Anzani engine of Blériot's Type XI monoplane was started. It was the beginning of one of history's epic flights.

At 04.41 hours the monoplane left French soil, flying over his escort destroyer. The wind was strong and he flew off course; he hadn't taken a compass. For several seemingly endless minutes he pondered his position, wondering whether to turn back or continue. Then, 20 minutes out, he saw the white cliffs marking Dover's

coastline and the castle, and realized he had flown too far east. Approaching the cliffs, he made a sudden turn westward, picking up violent headwinds that dramatically reduced his speed. But the opening appeared where he planned to land and he made his run in. Once again the wind caught him, but he was committed. He switched the engine off and the aircraft bumped down on the green grass of Northfall Meadow near the Castle at 05.17 hours. The Channel had been conquered.

The story does not end here. Not to be completely defeated, in the early hours of the 27th Latham set out from Cap Blanc Nez to make a second attempt at flying the Channel. Only 1.6km (1 mile) from the Dover coast, his engine failed and once again he went down into the water.

The two great rivals met again at the Reims air meeting that August. Blériot set speed records, bettered by Latham flying an Antoinette in April of the following year. Latham set a distance record, plus the first FAI accredited altitude record (though at half the height he believed he had managed over the Channel); Latham and the Antoinette VII reached 1,000 m altitude in January 1910 for the first time.

Left: Hubert Latham leaves Sangatte on his first cross-Channel attempt, accompanied by a French naval vessel.

Below: *Louis Blériot sets out over the Channel on the first ever aeroplane crossing of this stretch of water. It was probably the most important flight since the Wright brothers first flew in 1903.*

Chapter 4: Sponsorship and Air Racing

The early pioneering flights caused tremendous excitement, not only to those who were directly involved but also to newspaper readers around the world. The initial reports of these daring exploits created a widespread belief that man had now conquered the air and that very soon the sky would be full of new and exciting 'flying machines'.

The pioneers themselves viewed the situation very differently, being fully aware of the frailty of their machines and their very limited capability. But there was no lack of enthusiasm to speed the development of the aeroplane, and those involved in these first flights could gain considerable encouragement from the motorcar, which had become a practical means of transport in the closing decade of the 19th century, and was by now rapidly growing in sophistication.

This parallel development gave the early aviators heart. They could (and did) look closely at the proving of the motorcar and the stages which had speeded its development to practicality. Not surprisingly they discovered that motoring enthusiasts had engaged in competitive trials, the stress of which highlighted weak

components and poor design, and thus brought keen minds to bear on the solution of the problems involved. The aviators adopted a similar course of action and began contending against each other.

The Wrights in Europe

Progress was painfully slow in Europe; it was not until 9 November 1907 that Henry Farman, flying his Voisin-Farman I biplane, achieved a flight of more than one minute. But things were soon to be accelerated by an unexpected catalyst: Wilbur Wright himself and the Wright Model A.

Wilbur had arrived in France in the mid-summer of 1908. Basing himself initially at Hunaudières near Le Mans, he began assembling the aircraft and preparing for what he realized would be an important demonstration. This was made on the evening of 8 August. Conditions were perfect, cool and almost windless. As twilight approached, a crowd of pilots gathered to see a demonstration that, in their opinion, would probably be very similar to a display given by one of their number.

A sudden roar from the engine of the Model A turned

Below: *Wilbur Wright flying in France in 1908, his skills and those of his aeroplane proving so staggering to the gathered onlookers that they became the catalysts that spurred European aviators to greater achievements.*

all their heads to watch the take-off. By then Wilbur was already airborne and weaving graceful patterns in the sky. The onlookers were breathless. Almost before they had grasped the capability of this aircraft and Wilbur's mastery of the controls, he had throttled back and was setting the Model A gently but firmly on the ground. Their cheers of enthusiasm congratulated Wilbur for the first real demonstration these pilots had seen of the freedom and capability of powered flight.

It was precisely the push they needed to accelerate aviation progress in Europe. Competitive evaluation was soon seen to be the key to more rapid development of their aircraft with financial reward for achievement; the *Daily Mail* offered many sponsorship awards that stimulated aviation enthusiasts to make greater efforts. Meanwhile Henry Deutsch de la Meurthe and Ernest Archdeacon in France had offered a *Grand Prix d'Aviation* of 50,000 francs for the first pilot to complete a circular flight that exceeded a distance of 1 km. This was won on 13 January 1908 by Henry Farman flying his Voisin-Farman I biplane at Issy-les-Moulineaux, the 1 minute 28 second flight covering a total distance approaching 1.5km. The significance of a circular flight was the need for full control over the direction of flight.

The first aviation meeting

Following Louis Blériot's epic crossing of the English Channel on 25 July 1909 to pick up the *Daily Mail* prize of £1,000, the next important European event came on 22 August, when the first international aviation meeting began at Reims, one which lasted until 29 August. This brought together an assembly of no fewer than 38 competing aeroplanes, of which 23 succeeded in getting airborne.

In Great Britain, two months later, two flying meetings (one unofficial and one official) were organized at Doncaster and Blackpool respectively. A week later, another *Daily Mail* prize was won: £1,000 for the first British pilot to complete a circular flight of one mile in a British aeroplane. This important landmark was achieved by J.T.C. Moore-Brabazon (who had earlier been the first Briton to pilot an aeroplane) on 30 October 1909 flying the Short Biplane No 2, which covered the required distance in 2 minutes 36 seconds.

The first aeroplane meeting in the United States, which aroused much interest and enthusiasm, started at

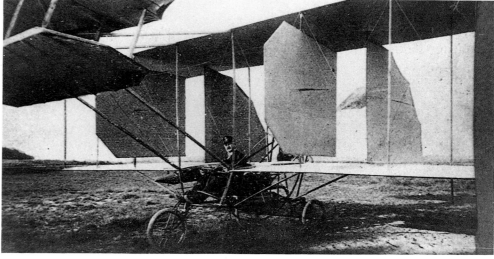

Dominguez Field, Los Angeles, on 10 January 1910. Just over three months later in Great Britain the first £10,000 *Daily Mail* prize was won by the French pilot Louis Paulhan. A huge sum in those days, it had been offered for the first pilot to fly from and to a point within 5 miles of the newspaper's London and Manchester offices respectively, and saw Englishman Claude Grahame-White and Paulhan (both flying Farman biplanes) competing in what history has dubbed the London–Manchester Air Race. Despite near-heroic attempts by Grahame-White to be first at Manchester (including making on 27–28 April the first recorded night flight in Great Britain), Paulhan got there first, at 05.32 hours on 28 April, landing at the Didsbury suburb of Manchester.

In the United States, during the period 6–12 September 1910, the *Boston Globe* newspaper sponsored an aviation meeting at Boston in which the Englishman Claude Grahame-White flew away with no fewer than five first prizes. In the following month he was again the winner when the first Gordon Bennett aeroplane race (one of 100 km) was flown at Belmont Park, New York. These successes in early American air events brought big financial reward, as had his efforts in Britain and European contests, bringing his winnings for 1910 to the staggering total (for its day) of £10,280. Much of the prize money went to the improvement of his flying schools.

Above: *German Karl Jatho, who had 'hop' flown before the Wright brothers in 1903, might have become the premier European aviator had it not been for a lack of finance. Nevertheless, his Model IV of 1909 (shown) achieved controlled and sustained flight and his Stahltaube monoplane of 1911 was the first successful aeroplane to adopt a basic steel tube structure.*

Left: *Following Wilbur Wright's excellent flights in France in 1908, the Short Brothers were approached at the instigation of Griffith Brewer to set up British manufacture of the Wright biplane. Seen here during a visit by the Wright brothers to Shorts in 1909 are (standing from left) Oswald Short, Horace Short, Eustace Short, Frank McClean, Griffith Brewer and others; (seated from left) J.T.C. Moore-Brabazon, Wilbur and Orville Wright, and Charles Rolls.*

Distance no object

The first major aviation event of 1911, and the first truly international air race held in Europe, was the Circuit of Europe which began on 18 June 1911 and continued until 7 July, when the French Lieutenant de Vaisseau Conneau reached the finishing point in his Blériot monoplane. The prize money totalled £18,300, attracting an entry of 49 aircraft, but only 9 of their number completed the course. Just over two weeks later, on 22 July, aircraft gathered at Brooklands, Surrey, for the beginning of another event sponsored by a £10,000 *Daily Mail* prize, the 'Round Britain' air race. The winner, once again, was the French Navy's Lieutenant de Vaisseau Conneau.

Pushing the seaplane

During 1912 there were few significant sponsorship activities, but the world's first meeting for hydro-aeroplanes (what we would now call seaplanes) was held at Monaco in March of that year. One of the judges

Below: The Royal Aero Club of the United Kingdom's reissued announcement of the unclaimed Daily Mail £10,000 prize for the first transatlantic flight without stop-over on land.

of that event was Jacques Schneider, son of a wealthy French industrialist.

Schneider had been a motoring enthusiast until suffering crippling injury in an accident, and now turned his interest to aviation. At Monaco he was surprised at the marginal performance and reliability of the contending aircraft. He came to the conclusion that competition could well encourage development of good passenger-carrying seaplanes that might, one day, provide the means for intercontinental air routes.

It was towards the end of 1912 before Schneider finalized his ideas, and he chose to announce these at the banquet held by the Aero Club de France on 5 December 1912, following the second Gordon Bennett race. He proposed a competition for hydro-aeroplanes, *La Coupe d'Aviation Maritime Jacques Schneider* (soon referred to internationally as the Schneider Cup), offering a trophy to the value of £1,000 (to be passed to consecutive winners) plus a cash prize of £1,000 for each of three successive years. The first contest took

---

Royal Aero Club of the United Kingdom,
3, CLIFFORD STREET, LONDON, W. 1.

Telegraphic Address : "Aerodom, London."
Telephone : Regent 1327-8-9.

"DAILY MAIL" £10,000 PRIZE.
Cross-Atlantic Flight.

(Under the Competition Rules of the Royal Aero Club.)

The Proprietors of the "Daily Mail" have offered the sum of £10,000 to be awarded to the aviator who shall first cross the Atlantic in an aeroplane in flight from any point in the United States, Canada, or Newfoundland to any point in Great Britain or Ireland, in 72 consecutive hours. (The flight may be made either way across the Atlantic.)

Qualification of Competitors.—The competition is open to persons of any nationality not of enemy origin, holding an Aviator's Certificate issued by the International Aeronautical Federation and duly entered on the Competitors' Register of the Royal Aero Club.

No aeroplane of enemy origin or manufacture may be used.

Entries.—The Entry Form, which must be accompanied by the Entrance Fee of £100, must be sent to the Secretary of the Royal Aero Club, 3, Clifford Street, London, W.1, at least 14 days before the entrant makes his first attempt.

No part of the Entrance Fee is to be received by the *Daily Mail*. All amounts received will be applied towards payment of the expenses of the Royal Aero Club in conducting the competition. Any balance not so expended will be refunded to the competitor.

Starting Place.—Competitors must advise the Royal Aero Club of the starting place selected, and should indicate as nearly as possible the proposed landing place.

All starts must be made under the supervision of an Official or Officials appointed by the Royal Aero Club.

Identification of Aircraft.—Only one aircraft may be used for each attempt. It may be repaired en route. It will be so marked before starting that it can be identified on reaching the other side.

Stoppages.—Any intermediate stoppages may only be made on the water.

Towing.—Towing is not prohibited.

Start and Finish.—The start may be made from land or water, but in the latter case the competitor must cross the coast line in flight. The time will be taken from the moment of leaving the land or crossing the coast line.

The finish may be made on land or water. The time will be taken at the moment of crossing the coast line in flight or touching land.

If the pilot has at any time to leave the aircraft and board a ship, he must resume his flight from approximately the same point at which he went on board.

GENERAL.

1. A competitor, by entering, thereby agrees that he is bound by the Regulations herein contained or to be hereafter issued in connection with this competition.

2. The interpretation of these regulations or of any to be hereafter issued shall rest entirely with the Royal Aero Club.

3. The competitor shall be solely responsible to the officials for the due observance of these regulations, and shall be the person with whom the officials will deal in respect thereof, or of any other question arising out of this competition.

4. A competitor, by entering, waives any right of action against the Royal Aero Club or the Proprietors of the *Daily Mail* for any damages sustained by him in consequence of any act or omission on the part of the officials of the Royal Aero Club or the Proprietors of the *Daily Mail* or their representatives or servants or any fellow competitor.

5. The aircraft shall at all times be at the risk in all respects of the competitor, who shall be deemed by entry to agree to waive all claim for injury either to himself, or his passenger, or his aircraft, or his employees or workmen, and to assume all liability for damage to third parties or their property, and to indemnify the Royal Aero Club and the Proprietors of the *Daily Mail* in respect thereof.

6. The Committee of the Royal Aero Club reserves to itself the right, with the consent of the Proprietors of the *Daily Mail*, to add to, amend or omit any of these rules should it think fit.

1st February, 1919.
For Entry Form, see over.

place at Monaco on 16 April 1913. The effects of the contests, despite the comparatively small prize offered, were so far reaching – and with an important but specialized effect on aircraft structural design and the development of in-line engines – that it was to take 19 years (13 September 1931) before the Trophy was finally won outright for Great Britain by Flt. Lt. J.N. Boothman flying the Supermarine S.6B in an uncontested event, averaging 547.305km/h (340.08 mph).

Records

Progress by the end of 1912 had been so rapid that Jules Védrines of France then held the world speed record at 174.06 km/h (108.16 mph) in a Deperdussin monoplane; Roland Garros of France had attained a height of 5,610m (18,405 ft) in a Morane-Saulnier aircraft, and a non-stop distance record of 1,010.9km (628.1 miles) had been set by M. Fourny of France flying a Maurice Farman.

By the time the third Aerial Derby took place at Hendon on 6 June 1914 there were already signs that some European nations might soon be at war. American W.L. Brock, flying a French Morane-Saulnier monoplane, won the event, taking the *Daily Mail* Gold Cup, Shell Trophy and a cash prize of £300 to become the first American pilot to win a major British competition.

In 1913, the *Daily Mail* announced a significant new prize: £10,000 for the first non-stop crossing by air of the North Atlantic. The flight could be made in either direction. One immediate response was from wealthy American businessman Rodman Wanamaker who ordered from the Curtiss company two flying-boats, one of which was being prepared to make the transatlantic flight attempt on 5 August 1914.

The day before the flight was due to begin, war was declared in Europe. Overnight, the great aerial sporting events of 1914 became a distant memory. The flight was cancelled; the two Curtiss machines became the prototypes for the patrol flying-boats which were to give honourable service during the war.

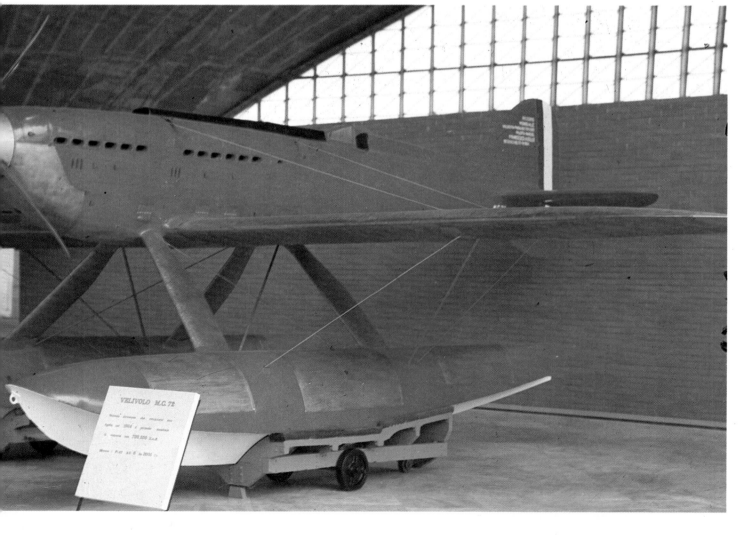

Above: *The Supermarine S.6B, the aircraft that gave Britain its third Schneider Trophy win in succession and outright possession of the Trophy.*

Above left: *Howard Pixton leaning on the wings of the Sopwith Tabloid, with which he brought the Schneider Trophy to Britain during the second contest in Monaco in 1914, achieving an average (and winning) speed of 139.66km/h (86.78 mph).*

Left: *Italian Macchi-Castoldi MC.72 racer, not ready in time to be used in the last ever Schneider Trophy race but setting a world speed record of 709.07km/h (440.60 mph) on 23 October 1934.*

Chapter 5: War in the Skies

The Great War of 1914–18 was the first major conflict to involve the massive use of air power. When the fate of the Allies hung in the balance during the German onslaught of spring 1918, aeroplanes played a decisive role in the outcome and the eventual defeat of the Central Powers.

In the last month of the war the Royal Air Force boasted no fewer than 22,171 aeroplanes and over 37,700 aero-engines, a far cry from the 179 Royal Flying Corps and 78 Royal Naval Flying Corps aircraft of August 1914, numbers including airships. But even these latter figures give a misleading impression of the true capability of the RFC in the summer of 1914. In 1913 it had been planned for the RFC to comprise seven squadrons of twelve aircraft each with a similar number of machines and pilots as a reserve for each squadron. Pre-war, however, these figures were never attained. In mid-year four RFC squadrons met at Netheravon. Foreign visitors were invited to inspect the camp, and incidentally included those from Austria-Hungary and Germany. The maximum number of machines able to be flown on any day was 30; this was a more accurate representation of the actual first-line strength of the RFC.

Full equipment and personnel levels with four of the RFC's squadrons were almost attained on the outbreak of war by conscripting civilian pilots of the Special Reserve and taking over some aeroplanes used by the Central Flying School. But this almost casual attitude to aeroplanes and their use in war in 1914 was soon to change as fighting intensified, and year by year production was stepped up. The new aeroplanes to come from British factories by May 1915 could be numbered in hundreds. Some 7,137 more followed between mid-1915 and February 1917, and deficiencies in number were made up by deliveries from France. The next ten months saw output rise four-fold to over 13,500 aeroplanes, and in the first ten months of 1918

nearly 27,000 machines were constructed. Overall wartime production in Britain by October 1918 had totalled 47,873 aeroplanes and 52,598 aero-engines. A massive new industry had grown from almost nothing.

Much the same was true of Germany, France and the other combatant nations. Germany had begun the war with a paper total of 246 Military Aviation Service aeroplanes and seven rigid airships, to which the Imperial Naval Air Service added 36 aeroplanes and one Zeppelin (five more flew before the end of the year). By the Armistice German production had also totalled nearly 48,000 aeroplanes, of which approximately 15,000 plus 27,000 aero-engines had survived to be surrendered to the Allies. Of these, about one-third were in front-line use. The French Aviation Militaire began the war with 160 aeroplanes and 15 airships, added to which were just eight naval machines. War production totalled 24,652 aeroplanes and nearly 92,600 aero-engines, of which 3,437 aeroplanes were active on the Western Front alone at the war's end. Austro-Hungarian and Italian production levels were also substantial, but the efforts of Russia and the American Expeditionary Force were sustained mainly from French and British production. There were, of course, notable exceptions, such as the large Sikorsky Ilya Mourometz bombers, Sikorsky S-16/S-20 fighters, and Anatra reconnaissance machines, to name but a few Russian types of importance.

Despite a much lower overall output of military aeroplanes than Britain, the part France played in sustaining the Allied cause throughout the war cannot be overstated. In addition to the deployment of Nieuports, Morane-Saulniers, Spads and other types by foreign squadrons, many aircraft built in other countries used French aero-engines. Gnome, Le Rhone and Clerget rotary engines were common to many British aeroplanes in particular; even the very British Royal Aircraft Factory B.E.2 series encompassed Renault-

Right: *During the First World War aeroplane construction suddenly became very big business with many companies both large and small previously employed in furniture and other manufacturing turning their hands to new skills.*

engined models. Almost the entire fleet of RFC aeroplanes at the outbreak of war carried French engines, and alongside the 530 new military aeroplanes produced by May 1915 for the RFC, Britain completed only 141 engines. But from as early as 1912 British efforts had been raised to design better aero-engines and this sustained programme began to pay off by 1915. British engine design centred on in-line models, leaving France to dominate the lighter and lower output rotary types throughout the war.

The tremendous improvement in the capability of warplanes during the course of the 1914-18 war was due in no small part to the development of better aero-engines. Huge increases in power without corresponding weight penalties allowed the design of ever-improved and, when required, much larger and faster aircraft, although techniques of airframe construction did not progress at the same rate. Most attempts to break away from traditional strut and wire bracing for wings remained experimental and only Germany fielded all-metal machines on active service. The production by Junkers of its armoured J.I close support biplane and D.I monoplane fighter helped establish for that company a lead in all-metal aircraft design that had great consequences to its position as a leading designer of post-war modern commercial airliners.

Pre-war achievements

The rapid developments of the war years did not arise entirely out of nothing; the years leading up to the Great War had seen the genesis of military aviation, and aeroplanes had seen active service in a number of lesser conflicts. The first officially recognized aeroplane flight

in Britain was made on 16 October 1908 by American-born Samuel Franklin Cody using the *British Army Aeroplane No 1*. In 1911 Britain then took the bold step of creating the nucleus of an air force proper by forming the Air Battalion of the Royal Engineers with five aeroplanes and an airship, which in turn led to the founding of the Royal Flying Corps on 13 May 1912.

In August 1912 the first-ever British military aeroplane trials were held, intended to find aeroplanes with which to shape RFC expansion. French as well as British machines took part. Winner of what was considered the most important trial – for speed – was Cody on a primitive biplane known as the Cathedral. Fortunately it was realized that its speed came from the huge 120 hp Austro-Daimler engine and from progressive design. The Army Aircraft Factory (the renamed

Above: RFC pilot cadets learn their skills using a B.E.2 airframe as an instructional tool.

Below: Cody with his Cathedral biplane, flown during the 1912 British military trials. Although the fastest aeroplane, it was rightly viewed as primitive and not selected for military service. (Science Museum)

8.7.18.

Balloon Factory) at Farnborough was not permitted to enter the trials, as it was deemed only a research organization. The fact that it had built its own B.E.1 covertly did not change matters, but when the even better B.E.2 appeared the War Office had to take greater notice.

For 1912 the B.E.2 was a remarkable aeroplane, modern in appearance and incredibly stable. While the one-off B.E.1 became the first Army aeroplane to receive a military serial under the new inter-service identification numbering system (as 201 – the Navy having numbers 1–200), the B.E.2 spawned production versions that were to be the stalwart of RFC/RAF reconnaissance squadrons throughout the coming war.

Another pre-war Royal Aircraft Factory experimental machine was the S.E.4, which demonstrated an incredible 211km/h (131 mph), while its F.E.2 was available at the outbreak of war for almost immediate production by others. This differed from the B.E.2 not only in its pusher configuration but by being designed from the outset as for air fighting, armed reconnaissance, ground attack and bombing. The factory never became a mass manufacturer as such – its designs put into production by other contractors – and the factory also progressed in aero-engine and propeller design, air armament and many other technologies. It subsequently became the Royal Aircraft Establishment, maintaining its special roles to the present day.

Main picture and below right: *Royal Aircraft Factory B.E.2a, the first service version of the B.E.2 and the first type of RFC aircraft to land in France after the outbreak of war. Suited to reconnaissance and light bombing, with the observer in the front cockpit, it had no fixed armament. By late 1915 B.E.2as and similarly unarmed B.E.2bs had been recalled from the Western Front as armed models took over in the face of increasing air opposition.*

Below left: *Junkers D.I. all-metal cantilever-wing fighter that appeared in March 1918. The 185 hp BMW IIIa in-line engine of the 41 production aircraft completed before the Armistice gave a speed of 187km/h (116 mph), while the corrugated skins provided great strength (but made it difficult to build quickly in quantity) and manoeuvrability was excellent. Corrugated skins became the trademark of Junkers aircraft post-war.*

Britain was not the only nation to found an air force at this time. Argentina did the same on 10 August 1912, Australia in September 1912, Austria much earlier, Belgium on 16 April 1913, Bulgaria in 1912, Chile on 11 February 1913, Denmark on 2 July 1912, France in April 1910, Germany on 1 October 1912, Greece in September 1912, Italy on 27 June 1912, the Netherlands on 1 July 1913, Portugal in 1912, Russia in 1910, Spain in March 1911, Serbia in 1913, Turkey in March 1912, and the USA with the establishment of the 1st Aero Squadron within the US Army on 5 March 1913.

The founding of specific air forces is not necessarily an indication of the start of military flying in these countries, as is seen from the events in the USA and Britain already detailed in this and earlier chapters; a great many events of major military importance had already taken place.

On 19 January 1910 Lt. Paul Beck of the US Army had dropped sandbags from an aeroplane while flying over Los Angeles in the first mock bombing experiment. On 30 June Glenn Curtiss followed this with another of greater significance, releasing his lead pipe dummy bombs from a height of 15m (50 ft) on to the outline of a battleship marked out with buoys on Lake Keuka. These, of course, were stunts, but served to show the vulnerability of land and sea targets to air attack. By then, however, genuine military flying using aeroplanes had begun.

On 9 June 1910 Lt. Féquant made the first reconnaissance flight in France, piloting a Henry Farman. Proper manoeuvres began in Picardie that September and it was from these that the aeroplane proved to have a unique role to play in warfare over and above that of the captive balloon. By 20 October a Permanent Inspector of Military Aeronautics had been appointed in France.

Early air armament experiments

The official line in many countries was that aeroplanes were suited to reconnaissance but little else, and for this armament was unnecessary. But there were a number of far-sighted people who held other views. On 24 July 1910 German August Euler received a patent for a special mount which enabled a rigidly-fixed machine-gun to be fired from an aeroplane. This was subsequently adapted to his *Gelber Hund* biplane for demonstration purposes. On the other side of the Atlantic, a Curtiss biplane was again used for armament experiments, when Lt. Jacob Earl Fickel, US Army, made history on 20 August 1910 by firing a rifle while in flight. In the same year Major Brooke-Popham of the British Air Battalion got himself into serious trouble with his superiors by fitting a gun to his Blériot monoplane. In 1911 Italian Capitano Guidoni released the first airborne torpedo, from a Farman biplane, while Lt. Myron Sidney Crissy and Philip Parmalee crewed the Wright biplane at San Francisco from which the first live bombs were dropped on 7 January 1911.

When on 2 June 1912 Captain Charles de Forest Chandler of the US Army manned the first ever machine-gun carried by an aeroplane (a Wright Model B), official interest in the experiment was unusually muted. The gun, the work of Colonel Isaac Newton Lewis, was promptly removed and the Colonel left the USA to set up production in Belgium. The Lewis gun in developed form later became the most used armament on British warplanes. All manner of other experiments, some official but others the brainchild of individual fliers,

Below: *Captain Charles de Forest Chandler holds a Lewis machine-gun that had been fitted temporarily to a Wright Model B piloted by Lt. Thomas de Witt Milling, College Park, Maryland, USA. Little official interest in arming the Army's aircraft followed and the Lewis gun was removed.*

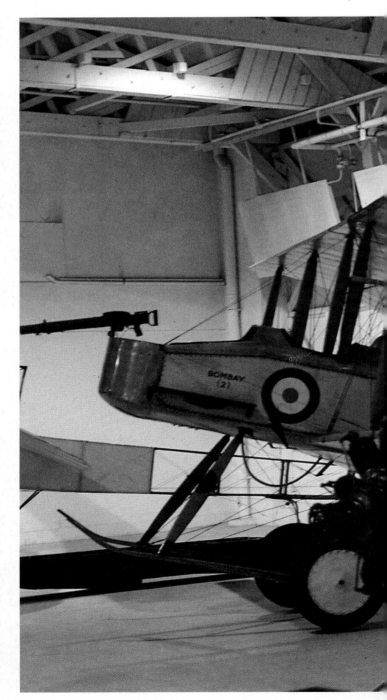

saw guns mounted here, there and everywhere, but always well away from the propeller. Officially, very few were taken seriously.

The interest of navies, especially those of the USA and Britain, in military flying played a major part in encouraging a wider view of the aeroplane's possible roles. American Lt. John H. Towers, who in 1919 led the Navy/Curtiss flying-boats that set out on the first staged crossing of the Atlantic, began trials in October 1912 to assess the suitability of aeroplanes to anti-submarine warfare. In the following month the British Admiralty ordered a fighting aeroplane from Vickers, which was displayed at the Olympia Aero Show in February of the next year as the Maxim gun-armed Destroyer E.F.B.1. Although this remained a proto-type, it began a series of designs that led directly to the RFC's and RNAS's first proper fighter, the F.B.5 Gun Bus of 1915.

The Gun Bus, like the contemporary Royal Aircraft Factory F.E.2a two-seater and the single-seat Airco D.H.2 fighter that followed to the Western Front, was a pusher-engined biplane with the crew occupying a short fuselage pod. This rather crude layout was necessary because British designers had not yet developed a synchronizing mechanism that would time machine-gun bullets to pass between turning propeller blades. Voisin in France also adopted this layout, producing a machine for bombing and ground attack. In its Type I to Type X forms, it lasted out the entire war and served with a large number of front-line squadrons.

But the armament problem that necessitated 'pusher'

Above: *Following the exhibition of its Destroyer E.F.B.1 (Experimental Fighting Biplane No 1) at the 1913 Olympia Aero Show, Vickers produced other experimental fighting prototypes of similar basic configuration. The E.F.B.5 had sufficient promise that the company decided to construct fifty as a private venture in 1914 before the outbreak of war, and the F.B.5 was officially accepted for RFC and RNAS service that summer.*

Left: *Replica of a Vickers F.B.5 Gun Bus two-seat fighting-scout.*

designs had already been tackled with varying degrees of success, although official circles were slow to take note. Raymond Saulnier in France was one such innovator, although his experimental synchronizing device to allow bullets to pass through the propeller arc required a constant propeller speed, making it impractical. Far more important was the work of German Franz Schneider, who in July 1913 patented a synchronization gear that worked at different propeller speeds. Schneider was employed by Luft-Verkehrs Gesellschaft, but it was not until he produced the company's E.VI two-seat monoplane in 1915 that his arrangement was put to proper test. But the E.VI remained a one-off. By then, however, Anthony Fokker had produced an armed version of his M 5K single-seat reconnaissance monoplane using his own synchronizing gear.

Aeroplanes afloat

Among the world's armed forces, it was often the navies that had the most far-sighted approach to flying. The US Navy, encouraged by outside influences, was the first to explore the possibilities of using aeroplanes from ships of the fleet. The *World* newspaper, having sponsored the bombing experiment by Glenn Curtiss in June 1910, planned another great demonstration. In conjunction with the Hamburg-American Steamship Line, it intended to have an aeroplane take off from the liner *Amerika* on 5 November 1910 on an experimental flight that could lead to faster air mail deliveries. A race then developed between this civil effort and the US Navy to be first to fly an aeroplane off a ship. After a series of delays the newspaper was beaten by the Navy, when on 14 November stunt pilot Eugene B. Ely took off in the Curtiss *Hudson Flier* from a hastily made platform over the bows of the stationary cruiser USS *Birmingham* at Hampton Roads in Virginia. The aircraft carrier was born!

On 18 January 1911 Ely made the first landing on to a ship, the USS *Pennsylvania* anchored in San Francisco Bay. Royal Navy Commander Charles Rumney Samson then made the first take-off from a moving ship, HMS *Hibernia* on 9 May 1912, but it was not until 2 August 1917 that British Squadron Commander E.H. Dunning

Left: *3.16pm on 14 November 1910: Ely pulls back on the controls as the* Hudson Flier *heads towards the water after taking-off from USS* Birmingham. *He recovers only after the propeller is damaged on contacting the water but lands safely at Willoughby Spit.*

Below: *Ely lands on the deck of USS* Pennsylvania *on 18 January 1911, the rope and sandbag arrester system bringing him to a quick stop.*

Above: *HMS* Hibernia *arrived off Portland for the May 1912 Naval Review carrying Short S.38 (rear) and S.41. The platform over the bow guns had been removed from HMS* Africa, *from which Samson had flown while the vessel was at rest in December 1911 and January 1912. From* Hibernia, *Samson made the first-ever take-off from a moving ship, on 9 May 1912.*

Right: *Squadron Commander E.H. Dunning slide-slips his Sopwith Pup fighter over the deck of HMS* Furious *to record the first-ever landing of an aeroplane on a moving ship, on 2 August 1917; fellow officers grab hanging straps on the Pup to bring it to rest.*

performed the first landing on to a moving ship, an event that finally made the aircraft carrier practical. This took place on board the new HMS *Furious*, the world's first proper aircraft carrier and on which Dunning had been appointed the first Senior Flying Officer. His second demonstration on the 7th ended in disaster, however, when his Sopwith Pup was carried over the bows and he was killed. But his loss was not in vain, and new methods of arresting aircraft landing on deck were devised and carriers quickly became part of the world naval scene.

Aeroplanes first go to war

In September 1911 Italy declared war on Turkey over the disputed North African territories of Cyrenaica and Tripolitania. An Expeditionary Force was hastily mustered and dispatched, which included seven French-built aeroplanes and two Austrian Taubes. All were unarmed. On 22 October Capitano Piazza of the Italian Air Flotilla boarded a Blériot monoplane and undertook a one-hour reconnaissance of Turkish positions between Tripoli and Azizia. This historic flight marked the baptism of aeroplanes to actual war. A second reconnaissance that day by another pilot flying a Nieuport showed the vulnerability of slow and low-flying machines when it returned with bullet holes from groundfire. However, the possibility of casualties had to be accepted if the machines were to be of use. On 25 October aeroplanes brought back news of a pending Turkish attack, allowing defence plans to be made.

As the days passed the aeroplanes became ever more useful. They began directing land and naval gunfire, and on 1 November Tenenti Giulio Gavotti flew a Taube over Ain Zara and Taguira Oasis, throwing out four 2-kg Cipelli hand grenades. The effect of even

these tiny weapons was tremendous. Air bombing had begun. The first torpedo dropped by Guidoni from a Henry Farman has already been mentioned, and in February 1912 Piazza undertook the first ever photographic reconnaissance sortie in war, flying over Suani-Beni Adem.

During the winter of 1911–12 the size of the Air Flotilla expanded with new supplies from Italy, including Drachen tethered kite balloons and airships. The latter allowed 'heavy' bombing attacks. Eventually Libya came under Italian occupation.

Another pre-war campaign is worthy of mention. In 1913 Mexico was in the throes of revolution, with government forces under attack and mercenaries aiding various factions. Aeroplanes flew here and there, occasionally making the headlines. One such flight into fame came on 10 May, when the Frenchman Didier Masson attempted to bomb warships at Guaymas. Then, in November, Phillip Rader supporting General Huerta and Dean Ivan Lamb helping Venustiano Carranza met in the sky. They pulled pistols and fired at each other but without effect, apart from adding their names to the history books by recording the first ever air-to-air combat.

In the following year the US government sent an expeditionary force to march against Vera Cruz following border incidents. During this, US Navy flying-boats undertook mine-countermeasures and reconnaissance missions after being catapulted from USS *Birmingham* and *Mississippi*.

Of course, other incidents involving aeroplanes took place before August 1914, and it has to be remembered that in the early part of the year French Capt. Hervé and his observer lost their lives at the hands of desert tribesmen during a colonial campaign in Morocco.

Above: *Nieuport monoplane with an 80hp Gnome engine operating in 1911-12 with the Italian Air Flotilla against Turkey.*

The Kaiser's war

Since 1905 Germany had prepared and honed the Schlieffen Plan to subjugate its two main enemies, Russia and France. The Kaiser seized the opportunity to mobilize during the summer of 1914 after a series of crises edged Europe towards war. On 28 June 1914 an assassin wanting Slav independence had gunned down Archduke Franz Ferdinand, heir apparent to the Austro-Hungarian throne. Heavy demands from Austria-Hungary had fallen on Serbia, in turn causing Russia to mobilize. The Kaiser had his opportunity.

On 1 August Germany declared war on Russia. The next day German forces flooded into Luxembourg at the start of a planned march through Belgium to strike at France, against which war was declared on the 3rd. On the 4th Britain declared war on Germany, and during the course of the month Austria-Hungary sided with Germany, and Serbia and Japan declared war on Germany. Other nations later joined the war. To Britain's call came the forces of its Empire, making the conflict truly a world war.

Over the Western Front

For the Allies, 13 August 1914 was chosen as the date for the first RFC aeroplanes to cross to France, and on that day Nos 2, 3, 4 and 5 Squadrons flew across the Channel with a mixed bag of French and British machines.

On the 14th Frenchmen Lt. Césari and Corp. Prudhommeau made the very first Allied bombing attack of the war, targeting the Zeppelin sheds at Metz-Frescaty. The success of individual French attacks prompted the move towards a dedicated bombing Groupe within the Aviation Militaire, and on 27 September 1914 it was formed using mostly Voisin pusher biplanes. French bombing raids on Germany thereafter caused the German Army to concentrate its depleted rigid airship strength on French targets initially, when the Naval Airship Division wanted to mount a joint raid on London.

A B.E.2a biplane and a Blériot monoplane of No 4 Squadron undertook the first RFC mission over enemy lines of the war, on 19 August. From then on

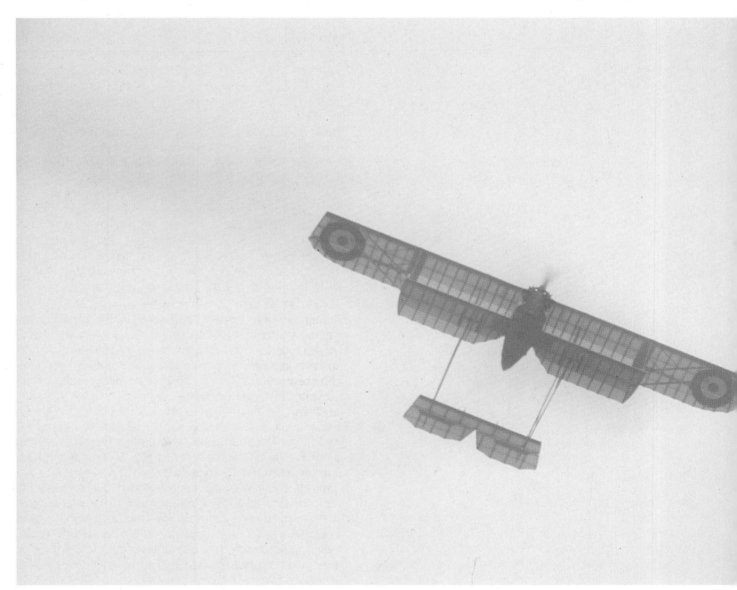

Right: *The French Caudron G.III was typical of the slow and almost defenceless reconnaissance aircraft flown on reconnaissance missions from the start of the First World War. Despite having a 'pod and boom' airframe usually associated with pusher-engined aircraft, the G.III mounted a tractor engine.*

As well-drilled German forces with modern armaments smashed through Belgium after free passage was refused and on into the fields of France, all was swept before them. The German people were elated at the early success, but the situation soon altered. Though lacking sufficient heavy guns, the Allies held the German advance during the First Battle of Ypres. By December the Central Powers were held at gunpoint across a Western Front of wire and trenches that ranged from the Franco-Swiss border to the North Sea. On the Eastern Front the Austro-Hungarian and German advance had also faltered into a bloody stalemate and this after aerial reconnaissance had assisted in the capture of 120,000 Russian troops and 500 heavy guns at the Battle of Tannenberg in the first month of war.

reconnaissance became the bread and butter duty of all air powers, the importance of this so aptly demonstrated when a French aeroplane spotted von Klück's forces moving towards the Marne on 3 September, allowing a defence to be planned in advance. But flying slow aircraft at relatively low levels over the enemy had its risks and on 22 August an Avro 504 belonging to No 5 Squadron was shot down over Belgium, the first RFC loss in action.

The parameters for flying successful reconnaissance missions had to be learned almost from scratch. Not only was there a need to increase the performance of aeroplanes expected to fly tens of miles behind enemy front lines, but there were benefits to both operations and crew morale if these were provided with reliable engines and the means to fight back if intercepted by an

armed enemy. Added to this, it was quickly realized that crews had to be taught certain skills if their missions were to be fully exploited. For a start, they had to understand the principles of ground warfare before they could appreciate what they saw from above and read the implications. The importance of photographic reconnaissance was another lesson, allowing daily updating of maps and enemy dispositions with an accuracy otherwise impossible to achieve.

Aerial photography was also useful to artillery units when preparing their targets, but when aeroplanes began direct spotting for the guns the results were not so pleasing. The inexperience of the flight crews, together with the use of Very lights or dropped messages to pass instructions, gave unpredictable results. Direct communication between air and ground was required, but this was a long time coming.

The first air victories

An air victory could be gained either by destroying the enemy's aircraft or by forcing it down. So it was that on 25 August 1914, Lt. Harvey-Kelly (the first RFC pilot to have landed in France on the 13th), in company with the crews of two other totally unarmed aircraft, forced a German two-seater to the ground. It was the RFC's first air victory. A German two-seater was also the first aeroplane to be shot down in the war, when on 5 October Frenchmen Sergent Joseph Frantz and Corporal Quénault managed to attack an Aviatik with their Voisin's Hotchkiss machine-gun while flying over Jonchery. There is an important distinction between this air victory and the actual first enemy aeroplane destroyed in air combat which took place on 26 August, when Russian pilot Capt. Petr Nikolaevich Nesterov had no choice but to ram his unarmed Morane into an Austro-Hungarian two-seater to bring it down (both crews losing their lives).

Above: *The Austrian Etrich Taube was widely built in Germany by various manufacturers before but especially after Igo Etrich gave up trying to enforce his patents in Germany. The bird-like monoplane flew reconnaissance and light bombing missions in the early stages of the war, the large German fleet being increased at the outbreak of hostilities by impressment of civil machines. Other operators included Austria-Hungary.*

Bombing offensives

At the beginning of the First World War about half the entire fleet of German military aeroplanes comprised Taube monoplanes. Designed in Austria by Igo Etrich and first flown in 1910, German manufacture of the Taube began in 1911. The very first bombs to fall on a capital city were dropped from a Taube flown by Leutnant Ferdinand von Hiddessen, on 30 August 1914. On this occasion one woman was killed and two other people injured at Quai de Valmy, Paris. With the five bombs was dropped a note boasting of the imminent arrival of German forces. Taubes even reached England, first striking at the Dover area in December.

Belgium had fewer than 20 aircraft in military service when Germany invaded and, with civilian machines hastily requisitioned, these undertook reconnaissance but were lost at an alarming rate. Those that survived formed the nucleus of a larger Allied presence around the Dunkirk and Ostend areas, from where RNAS aircraft ranged out on early bombing raids.

On the Eastern Front, although the Imperial Russian Flying Corps had begun the war with an aeroplane strength close in size to Germany's, many of the aeroplanes were old and practically worn out. The little it had in the way of an effective aircraft industry built under licence mainly French and German types plus a few British. The outbreak of war necessitated greater national effort to design indigenous aeroplanes, but to satisfy its immediate requirements many new machines came straight from France and America in 1915, the latter via the trans-Siberian railway. So, by the close of that year, the army and naval flying services were reasonably equipped. But effectiveness in operation was hindered by the huge distances over which spares had to travel, with the roads and railways already overwhelmed by the needs of the army. In 1916 Britain sent a mission to Russia to help upgrade the training of the air force, thereafter sending several hundred aeroplanes to assist in the fighting against Austria-Hungary and Germany.

The few indigenous aircraft produced by the Russians back in 1914 were generally mediocre. Surprisingly, then, it was a Russian designer who was to produce an aeroplane that, far from being average, was nothing short of a paralysing giant bomber. Igor Sikorsky had been a pioneer designer of both helicopters and aeroplanes. As Head of the Aeronautical Department of the Russian Baltic Railway Wagon Works in Petrograd, he had designed the *Le Grand*, a giant passenger-carrying biplane that had first flown at St. Petersburg on 13 May 1913. Not only was this the world's first four-engined aeroplane to fly but, such was its military potential, that from it was developed the *Ilya Mourometz* reconnaissance aircraft and bomber.

This military derivative was certainly no freak, but a carefully conceived long-range aircraft carrying a crew of up to 16 and a bomb load that varied as production increased to a maximum of 680kg (1,500 lb). The ten aircraft originally on order were quickly increased to 42 when war broke out, production eventually reaching 73

bombers. Service began in December 1914, with company pilots and engineers as the initial crews. The first bombing raid was undertaken against a target in Poland on 15 February 1915. Hundreds more missions were made.

Like Russia, Italy had been quick to see the merits of heavy bombing, with Caproni at the forefront of Italian multi-engined design. Having declared war against Austria-Hungary in May 1915, Italy used Caproni Ca 2s as the heart of its new strategic bomber force, which opened a sustained bombing offensive against Austria-Hungary on 20 August 1915. The aircraft flew over the Alps during the long missions. Capronis of this and later types also made night attacks and even became naval torpedo-bombers.

British bombing efforts received an incredible lift in late 1916 with the arrival of the RFC's first heavy bomber in the shape of the Handley Page O/100. Twin-engined, the O/100 had a range of about 1,125km (700 miles) and was capable of carrying a huge 907kg

Above: *Italy was a great exponent of strategic bombing during the First World War, with the Caproni company at the forefront of bomber production. The Ca 3 (illustrated) followed the Ca 2 into production in 1916 and 269 were completed for bombing and torpedo attack with Italian and French units.*

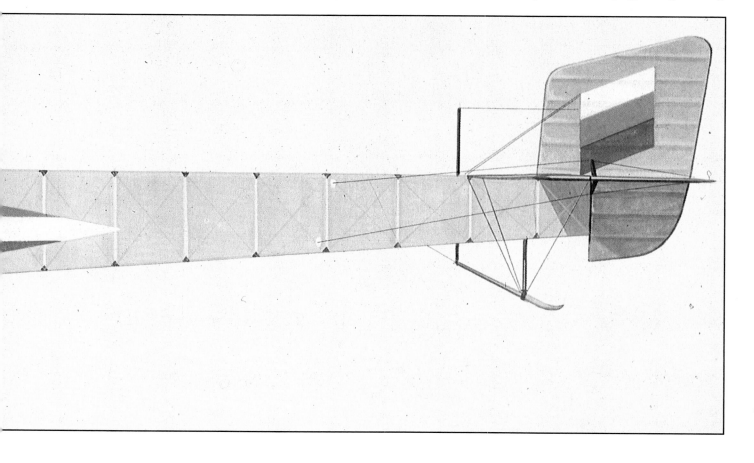

Left: *The Russian Sikorsky* Ilya Mourometz *reconnaissance-bomber, the largest operational aircraft of 1914 and initially flown on a strategic bombing mission in February 1915. Only three were lost during the war, one in a crash landing, one sabotaged and one shot down by fighters, the latter only after defending gunners had hit four of the enemy.*

(2,000 lb) warload. From it was developed the even better O/400. The impact of the O/100 was tremendous but losses sustained in daylight operations led to night missions. By then No 100 Squadron of the RFC had already stolen the honour of being the first British squadron formed specifically for night bombing; its small F.E.2bs began operations with two raids on the Douai fighter air base of the famed Richthofen Circus, on 5–6 April 1917. Strategic bombing proved so successful that on 5 June 1918 the RAF founded the Independent Force, intended specifically to concentrate on a strategic offensive against industrial and military targets within Germany, under the command of Major-General Sir Hugh Trenchard.

Other countries also employed sustained bombing operations during the war. Among the best remembered are the exploits of the giant Gothas flown by Germany, although purpose-designed bombers of varying sizes for German use also came from AEG, Friedrichshafen, Siemens-Schuckert, Zeppelin and others.

As German airships began to fail in their bombing role by mid-1917, mainly because of better air defences, so Germany turned to its new heavy bombing aeroplanes entering service in substantial numbers. No fewer than 21 Gothas opened mass German air raids on England, on 25 May 1917, with Folkestone and Shorncliffe among other towns receiving the full impact of the new weapons. On this occasion alone some 95 people were killed and 260 injured. Daylight raids on England lasted until August, by which time better British fighters recalled from the front to defend England had begun to inflict unacceptable losses. Missions switched to night, with the first mass Gotha raid in darkness striking at Dover on 3 September.

Above: *Handley Page O/400 heavy bombers in 1918, the best equipment of the Independent Force, RAF. Forty O/400s went on a single strike against targets in the Saar area in September 1918, recording the greatest bomber force to date.*

Right: *Handley Page O/400, identifiable from the earlier O/100 by its shorter engine nacelles and the extra bracing strut aft of these.*

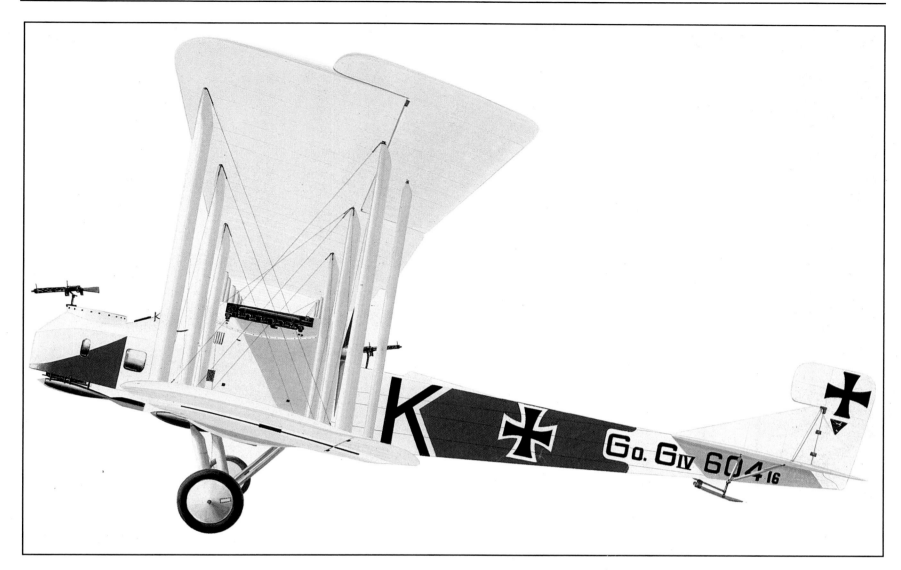

Above: *The German Gotha G.IV appeared in 1916, following limited production of the Gotha II and III bombers. G.IVs and G.Vs took over the main bombing offensive against Britain during May 1917 (from airships), switching to night raids from September. The main reason for their early success was that their two 260 hp Mercedes D.IVa engines allowed them to operate at 4,500-6,500m (15,000-21,300 ft) altitude, too high for defending fighters to reach in time without sufficient early warning.*

Right: *R (Riesen-flugzeug) series bombers were the largest deployed by the Germans during the First World War, dwarfing the G types and sometimes having up to six engines. Only 18 Zeppelin Staaken R.VIs were built by three manufacturers, 17 of them operating from the Ghent area.*

By 17 September even larger R-class bombers began operating against Britain, beginning with Zeppelin Staaken R.VIs. From February 1918 the R.VIs began to carry 1,000kg bombs (the largest of the war). Of course Britain was only one target for German bombers. It took a while for defences to become organized against these night attacks, but from January 1918 bombers raiding England began to be shot down (two Sopwith Camels of No 44 Squadron, RFC, gaining the first night victory over a Gotha). Added to losses in action were numerous accidents while landing after sorties. Bomber attacks on England ceased in May.

The French, the first to recognize the full potential of bombing, also produced large bombers, typically the Farman F.50, but for this nation its finest work was carried out by smaller machines. Probably the best of these was the Breguet 14, capable of carrying a 235kg (518 lb) warload and of flying at 195km/h (121 mph). By the Armistice, Breguet 14s had served with 55 French squadrons alone. This performance put it on a par with the British Airco D.H.9A, though both were considerably slower than the more lightly armed Airco D.H.4 that preceded the D.H.9A into service and which became such a favourite in America after the war.

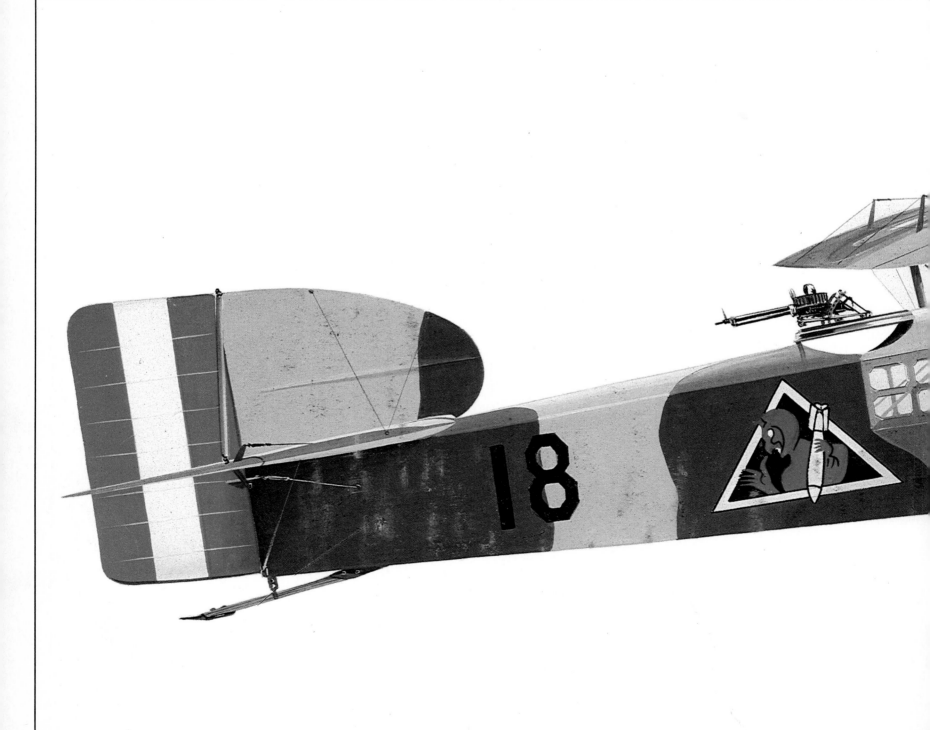

Left: *The Airco (de Havilland) D.H.9A light day bomber became a stalwart of the RAF for many years from 1918, the first few with 375hp Rolls-Royce Eagle VIII engines giving way to the main version with the planned US 400 hp Liberty in-line engine.*

Below: *French Breguet 14 light bombing (B2) and reconnaissance (A2) aircraft became operational in 1917, having been produced to replace obsolete 'pod and boom' Caudrons and Farmans. Examples served not only with French units but Belgian and American.*

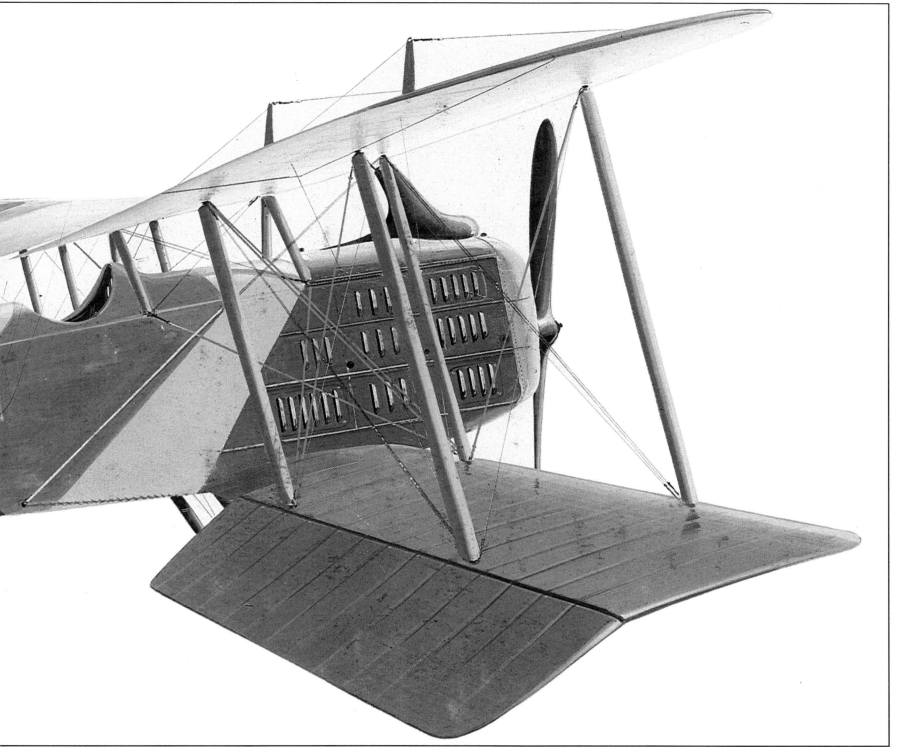

Right: *The last version of the Royal Aircraft Factory B.E.2 as the B.E.2e (shown here), evolved from the B.E.2c in 1916 and in consequence having an insufficient 90hp RAF 1a in-line engine and the movable Lewis gun in the forward cockpit where room to fire it was restricted.*

Contour fighting

Smaller warplanes were ideal for another form of attack, known as contour fighting. These sorties were mounted to disrupt communications, harass troop concentrations and reserves, and generally make the work of enemy land forces extremely difficult. Development of this form of air warfare was retarded to a degree by the lack of specialized machines, and perhaps the nearest to a perfect contour fighting plane was the German Junkers J.I of 1917–18. Although principally for close support, its all-metal armoured construction gave a measure of protection from ground fire that other aircraft lacked. This protection was also used on occasions to help it survive missions to fly ammunition and food to German trench troops cut off by the enemy. This aircraft was also equipped with radio communications.

Fighters

The majority of aircraft pushed into wartime service at the outbreak of hostilities in Europe had no permanent guns. Any pilot could carry tiny bombs in his cockpit to throw overboard if and when the opportunity arose, but there was an essential difference between this and proper armament. Those few machines that were armed had guns mainly for defence, and in the first days of aerial warfare air-to-air fighting usually took place by accident of meeting rather than deliberate policy.

Almost from the very start, aeroplanes used for reconnaissance showed themselves to be of far greater worth than an army's beloved cavalry or even armoured cars sent out on similar missions, covering huge areas far more quickly. By degrees the armies came to rely virtually entirely on aerial intelligence, and the ability of one side to prevent the other from gaining that intelligence was almost tantamount to 'blinding' it. And it was this need for supremacy of the skies that forced first the arming of reconnaissance aircraft and later the development of specialized fighters to destroy or escort.

All manner of ways were tried to arm aeroplanes, and in some early cases pilots were actively encouraged to carry personal pistols or carbines. Two-seaters were less problematical than single-seaters, as the observer could be given a gun on a flexible mounting to aim and fire in almost any direction away from the wings and propeller. For single-seaters, it was not so easy. One early solution was to build 'pusher' engined aeroplanes or fix a gun on the upper wing of a front-engined machine to fire outside the propeller arc, despite the

difficulties this imposed on the pilot when aiming. Officials in Britain, in particular, had faith in the flexibly-mounted front gun, not really understanding why pilots chose to leave the gun 'fixed' in one position and manoeuvre the whole aircraft to point the weapon.

1915 was the year that brought air fighting to the forefront. Raymond Saulnier had long been interested in arming military aeroplanes, and pre-war had invented a form of gun synchronization gear. The Morane-Saulnier Type L parasol monoplane used from the start of the war was one type of machine occasionally tried with a wing gun, achieving some success. But, still convinced of the need to fire at eye-level through the propeller arc, he devised a simple system involving deflector wedges attached to the propeller blades to prevent bullets damaging the propeller as they streamed through the arc. The first Type L equipped in this manner was handed over to Roland Garros, who for several days from 1 April 1915 claimed a number of enemy aircraft destroyed. Then, on the 19th, he was forced to land behind enemy lines and was captured before he could destroy his weapon system. The aeroplane was taken by the Germans for examination, prompting the consideration of a similar gun arrangement. Morane-Saulnier, meanwhile, continued for a while to fit deflector wedges to various machines.

A better system was devised in Germany, however, resulting in a fully successful synchronization (or interrupter) gear which timed the bullets to pass

between the turning blades without striking them. First fitted to the ill-fated LVG E.VI two-seater, an improved system was devised by Anthony Fokker and installed on his company's own small and highly manoeuvrable M 5K *Eindecker*. An armed Fokker M 5KMG was first used for trials at the Front and on 1 July 1915 Leutnant Kurt Wintgens shot down a French Morane-Saulnier while flying it. The initial production version of the armed *Eindecker* was the E.I, itself arriving at Douai on the Western Front for trials in July 1915. In the hands of Leutnant Max Immelmann it claimed its first Allied victim on 1 August. Improved and higher-powered E models followed. At first Immelmann, Oswald Boelcke

and Hauptmann Kastner had to share the first E.Is; but as more became available, other pilots trained and the air war over the Western Front took its first decisive turn. The first of many great German 'aces' were ranging unchecked.

The impact on the air war was immediate. Allied aircraft, unarmed or inadequately armed to defend themselves, were being shot out of the skies. Among the worst affected were the RFC's B.E.2s, so inherently stable for good reconnaissance and light bombing that they were sitting ducks to the highly manoeuvrable and faster *Eindeckers*. It was a time of crisis for the Allies. Valuable armed aircraft had to be diverted from other duties to escort bombers and reconnaissance aircraft on missions. The so-called 'Fokker Scourge' lasted through the winter of 1915–16, finally brought under control with deployment by the Allies' of the first purpose-designed armed single-seat fighters, like the Nieuport 11 *Bébé* biplanes (gun on upper wing) and the Airco D.H.2 'pushers'.

Below: *E.III, the most numerous production version of the famous Fokker* Eindecker *fighter, armed with one Parabellum or later Spandau machine-gun with interrupter gear. The 100hp Oberursel rotary engine provided only a 140km/h (87 mph) top speed, but the gun arrangement made it a deadly weapon against poorly defended Allied aircraft. But its reign of terror lasted only the winter of 1915-16.*

Eindecker. An armed Fokker M 5KMG was first used for trials at the Front and on 1 July 1915 Leutnant Kurt Wintgens shot down a French Morane-Saulnier while

Above: *Of 5,720 Sopwith 1½-Strutters built for fighter, bombing and reconnaissance roles, 4,200 were constructed in France. Their career on the Western Front began in early 1916 with the British services, French deployment not starting until a year later, by which time the design was past its best.*

Below: *The Nieuport 17 appeared on the Western Front in early 1916 as the latest French single-seat fighter derived from the Nieuport 11 and 16. First Nieuport 17s retained the old arrangement of having a single Lewis gun on the upper wing to clear the propeller arc, but later examples (as shown) adopted a Vickers gun.*

flying it. The initial production version of the armed *Eindecker* was the E.I, itself arriving at Douai on the Western Front for trials in July 1915. In the hands of Leutnant Max Immelmann it claimed its first Allied

ized forward gun. But the balance was short-lived. During the autumn the Germans began deploying new high-class fighters, typified by the elegant Albatros D.I and D.II biplanes with twin machine-guns and large engines to offer high speeds and stunning rates of climb.

The Allies had also received new single-seat fighters of outstanding quality, such as the Sopwith Pup and Spad VII, but the number of German machines proved overwhelming, with Britain also having to divert squadrons for air defence and French production

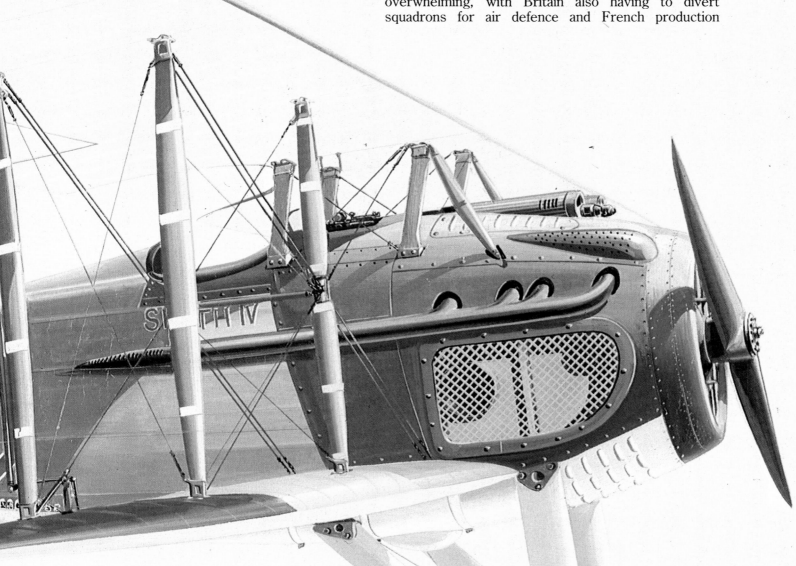

victim on 1 August. Improved and higher-powered E models followed. At first Immelmann, Oswald Boelcke and Hauptmann Kastner had to share the first E.Is; but as more became available, other pilots trained and the air war over the Western Front took its first decisive turn.

The impact on the air war was immediate. Allied aircraft, unarmed or inadequately armed to defend themselves, were being shot out of the skies. Among the worst affected were the RFC's B.E.2s, so inherently stable for good reconnaissance and light bombing that they were sitting ducks to the highly manoeuvrable and faster *Eindeckers*. It was a time of crisis for the Allies. Valuable armed aircraft had to be diverted from other duties to escort bombers and reconnaissance aircraft on missions. The so-called 'Fokker Scourge' lasted through the winter of 1915–16, finally brought under control with deployment by the Allies' of the first purpose-designed armed single-seat fighters, like the Nieuport 11 *Bébé* biplanes (gun on upper wing) and the Airco D.H.2 'pushers'.

Slowly the balance of air power between the antagonists was restored. The Bristol Scout, used since 1914, appeared for its final months of service in 1916 with a synchronized machine-gun, having previously sported many less successful forms of armament including duck guns. It was joined that year by the all-new Sopwith 1½-Strutter multi-purpose two-seater with a synchron-

stretched by its commitment to supply other Allied air forces. These difficulties culminated in the bitter air battles of 'bloody April' 1917, when the Allies were shot down in huge numbers over the Western Front. Among the terrible losses were again to be found B.E.2s, still being mass produced despite the obvious limitations of their deployment. New tactics also worked in Germany's favour, especially the adoption of 'circuses' that concentrated large formations of fighters in particular areas to stalk and engage the enemy on its own terms. The great exponent of this was, of course, von Richthofen, who honed the tactic to a fine art.

Above: *Follow-on single-seat fighter to the Spad VII, the Spad XIII entered service from May 1917, the typical 235hp Hispano-Suiza 8 Be in-line engine bestowing a 222km/h (138 mph) top speed. By the Armistice nearly 8,500 had been built for French, American, Belgian and Italian squadrons, with 10,000 more on order.*

Above: *The Fokker VII provided the last major challenge to Allied air supremacy over the Western Front.*

Right: *The Sopwith Camel was probably the best single-seat fighter of the First World War.*

Below: *Nieuport 11, with its Lewis gun mounted on the upper wing to fire outside the propeller arc.*

But again the Allies resisted total air defeat. New machines went into service in great numbers. Except for a slight hiccup with the arrival of the Fokker D.VII fighter in mid-1918, the Allies maintained air supremacy for the remainder of the war. American squadrons began arriving in France in February 1918 and began operational missions on 11 April, remembering that US pilots had earlier served as volunteers with the air forces of other Allied nations since 1915, including the famed French Lafayette Escadrille.

American domestic production was best suited to contribute trainers and flying-boats to the immediate war effort, so American pilots flew mainly French, British and Italian warplanes. Given the short duration of America's involvement in the war, encompassing the period when the Soviet–German peace treaty had stilled the Eastern Front and allowed Germany to commit massive forces to its spring 1918 offences, it is remarkable that 88 Americans became 'aces' (a title

Above: *The Sopwith Camel drew its name from its stocky appearance and a hump covering the breeches of the twin Vickers guns.*

Left: *Captain Albert Ball, RFC, who became the first great British fighter ace.*

Below: *One of the finest British single-seat fighters of 1917-18 was the Royal Aircraft Factory S.E.5A.*

awarded for five or more air victories) before the Armistice. Names like Captain Edward Rickenbacker and Second-Lt. Frank Luke thereafter lived in fame alongside those of German Rittmeister Manfred Freiherr von Richthofen ('the Red Baron'), Frenchmen Capitaine René Fonck, Lt. Charles Nungesser and Capitaine Georges Guynemer, Britons Captain Albert Ball and Major Edward Mannock, Canadian Major William A. Bishop and many others.

Anti-aircraft defence of cities

At the start of the war anti-aircraft defences were almost non-existent. This is not to say the Allies, and in particular Britain, were not concerned by the threat posed by Germany's long-range airships (see page 70). If anything, Britain had an exaggerated view of their capability. But needs must, and equipment priority had to be given to the fighting fronts, not least because, by attacking airships in their sheds, prevention was better than cure.

With the exception of the odd nuisance raid by Taubes and similar small machines, the Allies were not

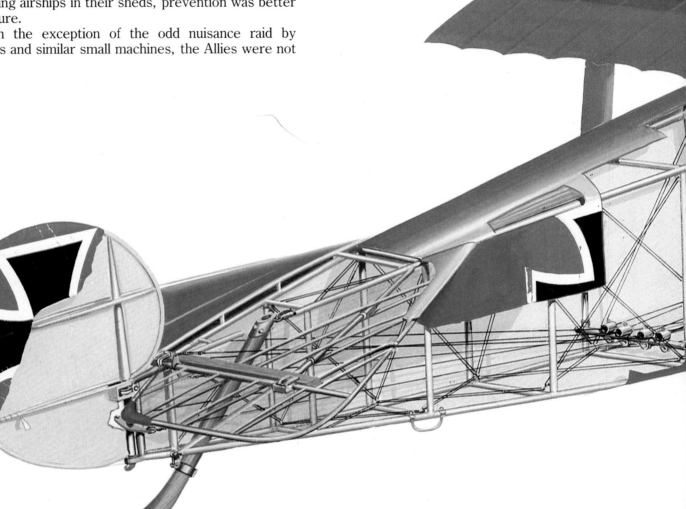

Right: With the success of the British Sopwith Triplane fighter in RNAS hands during 1917, German manufacturers attempted to produce equally successful triplanes. Fokker achieved this with its Dr.I, powered ironically by German or Swedish built versions of the French 110hp Le Rhone rotary engine (typically Oberursel UR.II).

immediately troubled by aeroplane bombing of cities. Neither had the expected Zeppelin menace materialized by the end of 1914. But in the following year airship attacks became a more serious problem.

In Britain, responsibility for home defence had passed to the Admiralty, who alone had not over-stretched their resources. Aeroplanes were withdrawn from the front for home defence, but in turn this meant that Fokker *Eindeckers* received even greater freedom of action on the Western Front than might otherwise have been the case.

Then in 1916 the Admiralty, having seen Britain through a most difficult period, passed control of home defence to the War Office, which provided the necessary equipment to organize more coherently. Squadrons of night fighters were based in key positions, and vulnerable areas received better and more numerous searchlights, guns and ammunition. The destruction of

Schütte-Lanz SL XI over Britain during the night of 2 September 1916 confirmed that the organization was working.

It had been expected that as airships became less successful in long-range bombing, so large aeroplanes would take over. As foreseen, Gothas and other types began arriving over Britain in early 1917, first in daylight and then at night. They wreaked heavy damage at little cost to themselves. A complete rethink of the defences for London and the South of England brought about a highly developed and unified system of aeroplanes, guns, searchlights and sound locators, backed by elaborate communications. Another innovation was the high-altitude tethered balloon apron, consisting of three balloons set 914m (1,000 yards) apart and connected by wire, trailing an apron of long steel-cable streamers through which aeroplanes could not fly safely. The other major combatant nations adopted

Below: *Le Prieur rockets carried by a Nieuport fighter for anti-airship duties.*

similar systems, including aprons, Venice putting up balloons with a less elaborate screen of cables to protect its architectural treasures.

The key component in anti-aircraft defence was, however, always the aeroplane itself, and this was to remain so until the advent of surface-to-air missiles after the Second World War. In this first of the world wars special weapons had been devised to make airship interceptions effective, ranging from steel darts dropped from above in the early days to incendiary ammunition and, later, Le Prieur type rocket projectiles fired from aeroplanes. In defence, as in every other avenue of air warfare, the application of new technologies had met each new crisis as it appeared. And while on the ground final victory had been won by attrition, in the air constant renewal of the machines of war to gain that extra little edge had been as important as weight of numbers.

Chapter 6: Airships

Back in October 1784 Jean-Pierre Blanchard had been the first to fit a propeller to a balloon in the hope of adding propulsion. This, he hoped, would overcome a fundamental problem, the inability to go anywhere other than the direction dictated by the wind. As a power source it failed, and balloonists resigned themselves to catching the right weather conditions if they intended to journey in a particular direction.

But right from the beginning of manned lighter-than-air flight there had been those who saw no point in aircraft that couldn't be controlled. They sought to overcome this by rethinking the basic design of the envelope. Thus the airship was conceived, a larger craft with an elongated envelope offering greater stability and lifting power, and the possibility of being directed and powered. A powered airship able to be navigated took the technical name 'dirigible', although the term 'airship' was more widely used.

Soon after the Montgolfiers had exhibited a balloon to the Académie des Sciences, an Academician named Monsieur Monge suggested linking a large number of manned spherical balloons together. The crews would cause their individual craft to ascend or descend and so 'snake' the chain through the air. It was never put to the test. Far more practical, but also rejected by the Académie, was the design for an airship by Lt. Jean-Baptiste Marie Meusnier of the French Corps of Engineers (in 1784). The envelope had two skins, the inner spherical envelope holding the hydrogen, while the outer maintained the elongated 'cigar' configuration using compressed air. Venting gas from the inner envelope to maintain the required altitude wouldn't, therefore, cause distortion in the craft's outer shape that might otherwise affect stability when landing. What undoubtedly caused its downfall in the eyes of the Académie was its tremendous size and the need to have no fewer than 80 men on board to work the large sails/propellers.

But the Meusnier idea of one gas-tight envelope inside another was adopted in a new way by the Robert brothers when they constructed their own cylindrical airship, which took to the air on 15 July 1784. This reversed Meusnier's concept by having a flexible air bag inside the main gas envelope, with vented air causing changes in altitude. In the event, the envelope had to be pierced during the first flight to relieve pressure and overall the airship was not a particular success. However, the importance of the craft from an historical viewpoint lay in the flexible inner air bag, a feature later called a *ballonet*. This was essential to the subsequent development of airships, used to compensate for variations in lifting gas volume and thereby maintain envelope superpressure and alter trim.

The expense and difficulty involved in constructing airships, which might have questionable flying capability compared to the known attributes of the simple balloon, caused a long lead-in period before the first successful craft appeared. It is to 1852, therefore, that historians look for the next milestone, while remembering that other designs had by then innocently come and gone. In that year Frenchman Henri Giffard gave the world its first airship capable of being steered, and one fitted with a 3 hp steam engine driving a propeller, so making this the first ever manned, powered and controllable aircraft. During its first flight on 24 September, Giffard navigated the 44m (144 ft) craft (a true dirigible) from the Hippodrome in Paris to Trappes, a journey of about 27km (17 miles). Average speed was a mere 8km/h (5 mph).

Two decades later Austrian Paul Hänlein produced a 50m (164 ft) airship with a 5 hp Lenoir four-cylinder engine fuelled by gas taken from the envelope. Although this might not seem a particularly practical solution to long distance flying, the engine actually consumed only a touch over 7m³ (250 cu ft) of gas each hour and the envelope capacity was 2,407m³ (85,000 cu ft). This is remembered as the first aircraft of any type to use an internal combustion engine. Unfortunately, Hänlein hadn't the capital to continue development beyond tethered flights.

Gaston Tissandier, one of the heroes of the Paris siege, had tried on several occasions to balloon back into the city, but to no avail. It can hardly come as a surprise, therefore, that he took great interest in navigable lighter-than-air craft. On 8 October 1883 he flew the first airship to use an electric motor (a Siemens using 24 batteries).

France first

The following year, 1884, was a watershed in the

Below: *Sectional drawing of French Lt. Jean-Baptiste Marie Meusnier's airship, with inner and outer envelopes and three large manually-turned propellers.*

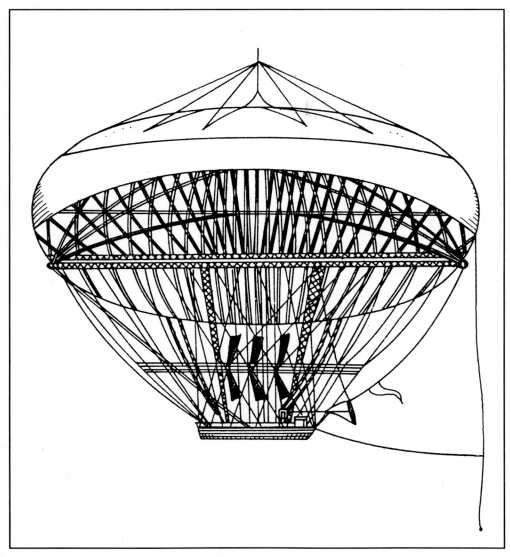

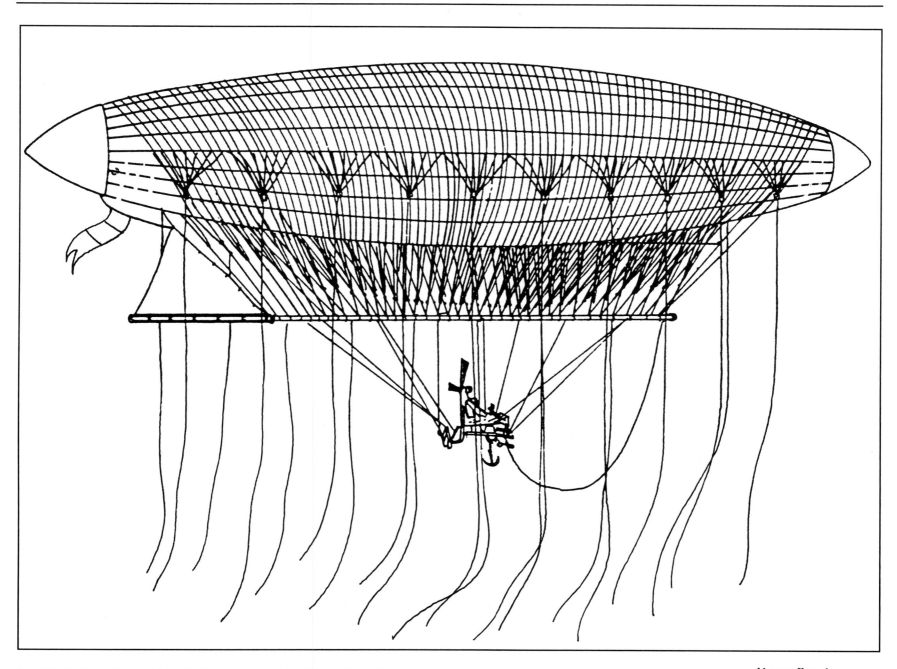

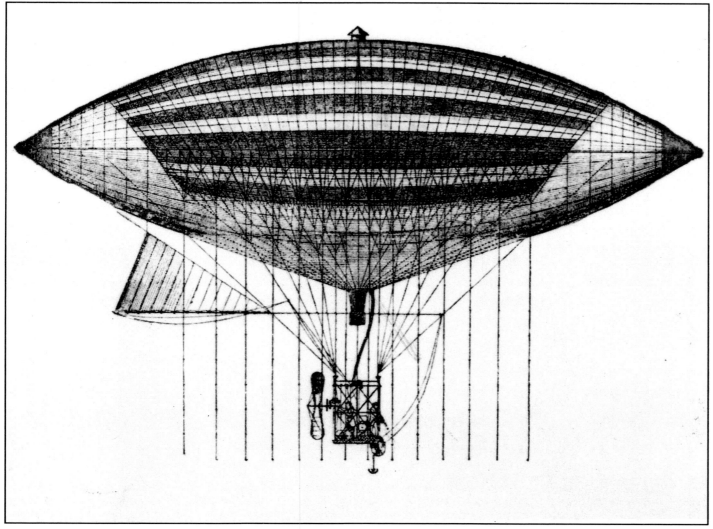

Above: *Frenchman Henri Giffard produced the world's first manned and powered airship capable of being navigated in 1852.*

Left: *Gaston Tissandier's electrically powered airship of 1883.*

development of airships and marked the ascendancy of France before Germany took the initiative. On 9 August that year Capitaine Charles Renard and Lt. Arthur Krebs of the French Corps of Engineers lifted off from Chalais-Meudon in the airship *La France* to make a circular flight of about 8km (5 miles). This lasted 23 minutes. For the first time a fully controllable airship had flown, and one capable of a reasonable 24km/h (14 mph) on the output of a 9 hp Gramme electric motor. The 'dirigible' as a practical flying machine for planned voyages in any direction had arrived.

Having developed the first petrol internal combustion engines, Germany was naturally the first to fit one to an airship, a 2 hp Daimler giving Dr. Karl Wölfert the necessary power source to send a mechanic on a short flight from Seelberg on 12 August. But this was just a small trial craft that followed eight years of earlier experiments; Wölfert had crashed in his very first airship in 1880. Experiments continued until 1897, when he and his mechanic were killed while testing the new *Deutschland* (on 14 June). The conflagration that resulted from the engine vaporizer setting the envelope alight and igniting the hydrogen into a great fireball was a sign of things to come.

Jules ROUFF & Cie Editeur:

Right: La France *became the world's first fully controllable airship, demonstrating a circular flight of about 8km (5 miles) in 1884.*

Zeppelins

The death of Wölfert might have been a severe blow to German ambitions had it not been for a certain elderly aristocrat of Württemberg by the name of Count Ferdinand von Zeppelin. Born on 8 July 1838, von Zeppelin had joined the Army in 1857, and as a young officer in his twenties travelled to America where the Civil War was raging. It was while in America that he had his first experience of lighter-than-air flying. He intended to make the Army his lifelong career, but in 1890 he lost his commission as a lieutenant-general after criticizing the Prussian ministry of war. Disgraced by the Army he loved, von Zeppelin now put all his efforts into the airship. Employing the skills of Theodore Kober – as von Zeppelin was an 'ideas' man, not an engineer – the *Deutschland* was prepared on paper. In 1894 it was submitted to an official technical commission arranged by the Kaiser and headed by Professor Hermann von Helmholz. It was rejected.

The *Deutschland* had been conceived to be a great flying cylinder, 117m (384 ft) in length and kept rigid by a metal framework of tubes and sheets. Passengers and freight were to be accommodated in separately linked modules, the whole pulled through the air by two 11 hp Daimler internal combustion engines like a giant aerial express train.

A totally new approach was needed, especially if he was to achieve official approval, and what better way to achieve both than to use the talents of Professor Müller-Breslau, who sat on the commission. Thus was conceived a new form of rigid framework, comprising a series of braced rings, designed for light weight and high strength, inside which could be housed the many individual hydrogen bags and over which the envelope could be attached. The classic 'cigar'-shaped Zeppelin had been born, but who remembers the name Müller-Breslau?

Already four years had passed since the Commission had rejected *Deutschland* but now plans moved ahead apace. That May the Joint Stock Company for Promotion of Airship Flight was founded, and in the following year (1899) construction of LZ 1 began in the specially fabricated floating hangar on Lake Constance.

From the outset, von Zeppelin had thought big, and LZ 1 was a magnificent 128m (420 ft) long, with a diameter of 11.73m (38 ft 6 in) and a volume of 11,300m³ (399,050 cu ft). Power came from two 16 hp Daimler engines, which later proved inadequate and allowed only 26km/h (16.5 mph), about half that anticipated. The day for the launch was fixed, and on 2 July 1900 the LZ 1 rose clear of its hangar. Not only were the engines underpowering the craft but control was ineffective. Somehow LZ 1 managed to alight safely and modifications were put in hand. The second flight took place on 17 October but control was still a problem. After a third flight the airship was scrapped in 1901. For a craft that used up all the finances of the company, it flew only for a little over two hours in total.

The huge investment needed to build a second airship delayed the start until 1905, but construction was rapid and the stronger LZ 2 emerged. The most important difference between this craft and LZ 1 was the adoption of two mighty 85 hp Daimler engines. The first flight of LZ 2 nearly ended in disaster and the crew and designers wore long faces as the airship was towed back to its hangar and temporary safety. A second flight was scheduled for 17 January 1906 and this time all began well. With the engines roaring, LZ 2 made a controlled ascent to 450m (1,500 ft) and cruised at a remarkable 53km/h (33 mph). Then it happened: first one motor failed and then the other, leaving the giant at the mercy of high winds. With courage the crew fought for control and eventually managed to alight at Kisslegg some 30km (19 miles) away. But the worst was not over, and during the dark hours a gale finished the airship off.

Using what remained of his private wealth, von Zeppelin tried one last hand and built LZ 3, which first ascended on 9 October 1906. At last here was a Zeppelin worthy of the name and, though not perfect, it flew well. With two 115 hp Daimlers it was even faster than LZ 2. It completed a 97km (60 mile) flight of two hours duration and in September of the following year amazed everyone with an eight-hour journey.

This was the breakthrough. The Army liked what they saw and thought it had military potential, but first

Below: *Zeppelin LZ 1 tethered over Lake Constance before its first flight on 2 July 1900, having been towed from its floating hangar. Count von Zeppelin is at the controls.*

Above: *Zeppelin LZ 3, the first rigid airship to fly well and later sold to the German Army as Z 1.*

Right: *Zeppelin LZ 4, destroyed on 5 August 1908 during a long-endurance Army trial flight.*

wanted certain guarantees. Clearly such a large airship was most useful for long-range patrolling and so before purchase LZ 3 had to show that it could fly for a full day and night, during which 700km (435 miles) had to be covered to an appointed destination and back to the assigned station. In other words, a fully controlled long-endurance mission.

Von Zeppelin viewed this as beyond the capabilities of the LZ 3 but offered to construct a further airship to meet those requirements. LZ 4 was of similar length to LZ 3 but had approximately 20 per cent greater volume, and its slightly lower-output Daimler engines gave it marginally increased speed. Finished by mid-1908, it made an experimental flight to Switzerland at the beginning of July before setting out on the full Army trial on 4 August. All began well, but 11 hours into the flight an engine broke down. Putting such a huge craft down on an unprepared track of land was not easy and it alighted instead on the Rhine. After fixing the engine and lightening the payload, LZ 4 set off again for Mainz and, having reached there, turned back. But fate had more problems in store. As the crew settled to a comfortable cruise, engine failure again forced a landing. While repairs were underway a storm broke, catching the airship and ripping it loose. It caught fire and fell to earth, a damp smouldering heap.

In the wreckage at Echterdingen lay von Zeppelin's hopes. But he had become something of a national hero and quite unexpectedly huge sums of money voluntarily donated by the public flooded in. Suspicious of Prussian government officials who tried to take control of the donations, von Zeppelin established the Zeppelin Foundation for the Promotion of Aerial Navigation. With the money he constructed LZ 5, a sister ship to the unfortunate LZ 4, and this craft plus the earlier LZ 3 were bought for the Army in 1909, becoming Z II and Z I respectively. Z I served out a full life until deletion in 1913, whilst Z II was destroyed after a forced landing in November 1910.

The later LZ 14 became the first German Navy Zeppelin, as L 1, having first flown on 7 October 1912 and completed a 1,450km (900 mile) proving flight a

week later. Much the largest of the early Zeppelins, with a length of 158m (518 ft) and a volume of 22,475m^3 (793,700 cu ft), it had three 165 hp Maybach engines to offer 80km/h (50 mph). Such was its capability for patrolling large areas of the North Sea that a five-year programme was instituted by the Navy in January 1913 to see the construction of ten new airships and a new station at Nordholz. Thus, in a stroke, the foundations were laid that made the German Naval Airship Division by far the greatest operator of rigid airships in the coming world war.

Like von Zeppelin himself, this Airship Division had to endure early hardships and tragedies that threatened its very existence: L 1 went down in the North Sea during a storm with the loss of 14 lives on 9 September 1913, and L 2 (the first Zeppelin designed to be capable of carrying bombs to England) caught fire over Johannisthal with the loss of 28 lives only five weeks later. But the military service did survive and by the end of the First World War it had operated 69 Zeppelin and Schütte-Lanz airships, although many of these and about 40 per cent of its personnel had been lost (the highest percentage of any military service). The enormity of this loss compares to just 16 officers and 32 other ranks killed within the British Airship Service during the war.

Before leaving the military aspect of early German

Above: German Naval Airship Division Zeppelin LZ 45, carrying the military designation L13. First flown on 23 July 1915, it was commissioned two days later. Among the most successful wartime Zeppelins, it flew 159 times, including 17 bombing raids and 45 scouting patrols, ending its career in April 1917 when it was decommissioned and dismantled that December.

Below: Zeppelin LZ 14, as German Naval airship L1 on manoevres with the fleet.

airships, further mention has to be made of Dr. Johann Schütte, whose Schütte-Lanz company specialized in constructing rigid airships with wooden framework. The SL 1, first flown on 17 October 1911, was purchased by the German Army, as was SL 2. On the latter craft, which was completed in February 1914, the company introduced advances well beyond those incorporated into contemporary Zeppelins. Notwithstanding the plywood girder structure, SL 2 featured efficient cruciform tail surfaces, a highly streamlined hull, and many other design initiatives which, unfortunately for the company, were allowed to be used by von Zeppelin as well once the government took control of the patents after war broke out. SL 2 carried out excellent work on both Western and Eastern Fronts before a storm ended its career in 1916. SL 2 is considered by historians to have been the first truly modern dirigible. The first naval Schütte-Lanz was SL 3, which also lasted into 1916, having been launched in 1915.

Other countries

The purpose behind the development of airships in the first instance had been to produce aircraft capable of being navigated. Only then would flying have real benefits. The circular flight by *La France* had brought that day close, and when Alberto Santos-Dumont flew his tiny 33m (108 ft) *No 6* airship around the Eiffel Tower in Paris on 19 October 1901, controlled flying was again evident.

While von Zeppelin reflected over the loss of LZ 1, he must have been inspired (or exasperated) at further French success when, on 12 November 1903, the Lebaudy brothers coaxed a 60km (37 mile) flight between Moisson and Champ-de-Mars from their semi-rigid *Le Jaune*. (A semi-rigid is an airship with a single structural member along the envelope to carry and distribute loads and help maintain envelope shape.) The second Lebaudy airship appeared in 1904, featuring a volume of 2,660m^3 (93,940 cu ft) and powered, ironically, by a 40 hp Daimler. This was bought by the French Government and became the first ever military airship. Many other Lebaudy airships followed.

By then non-rigid airships (without any rigid framework) were also doing well, the famous *Société Astra des Constructions Aéronautiques* balloon company producing many airships from 1907, beginning with the *Ville de Paris* that was presented to the French Army for use from Verdun by Henry Deutche de la Meurthe. Non-rigids were also the trade of Maison Clément-Bayard.

Of course, other countries too had built airships by 1910, including Austria, Belgium, Great Britain, Italy, Japan, Russia, Spain, and the USA, but none were of the large rigid type. Britain was the first of these countries to place an airship in army service, its *Dirigible No 1*, popularly named *Nulli Secundus*, having first flown on 10 September 1907 with Colonel John Capper, Captain W. A. C. King and Mr. Samuel Cody on board (accommodated in an open gondola that also carried the 50 hp Antoinette engine). But Britain had to wait until September 1911 for its first large rigid airship to appear, the Vickers R1 *Mayfly* even then being wrecked at Barrow in a handling accident before a single flight had been made. In the event, while eight other rigids did appear in Britain between 1916 and 1918, late plans to begin an offensive campaign against Germany using airships were thwarted by the Armistice. And so it was to patrol non-rigids that Britain owed most of its 87,700 wartime flying hours by the Airship Service.

Far left: *In 1901 Alberto Santos-Dumont gave a good demonstration of controlled airship flying by navigating his airship No 6 around the Eiffel Tower, Paris.*

Below: *The* Nulli Secundus II, *a rebuilt version of its predecessor, and launched in July, 1908.*

The first airline

Returning briefly to 1909, von Zeppelin had anticipated further immediate orders for his airships from the Army after the sale of LZ 3 and 5, and constructed the LZ 6 against this likelihood. However, Army trials had unexpectedly favoured smaller semi-rigids and non-rigids of the types being manufactured by the German Military Airship Works and August von Parseval, despite their shorter range. The Count was left with a giant airship on his hands. To make use of it, and get the Army to see the folly of its ways, he established *Die Deutsche Luftschiffahrt Aktiengesellschaft* on 16 October. Better known as Delag, it was the world's first commercial airline company. Persuaded of the benefits, various German cities stumped up most of the money for the enterprise, each also preparing a shed. Yet once again the road to success was to be hard won.

Delag passenger flying began with LZ 6 in 1910, making this the world's first commercial aircraft, but by the late summer it was a burnt-out wreck lying in its shed. LZ 7 *Deutschland*, the airline's second craft, had already by then become the victim of a storm at Teutoburger Wald. Delag's third airship was LZ 8 *Ersatz Deutschland*, launched in 1911 but destroyed in a docking accident that May. Fortunately, none of the passengers on board LZ 7 and LZ 8 were injured.

The situation again looked extremely bleak for the Count, who gambled once more with the construction of LZ 10 *Schwäben*. Appearing on 15 July 1911, and with Dr. Hugo Eckener at the helm, it began a long run of successful flights that lasted until 28 June 1912 when it caught fire in its shed at Düsseldorf. By then LZ 11 *Viktoria Luise* was in regular service, and later came LZ 13 *Hansa* and LZ 17 *Sachsen*. *Hansa* was used by Delag to begin the first international services on 19 September 1912, linking Hamburg with Copenhagen in Denmark and Malmö in Sweden.

Delag continued operating until November 1913, by which time over 34,000 passengers had been carried without fatality. Because of their generally similar configuration to military Zeppelins, the Naval Airship Division made use of Delag craft from the outset for training, sometimes flying actual services. After the Armistice of 1918, Delag reopened its airship services on 24 August 1919 using the new LZ 120 *Bodensee*, linking Friedrichshafen with Berlin. However, this was closed by the Allied Control Commission on 1 December after 103 flights had carried 2,400 passengers and 30,000kg (66,140 lb) of freight. In the following year the airship was passed to Italy. A further airship intended for Delag, LZ 121 *Nordstern*, was taken over by France in 1921.

Right: *Delag passenger-carrying Zeppelin LZ 10* Schwäben *above its shed at Düsseldorf.*

Right: *With the intention of renewing Delag's passenger services after the First World War, Zeppelin LZ 120* Bodensee *was built to fly between Friedrichshafen and Berlin.*

Airships at war

The Italian Air Flotilla took the first aeroplanes to war in October 1911 in its dispute with Turkey over territories in North Africa (see page 53). It increased its air power during that winter with the receipt of extra aeroplanes and airships. The airships were widely used for reconnaissance and were also employed for what might then have passed for 'heavy' bombing.

German use of airships, as predicted by the British, was immediate and effective on the outbreak of the First World War. On 12 August 1914 Naval Zeppelin L 3 (LZ 24) found the Dutch battleship *de Zeven Provincien* and accompanying destroyers near Terschelling Island. But it was for their bombing raids against England that Zeppelins are best remembered.

The fear that German long-range airships would strike at targets in England as well as perform important long-endurance patrols over the North Sea was uppermost in British minds on the outbreak of war; it had been foreseen once Delag began operating successfully in 1912. It therefore became high priority to destroy them.

A fortnight after the first RFC aeroplanes flew to France, it became the turn of the first Royal Naval Air Service (RNAS) aircraft, a collection of eleven varied machines belonging to Wing Commander Charles R. Samson's Eastchurch Squadron. Not a single aeroplane had fixed armament. The only armed aircraft belonging to the squadron was the Astra-Torres *No 3* airship, and this was soon returned home. But it was this squadron that first took the fight to the Zeppelins, when on 22 September four pilots flying biplanes left their base in Antwerp with hand-held 9kg (20 lb) Hales impact bombs intent on dropping them on the German airship sheds at Cologne and Düsseldorf. Only the Avro 504 flown by Flight Lt. Collet found its target at Düsseldorf, but all three bombs proved dud. Despite the failure of the missions, this is still remembered as the first British air attack on Germany.

On 8 October, with the German Army just a day away from Antwerp, the squadron took another opportunity to hit the same two airship bases. One Sopwith Tabloid was assigned to each. Squadron-Commander D. A. Spenser-Grey flew into mist and was unable to locate the Cologne sheds and bombed the railway station instead, but Flight Lt. R.L.G. Marix had better luck. Flying low to ensure accuracy, he dropped Hales bombs from 180m (600 ft). The effect was incredible. The shed housed Army Zeppelin Z.IX (LZ 25) and it burst into a great fireball hundreds of feet high. Marix's aeroplane, however, was hit by machine-gun fire. When the Tabloid could limp no further, he landed and covered the last 30km (18 miles) of the return journey to base on a bicycle.

The 8 October attack had been a devastating blow for the Army's airship fleet. It had already suffered the loss of four Zeppelins – including Z VI, Z VII and Z VIII to groundfire while making low-level reconnaissance flights. Now left with only two Zeppelins – one being an old Delag ship – and the single SL 2, the striking power of this service had been crippled after only two months of war.

Not so the Naval Airship Division, and it was to its Zeppelins that attention turned. In the first formation strategic bombing mission in the history of warfare, three RNAS Avro 504s set out from Belfort in France for Friedrichshafen on 21 November 1914. Each aircraft carried four Hales bombs, and with these the pilots damaged L 7 (LZ 32) and blew up the associated gasworks. Flight Commander J.T. Babington and Flight Lt. S.V. Sippé returned safely but Squadron Commander E.F. Briggs received a head wound and was taken prisoner. L 7 was subsequently repaired and returned to service, finally being shot down in flames on 4 May 1916 by British naval vessels.

It had been the plan of the German Admirals to strike

Above: *French Astra-Torres non-rigid airship with two Renault engines, used for coastal patrol.*

at Britain with long-range airships should war ever present the occasion – given that their surface ships were probably unequal to the task against the might of the Royal Navy. But the belief that they could inflict some kind of total disaster on the enemy's homeland using airships was ridiculously optimistic. The German Army and Navy had vied to be first to fly airships against Britain. And when the Army lost the bulk of its rigid fleet in the early months of the war it requested the use of naval machines, which naturally the Naval Airship Division resisted.

Plans and counter plans had been drawn up for attacks from the very first month of war, but the Kaiser was having none of it, supported by Admiral von Pohl who saw no good in putting the Naval rigids at risk when they were needed for vitally important patrols over the North Sea in support of the High Seas Fleet. Frustration set into the Naval Airship Division as good weather passed by. By December 1914 even the Army began putting up barriers to the Division's hopes, not wishing to miss the first England raid and, anyway, hoping to enlist the Division's aid in hitting French towns in retaliation for aeroplane bombing missions on Germany.

But continued pressure on von Pohl forced him to seek an audience with the Kaiser in early January 1915 to raise the possibility of attacks against England. The pill was sweetened by the promise to keep the raids strictly to military targets in London and the lower Thames, with as little destruction of historic buildings

Below: *A well-preserved Avro 504 of the type used to bomb the Friedrichshafen Zeppelin sheds in November 1914.*

and civilian dwellings as possible. Von Pohl advised against waiting for the Army to gain the means to assist. The bait was taken, but with the proviso that London was not targeted at all but rather the coast and those areas of the lower Thames of military importance. It was a start and hurried final plans were drawn up.

Rising like great whales from Nordholz and Fuhlsbüttel, L 3, L 4 and L 6 set out on this historic first airship raid on England of the war on 19 January 1915. L 6 soon suffered engine problems and returned to base, but the remaining two dropped high-explosive and incendiary bombs on Great Yarmouth, Sheringham, Thornham, Brancaster, the wireless station at Hunstanton, Heacham, Snettisham and King's Lynn, leaving in their wake four dead and 15 injured. The effect on British morale was not as expected, and calls rose from the people for aeroplanes capable of striking back, leading eventually to the operational use of aircraft like the Handley Page O/100 of 1916, the first viable heavy night bomber.

On 3 May Naval Zeppelin L 9 (LZ 36) carried out an attack on four surfaced British submarines from an altitude of about 1,000m (3,280 ft), remarkably managing to damage one. That same month the Kaiser finally gave permission for London to be targeted, as long as the raids took place east of the Tower, well away from his royal relations. On the 31st the Army took the initiative and LZ 38 dropped 1,360kg (3,000 lb) of bombs on north-east London, causing the death of seven and injuring 14 more. A news blackout was ordered by the British Admiralty to prevent panic. The Naval Airship Division's first attack intended for London was on 4 June, using L 10 (LZ 40) and SL 3, but poor navigation brought most damage to Gravesend. Three months later L 10 was destroyed and its crew were dead.

For the RNAS, charged with air home defence, dealing with the airships was every bit as hard as for the gun and searchlight batteries on the ground. The airships often appeared at night, flew high and quietly, and could take considerable damage because of their multi-cell gas arrangement. It became a war of cat and mouse, and even when aeroplanes managed to approach, they had insufficient armament to finish the job and could expect fierce return fire from airship machine-gunners.

The loss of airships in 1914 had taught the German Army lessons regarding the folly of low flying and, if these needed renewing, on the night of 17–18 May 1915 LZ 38 and LZ 39 were intercepted at 610m (2,000 ft) and 3,050m (10,000 ft) altitude respectively by RNAS aeroplanes. LZ 39 sustained damage but LZ 38 escaped when the guns on the attacking Avro 504 jammed. The most important aspect of these particular interceptions was the use by the British aeroplanes of new incendiary ammunition, expected to pierce and ignite the gas bags. But the ammunition hadn't stopped LZ 39 and new explosive bullets were needed.

Among the RNAS pilots in action against the Army Zeppelins that May was Flight Sub-Lt. R.A.J. Warneford of No 1 Squadron who later, on the early morning of 7 June, set off to bomb the airship sheds at Berchem St. Agathe in an 80 hp Morane-Saulnier Type L with no gun armament. At Ostend he caught sight of LZ 37, one of three airships on a raid to London. Warneford changed direction. Seeing him coming, the airship tried to gain height. Warneford followed. At 3,350m (11,000 ft) he found himself just above LZ 37, machine-gun bullets all round. Knowing he would survive only one pass, he dived for the target, throwing out six Hales bombs as he went. The sixth exploded, igniting the airship and sending it burning to the ground. It fell on a suburb of Ghent, killing two nuns. Only one member of Oberleutnant van der Haegen's crew survived. LZ 37 had been the very first airship destroyed in an air attack and Warneford was awarded the VC and Chevalier of the Legion of Honour, but was killed ten days later in a flying accident.

The strain of long missions against a better prepared enemy began to show on airship crews. L 15 (LZ 48) was hit by explosive darts fired from an RFC B.E.2c and then anti-aircraft fire as it tried to limp away (on the night of 31 March–1 April 1916), eventually coming down at Fundress, making this the first Zeppelin destroyed over Britain. And Lt. W. Leefe Robinson RFC gained the VC on the night of 2 September that year when he shot down Schütte-Lanz SL XI over British soil.

Originally confident of their immunity, airship crews slowly became demoralized as others of their rank fell victim to attack, their once secret paths in the dark night sky lit by more competent searchlight batteries and phosphor shells.

The destruction of SL XI is widely believed to have prevented a planned huge London raid, although on the night of 23–24 September 11 airships did press attacks on London and elsewhere. Two of these were shot down, at Little Wigborough and Great Burstead.

During the course of the war the German Army and Navy had to contend also with airship losses through non-combat causes. Some caught fire while being inflated, and others were lost in bad weather or destroyed on landing, but of all Naval Airship Division Zeppelins no fewer than 14 were shot down. The last airship raid on England to cause injury took place on 12 April 1918. Altogether Britain had sustained 51 such attacks, from which 557 people had died and many more had been injured.

Were the airships successful? Despite the emphasis given to raids against Britain by historians, sea reconnaissance remained the most important function of the German Navy's airships during the whole of the war. In this they were well qualified. The raids against Britain alone would not have justified their cost in terms of construction, the loss of crews or the damage done. At the Armistice the Division had nine or ten Zeppelins remaining. In a final act of defiance, and to prevent them going to the Allies under the terms of the Versailles Treaty, on 23 June 1919 German crews at Nordholz wrecked six of these Naval Zeppelins. The story was over.

The last of the many

America, which had given the world the nickname 'blimp' for non-rigid airships – derived from B Class limp – discovered the inert gas helium and used it initially on the Goodyear C.7 coastal patrol and convoy 'blimp' (first flown on 1 December 1921). At last crews were safe from the explosive nature of hydrogen. The first rigid airship to use helium was again American, the US Navy's ZR-1 *Shenandoah*. This was designed using information gathered from Zeppelin L 49 (LZ 96), which had force landed in France on 20 October 1917. ZR-1 lifted off for its maiden flight on 4 September 1923, from Lakehurst, New Jersey. Performance was disappointing as it had not been designed to use helium. Unfortunately, after 55 other flights ZR-1 was lost with many lives in a storm on 3 September 1925.

Anxious to expand its rigid airship programme, the US Navy had previously planned to purchase the new

Facing page, top: Naval Airship Division Zeppelin L9 (LZ 36), commissioned in March 1915 and flown 148 times before being destroyed by fire in an inflation accident in its shed at Fuhlsbüttel.

Bottom: *Painting entitled* The Glorious Achievement of Lieut. Warneford VC, *depicting the destruction of LZ 37 over Ghent on 7 June 1915.*

Below: *The US Army TC-1 was an early helium-filled 'blimp' of 1922, used for training.*

Right: *The US Navy's helium-filled airship, ZR-1 Shenandoah. First flown on 4 September 1923 at Lakehurst, it was lost in a storm over Caldwell, Ohio on 3 September 1925.*

R-38 from Britain as the ZR-2 and take over two ex-German Navy Zeppelins. R-38, the largest airship ever built up to that time, broke up in August 1921 with heavy loss of life. The US Navy was equally unlucky with its Zeppelins, as these were among the airships wrecked by German crews at Nordholz in 1919.

Instead, the Inter-Allied reparations commission ordered a new replacement directly from the Zeppelin company, and LZ 126 becoming ZR-3 *Los Angeles.* Initially filled with hydrogen (later helium), it crossed the Atlantic between 12 and 14 October 1924 and accumulated 5,368 flying hours in more than 300 flights

Below: *The remains of Shenandoah.*

prior to an honourable retirement in 1932.

Construction of LZ 126 actually saved the German Zeppelin company from going out of business. Later, with Goodyear, it co-founded Goodyear-Zeppelin Corporation of Akron, Ohio, which (in 1928) was awarded the contract to build two new rigid scouting airships for the US Navy. These became the highly successful but ill-fated USS *Akron* and *Macon*, commissioned in 1931 and 1933 respectively. Unlike any other airships ever built, each was designed from the outset to carry four Curtiss F9C-2 Sparrowhawk biplane scout-fighters, stowed in internal hangars when not needed and

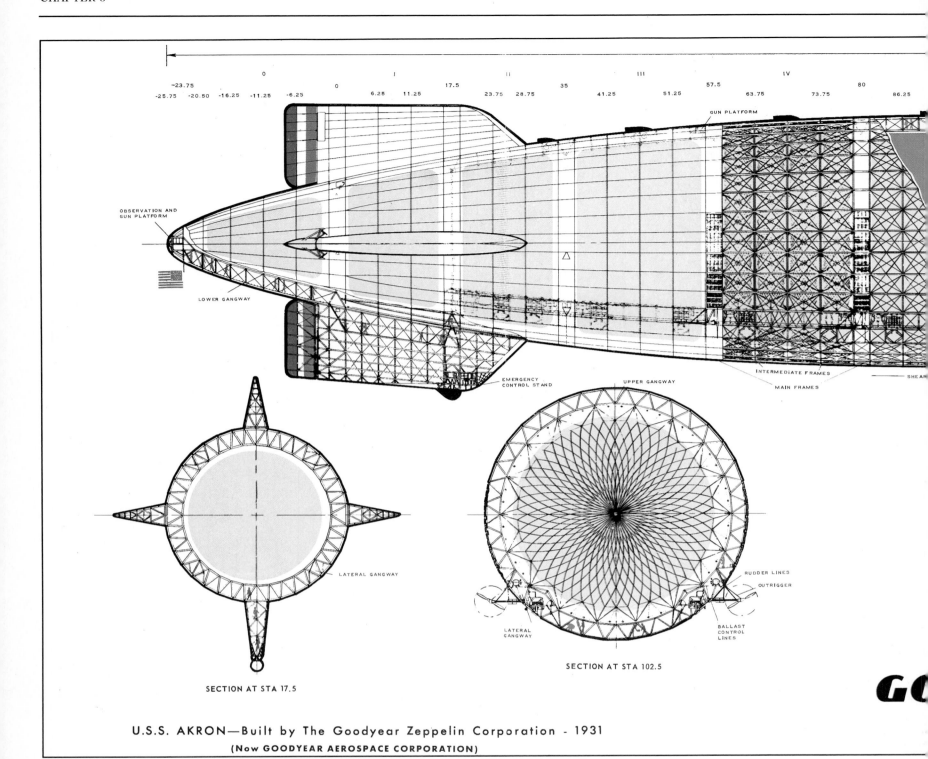

SECTION AT STA 17.5

SECTION AT STA 102.5

U.S.S. AKRON—Built by The Goodyear Zeppelin Corporation - 1931
(Now GOODYEAR AEROSPACE CORPORATION)

Right: *The first US Navy carrier airship was* Akron, *followed by* Macon *(illustrated) of 1933 commission.*

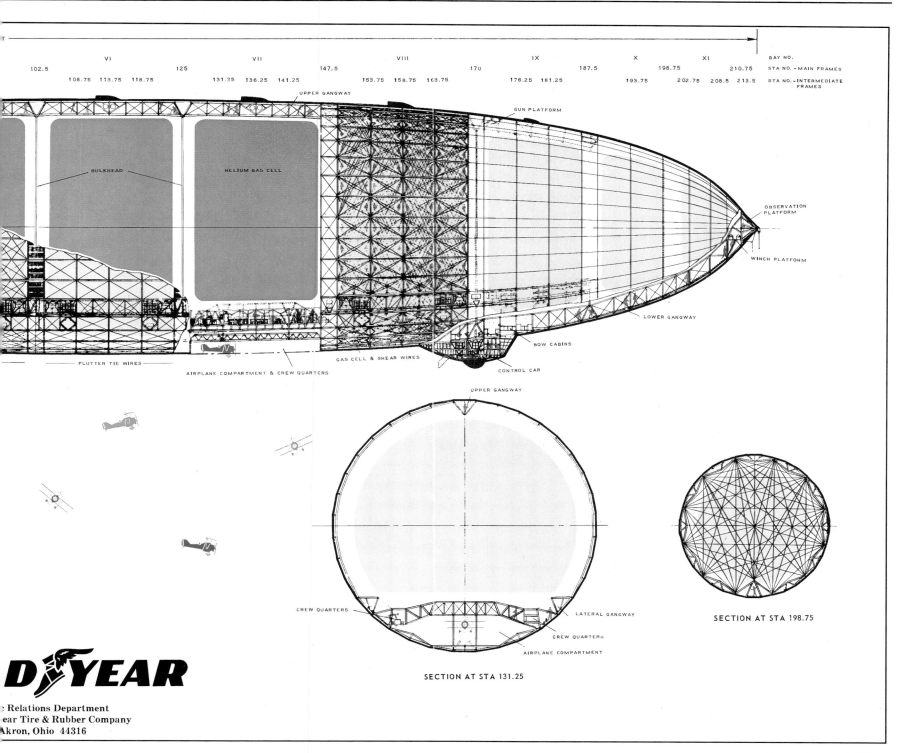

BAY NO.

| | VI | | | | VII | | | VIII | | | IX | | X | | XI | | STA NO. – MAIN FRAMES |

102.5   125   147.5   170   187.5   198.75   210.75

108.75   113.75   118.75   131.25   136.25   141.25   153.75   158.75   163.75   176.25   181.25   193.75   202.75   208.5   213.5   STA NO. – INTERMEDIATE FRAMES

UPPER GANGWAY

GUN PLATFORM

BULKHEAD   HELIUM GAS CELL

OBSERVATION PLATFORM

WINCH PLATFORM

LOWER GANGWAY

BOW CABINS

CONTROL CAR

FLUTTER TIE WIRES   GAS CELL & SHEAR WIRES

AIRPLANE COMPARTMENT & CREW QUARTERS

UPPER GANGWAY

CREW QUARTERS   LATERAL GANGWAY

CREW QUARTERS

AIRPLANE COMPARTMENT

SECTION AT STA 131.25

SECTION AT STA 198.75

D·YEAR

Relations Department
ear Tire & Rubber Company
kron, Ohio 44316

Above: *Layout of USS* Akron, *courtesy and copyright of The Goodyear Tire & Rubber Company.*

U.S. NAVY

Left: *USS* Macon *in flight near Manhattan Island.*

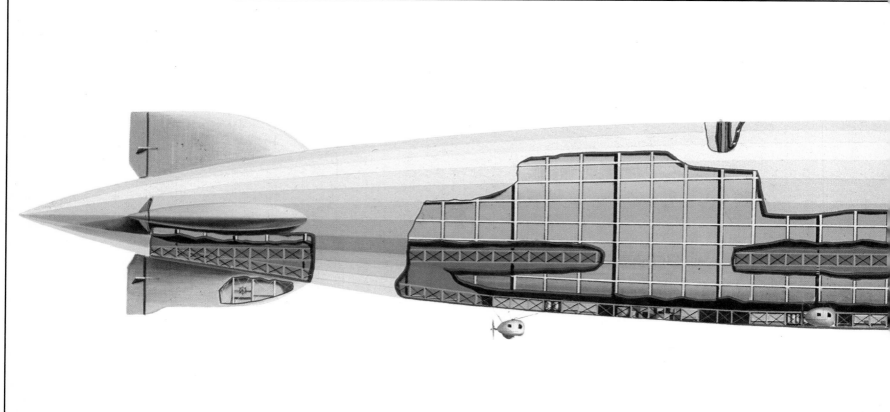

Top: *The last airships in operational service with the US Navy were Goodyear ZPG 3-Ws for airborne early warning. These were also the largest of the Navy's non-rigids, seen here docked to mobile masts.*

launched and recovered by special trapeze. *Akron* was lost in the sea off New Jersey in a storm during the dark hours of 3–4 April 1933. *Macon* was also lost at sea, on 11 February 1935. The US Navy ended rigid airship operations after this, but continued flying blimps until 1962 (the last ones being airborne early warning Goodyear ZPG 3-Ws).

After constructing *Los Angeles* for the USA, Zeppelin built the LZ 127 *Graf Zeppelin* for German use, the first of two airships bearing this name. Launched in 1928, it was the first airship to circumnavigate the world – between 8 and 29 August 1929 – starting and finishing at Lakehurst in the USA and flying via Friedrichshafen, Tokyo and Los Angeles. Captain for the flight was Dr. Hugo Eckener himself. The most successful airship

ever, during its passenger-carrying career it covered more than a million air miles and gave some 13,100 people one of the few remaining chances to fly commercially by lighter-than-air. It was finally scrapped in 1940, along with LZ 130 *Graf Zeppelin II*, which had only been launched on 14 September 1938. LZ 130 is remembered as the largest of all airships, 245m (803 ft) long and with a volume of 199,981m³ (7,062,270 cu ft). LZ 130 made its last 'official' flight on 20 August 1939, but a radar spying mission against Britain followed. The new LZ 132 was never completed, but it would have been even larger, with an 8½ million cu ft volume.

The era of the giant passenger-carrying airship ended with disasters so horrific that confidence never recovered. Britain's last two rigid commercial airships

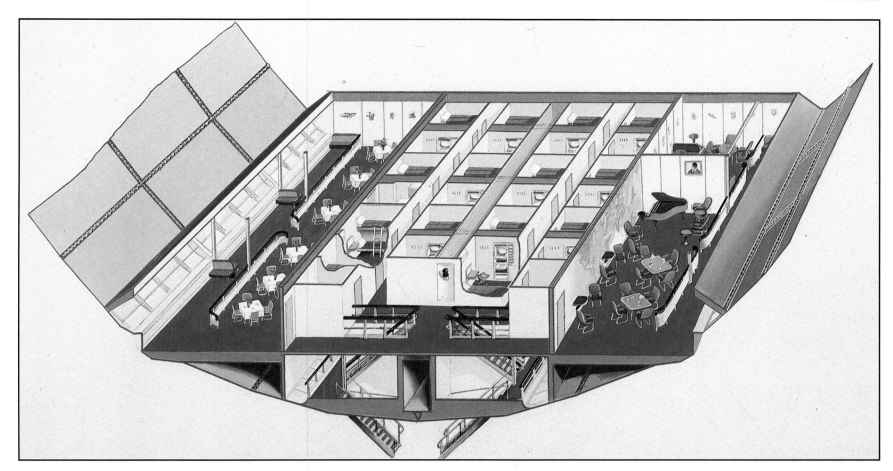

Above: *Passenger salons and berths of a passenger-carrying Zeppelin airship.*

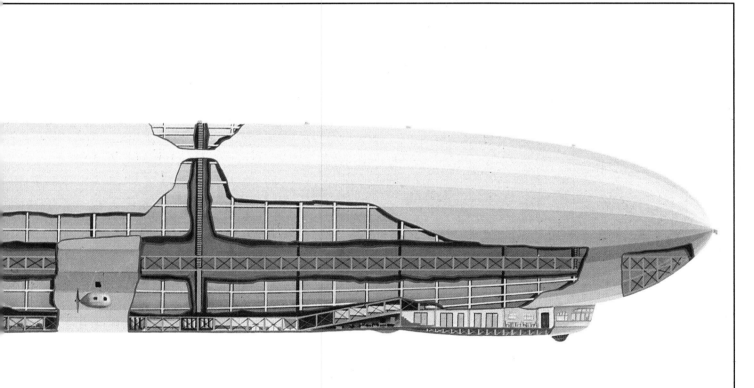

Above: *Passenger salons and berths of a passenger-carrying Zeppelin airship.*

Left: *Sectional drawing of LZ 127 Graf Zeppelin.*

Below: *R100, launched in 1929, taken out of service in 1930 after the R101 tragedy, and sold for scrap in 1931 for just £450.*

were the R-100 and R-101. The former was the brainchild of Barnes Wallis and featured his strong geodetic form of airframe structure. During a trial on 16 January 1930, it recorded a speed of 131 km/h (81 mph), the highest ever for a rigid airship. On 29 July the R-100 left Cardington on a flight to Montreal, Canada, the journey taking just 78 hours 51 minutes. Between 13 and 16 August it returned, cutting the time down to 56½ hours. This double crossing promised a great future that lay before it – but it was not to be. On 5 October the larger British R-101 airship left Cardington for a flight to Egypt and India. It never made it. Hardly into the journey, it crashed to the ground at Beauvais in France after making two unexpected dives, and burst into flames. With it went Britain's rigid airship future.

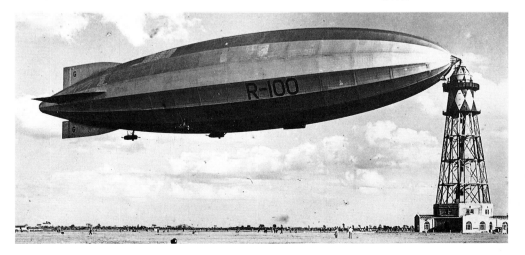

Above: *The British rigid airship dream was buried with the ashes of the R101 on a French hillside near Beauvais on 5 October 1930.*

Right: *The final and most spectacular conflagration of a rigid airship happened on 6 May 1937, when the German Hindenburg burst into a fireball for no apparent reason as it came in to dock at Lakehurst, New Jersey after a successful flight from Frankfurt, Germany. Water is seen falling from the ballast tanks. (US Navy)*

Left: Hindenburg's *final moments, its nose still high off the ground but engulfed in flame. (US Navy)*

Germany remained a staunch believer in rigid airships and continued highly successful operations through the 1930s. The first commitment to that belief after the British tragedy was the construction of the LZ 129 *Hindenburg*, a sister to the subsequent LZ 130. Begun in 1934, it was a fine ship, large, fast and highly furnished for the comfort of passengers. Safety was her watchword; the engines used crude oil, crew walkways were rubber coated to avoid sparks, the smoking lounge was completely fire-proof, and passengers and crew were not permitted to bring on board their own cigarette lighters. It did lack one attribute, however: the Americans refused to sell Germany helium.

Launched on 4 March 1936, *Hindenburg* began its first transatlantic flight on 6 May, taking only 61 hours 50 minutes to reach Lakehurst. The return to Friedrichshafen was covered in an amazing 49 hours 3 minutes. It was always greeted as something special, often attracting a flotilla of onlookers. Then the worst happened. When approaching its mooring at Lakehurst on 6 May 1937 after a successful transatlantic flight from Frankfurt, it suddenly, unbelievably, caught fire, the flames quickly running along the length of the envelope to engulf the complete ship. The huge fireball slowly drifted to the ground. As it collapsed, the last survivors jumped free of the gondola in the hope of crossing the open ground before the burning mass fell on top of them. Many owed their lives to the fact that, to the last, the airship had tried to stay off the ground. Amazingly, only 35 of the 97 people on board were killed. In this, the last great airship disaster, hopes for the future of commercial lighter-than-air travel died. Dr. Hugo Eckener sat on the Board of Inquiry, which judged that leaking gas from the stern had been ignited by static electricity. Eckener had seen the Zeppelin through its whole span of life, nearly four decades, the good times with *Schwäben* and *Graf Zeppelin* and the bad times in war and peace.

Epilogue

In the 1990s airships of a much smaller and safer generation fly regularly. They do not pretend to be the great passenger carriers of the past and, anyway, there would be no place for such giants in an age of fast jet travel. Most are for air advertising; some take handfuls of passengers on short but exciting sightseeing journeys. Even the US Navy is considering reintroduction of small airships for specialized military missions.

Left: *One of the new generation of non-rigid airships, the British Airship Industries Skyship 500 first flew in 1981 and is high-tech in every sense.*

Chapter 7:
Birth and Re-birth

The First World War ended on 11 November 1918, having shattered the fabric of European society and witnessed slaughter on a scale never before seen. The most beautiful and fertile regions of Europe had been reduced to wasteland; millions were dead, and those who returned home in victory or defeat faced uncertain futures. The Allies were determined to exact a heavy price on German militarism. For those in sympathy with Russians fighting a civil war against the Bolsheviks, peace was still some time away. Here an irony of war and peace was self evident: the very same revolutionary government in Russia that had signed a peace treaty with Germany in March 1918 now faced opposing countrymen backed not only by small forces from the Allies but also a few of Germany's surviving air 'aces'.

The re-start of airlines

The first passenger service, the Delag Zeppelin line, had already appeared before the war (see page 78). The first airline to operate scheduled aeroplane services was also of pre-war origin, the St. Petersburg–Tampa Airboat Line based in Florida, USA, which began operations on 1 January 1914 using a Benoist flying-boat. But this lasted only four months.

As a remarkable act of faith in the future of aeroplanes and the outcome of the war, on 5 October 1916 the first British airline was registered by George Thomas Holt as Aircraft Transport and Travel Ltd. Similar steps were being taken abroad, with Germany forming Deutsche Luft-Reederei (DLR) in December 1917. DLR had to wait until 5 February 1919 to start scheduled domestic operations between Berlin and Weimar, while in Britain civil flying was not permitted until publication of the Air Navigation Regulations on 1 May 1919. However, this may be slightly misleading, as AT&T organized earlier operations under military guise: in February 1919 AT&T had begun food and clothing mercy flights between Folkestone and Ghent in

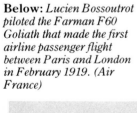

Below: *Lucien Bossoutrot piloted the Farman F60 Goliath that made the first airline passenger flight between Paris and London in February 1919. (Air France)*

Belgium, but using RAF pilots flying Airco D.H.9 converted light bombers. It should also be remembered that France was responsible for undertaking the first airline passenger flight between Paris and London, on 8 February 1919, beating the British ban on civil flying by carrying only military passengers in the Farman F60 Goliath.

The race begins again

When the war ended it may have been assumed that the aeroplane had improved immensely during four years of combat use. In fact it was aircraft engines which had improved the most, the additional power available making acceptable the performance of drag-inducing biplane structures that showed little change for the better.

Clearly, the financial 'carrot' that had prompted pre-war developments would need to be revived if aviation was to leap forward. The *Daily Mail* transatlantic prize was still on offer, and proved to be the first to fall on 14–15 June 1919. This achievement was gained in a Vickers Vimy bomber, flown from St John's, Newfoundland, to Clifden, County Galway, Ireland, by Capt. John Alcock and Lt. Arthur Whitten Brown in a total flight time of 16 hours 27 minutes. The significance of this dangerous flight can hardly be overstated, and both men received knighthoods. The Vimy ended its flight nose-down in a peat bog! Of course, by then the Atlantic had already been crossed by aeroplane between 8 and 31 May 1919, although the US Navy Navy/Curtiss NC-4 flying boat under the command of Lt. Commander A.C. Read had done so in stages in a flying time of 57 hours 16 minutes. The accompanying NC-1 and NC-3 had failed to make it to Plymouth.

On 12 November 1919, another Vimy took to the air from Hounslow, west of London, crewed by the Australian brothers Capt. Ross Smith and Lt. Keith Smith and two other airmen. Its destination was

Darwin, Australia, and it successfully reached its target on 10 December in a total flying time of 135 hours 55 minutes, and winning for the Smith brothers the sum of £10,000 from the Australian government, as well as knighthoods from the British.

The third of these long-distance Vimy flights was less successful. Lt. Col. Pierre van Ryneveld and Sqn. Ldr. Christopher Quintin Brand took off from Brooklands, Surrey, on 4 February 1920 for South Africa. By the time they reached Cape Town they had crashed two Vimys, and completed the flight in a war surplus D.H.9 borrowed from the South African government.

This same year – 1920 – saw in the United States the first Pulitzer Trophy air race, flown on 25 November 1920 at Mitchell Field, Long Island, NY. This, the very first of the renowned US national air races, was won by Capt. Corliss Moseley of the US Army Air Service flying a Verville-Packard 600 at an average speed of 251.9km/h (156.5 mph). Two years later in the UK the

King's Cup (George V) air race was inaugurated, flown first during 8–9 September 1922, and won on this occasion by Captain F.L. Barnard who was flying the Instone Air Line D.H.4A *City of York* from Croydon to Glasgow and back at an average speed of 199 km/h (124 mph).

The year 1923 saw competition of a different kind in the UK, with the *Daily Mail*, the Duke of Sutherland and the Abdulla Company putting up prizes of £1,000, £500 and £500 respectively to encourage the development of a practical single-seat and economical light aircraft. Competition was keen, and it is interesting to note that an award for the longest distance flown on one gallon of petrol was shared between two aircraft, both of them achieving a distance of 140.8km (87.5 miles). In the following year the British Air Ministry offered a prize of £3,000 for a practical and efficient two-seater light plane, the prize going to the Beardmore Wee Bee monoplane.

Above: *15 June 1919. Alcock and Brown's Vimy when it landed at Clifden, Ireland after their transatlantic flight.*

Far left: *Captain John Alcock.*

Left: *Lt. Arthur Whitten Brown.*

Atlantic again

In the United States, meanwhile, Raymond Orteig had offered an award of $25,000 in 1919 for the first person to fly solo across the North Atlantic. After many famous and not so famous pilots lost their lives trying, this prize and the fame that accompanied it was finally won in 1927 by Capt. Charles Lindbergh flying the Ryan NYP (New York to Paris) monoplane *Spirit of St Louis*. Not only was this a remarkable achievement for both man and machine, but one so well reported during the event that millions of people around the world found their hearts captured by aviation. Remarkably, Lindbergh was then the 92nd to cross the Atlantic by air.

Razzle-dazzle

In 1929, the first of the famous US National Air Races took place which, with their noise, excitement and razzle-dazzle, had the American public 'hooked' on this new sporting activity until the start of the Second World War in Europe introduced more urgent considerations. First of the major events was the Thompson Trophy Race, inaugurated at Chicago, Illinois, during August, a closed-circuit round-the-pylons race that thrilled the crowds. It was to become an annual event.

Rather more serious in outlook was the long-distance Bendix Trophy Race, flown for the first time on 4 September 1931 between Burbank, California, and Cleveland, Ohio. The inaugural race was won by the legendary 'Jimmy' Doolittle flying a Laird Super-Solution biplane, and the Bendix also became an annual event until the outbreak of war. It was resumed after the war, and in 1946 introduced a special section for jet-powered aircraft.

The airlines take off

The start of airline services proper and their development, especially in Europe, were inextricably entwined with the military; ex-warplanes were available for immediate conversion into makeshift airliners, and there was certainly no shortage of ex-military pilots. But there was more to it than that. Many of the great long-distance flights along routes later to be exploited commercially were pioneered by military crews in military aeroplanes. For example, between 28 July and 8 August 1918 Major A.S. MacLaren and Brig.-General A.E. Borton flew a Handley Page O/400 bomber from England to Egypt. And from 29 November to 12

December that same year Borton, in company with Captain Ross Smith and Major-General W. Salmond, continued on to link Egypt with India. Similarly, Britons Alcock and Brown used a Vickers Vimy bomber to make the first ever non-stop transatlantic flight (see page 90) following the very first air crossing of the Atlantic (but in stages) by a US Navy/Curtiss NC-4 flying-boat under the command of Lt.-Commander A.C. Read (8–31 May 1919).

Air mail also played a part in developing airlines, though at first the connection may be unclear. Italian military airmail services started in May 1917, followed by the French in August 1917. An international military operation between Vienna and Kiev was struck up in March 1918, followed by airmail-carrying by the USA and Canada, and Switzerland in January 1919, and a London–Paris service by Britain that same month.

The experimental airmail run by the US Army in America from 15 May 1918 was a milestone that led to the first stage of an elaborate transcontinental airmail service inaugurated on 15 May 1919 between Chicago and Cleveland. The full coast-to-coast transcontinental service took until 22 February 1921 to come into fruition. The revenue from carrying mail would later be lifeblood to fledgeling US airlines, even leading to special aeroplanes being designed for the purpose, following the US government's decision of 1926 to turn over the transcontinental service to private enterprise.

Meanwhile, William Boeing and Edward Hubbard had made their own bit of history by starting US international airmail services on 3 March 1919, flying between Seattle, USA, and Victoria, British Columbia, Canada. The aeroplane used was a Boeing CL-4S. But even more important than this was the Swiss military airmail route using Haefeli DH-3s between Zürich and Berne, which spawned an early but short-lived passenger service.

The British London to Paris service that began on 10 January 1919 was strictly a military affair and was of great importance for several reasons. Run by No 2 (Communications) Squadron, RAF, using D.H.4 bombers converted to have enclosed accommodation for two passengers, it transported VIPs as well as mail between the two capitals during the period of the Peace Conference in Versailles. The Treaty itself was concluded on 28 June 1919, and thus the service ended that September after 749 flights.

Below: To many, the US National Air Races immediately conjure thoughts of the seven exciting Gee Bee racers created by Zantford 'Granny' Granville. The basic design concept was to put the most powerful engine possible into the minimum of airframe, producing extremely fast if rather unstable racers of extraordinary appearance. The 800hp Wasp-engined Super Sportster (illustrated) won the 1932 Thompson Trophy Race at an average of 406.6km/h (252.6 mph) in the hands of Jimmy Doolittle.

The Farman brothers, who had been responsible for the first Paris–London airline passenger flight, also inaugurated the first sustained and regular international commercial passenger services on 22 March 1919, flying between Paris and Brussels.

The Versailles Treaty – war and peace

The terms of the Treaty were intended by the Allies to ensure that never again would Germany have the capacity to wage international war. The German Army was prohibited a strength above 100,000 and, to emphasize its defensive nature, no General Staff was allowed, conscription was forbidden, and a long term of service was mandatory. Similarly, Navy strength was cut to just 16,500 officers and men, a total of only 24 capital warships was allowed, plus twelve torpedo boats but no submarines.

But the Treaty came down most heavily against German aviation. A blanket abolition was ordered of German military and naval air forces, without exception. All aeroplanes, aero-engines, airships and other equipment had to be surrendered in total. At a stroke, military flying in Germany had died. Some design and manufacture of civil aeroplanes was allowed, but strictly limited in scope by restrictions on engine power. Any aircraft with military potential, albeit in civil use, would not be allowed. Government subsidies for aircraft construction were forbidden, as was any kind of military training.

One immediate effect of these harsh conditions was to put an end to Delag's new post-war airship operations, as the Zeppelins' obvious military potential had already been demonstrated in the war. More important to the birth of commercial aviation were the prospects for Junkers' new F 13. This was the first new civil aircraft built in Germany after the war, first flying just three days before the Treaty was signed. Junkers had put all its experience of metal construction and canti-lever wings into this little machine, making it the world's first purpose-built all-metal airliner.

Carrying two crew plus four passengers in an enclosed cabin, the F 13's 160 hp Mercedes D.IIIa engine offered impressive performance. (Initial production aircraft used the 185 hp BMW IIIa engine and late machines the 310 hp Junkers L.5). But the Allied Commission of Control stopped F 13 sales (even to America) and halted production, judging it an aeroplane with military potential. However, as it became difficult to conceive of any aircraft *without* military potential of one kind or another, in early 1920 the Commission backed down and the F 13 went into production, soon to find markets in Europe and all over the world. Production lasted until 1932, by which time 322 had been constructed.

Airlines and services develop

Britain's first purpose-built airliner was a far more modest effort, the de Havilland D.H.16 biplane, though it managed excellent work with AT&T and later KLM (leased). London Airport opened in July 1919 and on 25 August AT&T began a daily service between London and Paris, the first scheduled international aeroplane service in the world. Simultaneously, airlines were started all over Europe and on other continents, mostly with converted military machines.

Following the founding of KLM, the Royal Dutch airline, on 7 October 1919, AT&T and KLM co-operated to establish an Amsterdam–London service, begun on 17 May 1920. Meanwhile, on 13 August 1919 the League of Nations founded the Paris Convention to regulate international flying.

AT&T made its last commercial flight on 15 December 1920. The day before, a British operated O/400 airliner (converted from a bomber) had crashed in fog at Cricklewood; this was Britain's first fatal accident on a commercial service. The Daimler Airway succeeded AT&T, and it was a D.H.18 of this airline that collided with a Farman Goliath of Grands Express Aériens over Thieuloy-Saint-Antoine in France on 7 April 1922, the first time airliners on scheduled services had been involved in an air collision. Seven people were killed. On 31 March 1924 Daimler, Handley Page Transport, Instone Air Lines and the British Marine Air Navigation Company merged to form Imperial Airways, Britain's new national airline. On 6 January 1926 two German airlines merged to form Deutsche Luft-Hansa, Germany's national airline, with the government taking a 37.5 per cent shareholding. Other early national airlines included Dobrolet, founded in the Soviet Union in March 1923, the forerunner of Aeroflot, and Belgium's Sabena, formed on 23 May that year.

Despite the often very simple conversion of warplanes into airliners, the absence of any real training of

Below: *de Havilland D.H.18 operated by Britain's first commercial airline, Aircraft Transport & Travel Ltd.*

staff, the use of hangars left over from the war, and virtually no airfield aids beyond windsocks and oil flares to indicate wind strength and direction, the early airlines were quite successful and safe. Comfort was another matter, and occasionally passengers were expected to endure the open air, wearing leather coats and hats or sit among the internal bracing of converted bombers.

Meanwhile, in 1922, Daimler had begun offering in-flight food, taken to new heights of service by Imperial Airways and France's Air Union later in the 1920s, served by a steward. Boeing Air Transport put a trained nurse on its Model 80 San Francisco–Cheyenne route from 15 May 1930, thereby introducing the air stewardess.

Flying aids

The tragedy of the April 1922 collision had been caused by both pilots following a road in bad weather. Navigation by geographical features was commonplace, and to help aircrews it was not unusual for railway stations to have their names painted in clear lettering on their roofs. The rarity of collisions undoubtedly reflected the fairly low volume of commercial air traffic at this time, but clearly proper plans for safety were needed.

Two-way radio and radio direction-finding by ground stations allowed an early form of air traffic control, but passengers were by necessity flown in daylight and bad weather often cancelled operations. But commercial success rested on achieving more air movements, which in turn encouraged the development of aids to allow bad weather travel and then even night flying. Innovations included electric flight direction beacons (first introduced in the USA on 21 August 1923), location beacons at airports, and other lights to mark obstructions, airport boundaries and approaches. It was a start, and from these came other aids for safer air travel, including Germany's Lorenz beam-following system for airport landing and America's radio beacon air navigation system. The Lorenz system can be seen

as the forerunner of today's Instrument Landing System (ILS). Neither should one forget Britain's development of radar when discussing the evolution of air safety, although it did not come into commercial use until after the Second World War.

New airliners

The temperamental nature of aircraft in the early 1920s, especially their aero-engines, and the difficulties posed by bad weather, had forced the introduction of emergency landing grounds along the busiest routes. But unscheduled landings caused delays and lost revenue. In the search for increased profits, each facet of these and other operating problems was tackled methodically. An important breakthrough came with the production of new high-output air-cooled radial engines, typified by the British Bristol Jupiter. These helped reliability, but the airlines also needed to carry more passengers to make ends meet.

Now came a great leap forward. Manufacturers took the lead and added to their product lines new larger airliners powered by two or three of the new radials. Among the first were the 18–20 passenger Armstrong Whitworth Argosy and 14-passenger de Havilland D.H.66 Hercules, used by Imperial Airways from 1926–27. These were biplanes, the former first used on the Croydon–Le Bourget route and the latter on the airline's Cairo–Karachi service, but contemporary monoplanes of more advanced designs were also appearing. From Fokker in the Netherlands came the F.VIIa-3m, Junkers in Germany produced a succession

Centre: *Among the excellent flying-boats built by Dornier was the unsuccessful but historic Do X, which first flew on 25 July 1929. It was a twelve-engined giant, with a wing span of 48m (157 ft 6 in) and accommodating a crew of 10 and 150 passengers. Then the largest aeroplane in the world, one prototype began a flight between Germany and New York on 2 November 1930, arriving after many mishaps on 27 August 1931. Needless to say, it did not go into commercial service.*

Below: *The luxurious passenger salons in the Dornier Do X.*

of streamlined aircraft, and Ford in the USA developed its famous Tri-Motor.

Multi-engined airliners had the added benefit of improving safety when crossing water, as an engine failure would not precipitate ditching. But for the long sea routes there was nothing to touch the new flying-boats. In many respects, these introduced levels of luxury unique in air travel. Their cavernous hulls were ideally suited to well-appointed sitting and sleeping quarters needed for long journeys. Again Europe was at the forefront; British, French, German and Italian flying-boats only truly rivalled in the mid- to late 1930s, when American manufacturers produced an ultimate range of very impressive large machines for transatlantic and trans-Pacific operations.

Partly because of its Empire, but encouraged no doubt by a falling percentage of European air traffic in the mid-1920s, Britain had taken a major role in establishing long-distance routes. While the aeroplanes used had to be sturdy, passengers too had to show considerable fortitude. When Imperial Airways opened a commercial route between London and India on 30 March 1929, passengers first flew to Switzerland in an Argosy landplane, then took a train to Genoa (Italy), from there going by air in a Short Calcutta flying-boat to Alexandria in Egypt, and finally hopping on a Hercules for the last crossing to Karachi. The journey took a full seven days and cost £130 one way.

Through the 1930s flying-boats remained the masters of long-distance commercial aeroplane travel over water, but this was soon to change. To the requirements of US airlines, American manufacturers had begun designing a series of large, four-engined modern landplanes, the first of which appeared shortly before the outbreak of war in Europe. Intended mainly for domestic services in the US, their speed, range and high seating capacities made them suitable also for international and even intercontinental routes. The Second World War delayed their commercial inauguration, but after the war they soon put large commercial flying-boats out of business. Some introduced cabin pressurization, allowing passengers to be carried in smooth flight above the worst of the weather.

The United States of America became the leader in the development and manufacture of modern airliners, and has managed to hold the position ever since. In some respects this can be viewed as the air component of the nation's inter-war and post-war drive to outperform Europe industrially. Boeing started the ball rolling with its first commercial monoplane, the Model 200 *Monomail*. First flown on 6 May 1930 and designed for high-speed mail carrying, it was the first aircraft to combine an all-metal airframe with cantilever low-mounted wings and a retractable undercarriage.

On 8 February 1933 Boeing flew its new Model 247 airliner, having produced an experimental bomber along the same lines, the B-9 of 1931. Though seating only ten passengers, its many modern features included all-metal construction, cantilever low wings, retractable undercarriage, Pratt & Whitney R-1340 Wasp radial engines in low-drag ring cowlings, pneumatically operated rubber de-icing boots on the wings and tail, fully enclosed flight deck, a thermostatically controlled cabin heating/cooling system, and a high standard of cabin fittings. The final production aircraft, plus updated models, even had controllable-pitch propellers. Sixty-one were built, operating from 1933, having been ordered initially for the airlines comprising Boeing Air Transport System.

Boeing's rival in this class of airliner was the 12-seat DC-1 from Douglas that had first flown only months after the Model 247, on 1 July 1933. Its development had been prompted by TWA, who had been unable to secure delivery of early Model 247s. Only one DC-1 was built, but the more powerful and longer 14-seat DC-2 went into series production, and by 1935 Douglas was producing one every three days to meet demand.

Douglas stole Boeing's thunder with the DC-2, but even better things lay around the corner. American Airlines required a sleeper airliner for its long transcontinental service. Clearly the DC-2 was too small to be economical and Douglas somewhat reluctantly designed a slightly larger version, as the Douglas Sleeper Transport, the DST or DC-3. This provided accommodation for 28 seated passengers or 14 sleeping berths. The prototype first flew on 17 December 1935, the 22nd anniversary of the first flight by the Wright brothers. American Airlines introduced it on its New York–Chicago run on 25 June 1936, leading to transcontinental operations that September. It was an enormous success. Orders came flooding in. During the Second World War it became a standard transport with the Allies, and remained in production until 1947, when nearly 11,000 had been built.

Left: *An important stepping stone in the development of the modern airliner was the Boeing Model 200 Monomail mailplane, that company's first commercial monoplane and featuring an all-metal airframe, cantilever low-mounted wings and a retractable undercarriage.*

Above: *The fourteen-seat Douglas DC-2 filled the gap left by the unavailability of the Boeing Model 247, leading to the even more successful DC-3. This DC-2 found its way into military service.*

Left: *Sixty Boeing Model 247s had been ordered for the airlines comprising Boeing Air Transport System before the prototype flew, and the newly founded United Air Lines began operations in 1933. But, as the production schedule slipped, Boeing found it could not satisfy the many enquiries for the airliner and Douglas filled the gap.*

97

They shall not be forgotten

The inter-war period of 1919–39 witnessed the rebirth of civil flying, encouraged by the design of specialized light aircraft for aero clubs, typified by the de Havilland D.H.60 Moth two-seater biplane. Clubs made aeroplanes available to ordinary folk who wanted to learn to fly but could never afford their own machines. Popularization also came from air meetings and flying competitions, but there were other attractions. Throughout the inter-war period flights of great daring were made, sometimes by military crews but most spectacularly by intrepid civilians often as ordinary in their previous lifestyles as the small aeroplanes they chose to pilot.

Alcock and Brown instantly became the first megastars of post-war route-proving. Australia again featured in the news in 1919 when Capt. H. Wrigley and Lt. A. Murphy crossed the continent between 16 November and 12 December. No big bomber for them, but a little B.E.2e.

In an epic staged flight that caught the imagination of millions, Lt. William D. Coney of the US Army Air Service became the first person to fly solo across the US continent from coast to coast, spending 22 hours 27 minutes in the air between 21 and 24 February 1921. A

year later, on 13 March 1922, Portuguese pilots Captain Gago Coutinho and Captain Sacadura Cabral began a staged flight over the South Atlantic in a Fairey IIIC, finally reaching Brazil in the replacement Fairey IIID, *Santa Cruz*, on 16 June. A little later, on 4 September, Lt. James H. Doolittle flew a D.H.4B across the US, the first time the 3,480 km (2,163 mile) journey had been achieved in a single day. A non-stop flight had to be the next 'first' across the US continent, and this was achieved by Lt. O. Kelly and Lt. A. Macready of the US Army Air Service in a Fokker T-2 between 2 and 3 May 1923.

A certain amount of rivalry developed between the US Navy and Army Air Service when it came to long distance flights. The Navy had been the first to fly the Atlantic in stages and the Army's continental crossings had not achieved quite the same prestige. The answer came in 1924, when Army Douglas DWCs (Douglas World Cruisers) made the first circumnavigation of the world. Four had left Seattle on 6 April. Accidents en route reduced their number, and two finally made it back on 28 September after covering a distance of 44,340km (27,553 miles).

Although van Rynevald and Brand had reached Cape

Above: Fokker F.VIIA-3m Josephine Ford *which reached the North Pole in 1926.*

Right: Of the four US Army Douglas DWCs that set out to make the first staged round-the-world flight in 1924, only Chicago *and* New Orleans *completed the journey. (US Air Force)*

Town in 1920, a more important flight from England was made by Alan Cobham and his mechanic A.B. Elliott, in a de Havilland D.H.50 between 16 November 1925 and 17 February 1926. Cobham specialized in return flights, and on 13 March they duly arrived back in England. Three months later, with the de Havilland converted into a seaplane, Cobham and Elliott set out for a two-way journey to and from Australia.

Cobham, whose many important flights had included one between London and Rangoon and back between 20 November 1924 and 18 March 1925, will always be remembered in history as the man who blazed the routes that helped Imperial Airways establish their famous Empire services.

1925 also witnessed attempts to reach the North Pole by air. The extraordinary Norwegian explorer, Roald Amundsen, who in 1911 had reached the South Pole by land, was joined by American Lincoln Ellsworth and four others on 21 May 1925 when two German Dornier Wal flying-boats set off bound for the Pole. On this occasion luck was not on their side.

While Amundsen was putting together a second expedition, this time by airship, US Navy Lt. Cdr. Richard E. Byrd and Floyd Bennett planned a rival attempt. Byrd, who was used to Arctic flying with the Navy and had designed the navigation equipment taken by the NC flying boats on their 1919 transatlantic flight, set off for the North Pole on 9 May 1926 in a triple-engined Fokker F.VII named *Josephine Ford*, just two days after Amundsen had arrived in Spitzbergen with his Italian airship *N.1 Norge*. But the aeroplane flight was successful, making the journey in 15¾ hours. Amundsen had to be content with the honour of making only the second air journey to the North Pole (though the first by airship) which he did between 11 and 14 May. During 28–29 November 1929 Byrd also led the first flight over the South Pole, this time using the Ford 4-AT Tri-Motor *Floyd Bennett*, named after his friend who had died of pneumonia before the expedition. Sadly, by then Amundsen too had died, in a seven-nation attempt to rescue the Italian General Umberto Nobile (designer and commander of the *N.1*) who had set out in the airship *Italia* for another North Pole flight. Nobile and half his crew survived.

Britons T. Neville Stack and B.S. Leete flew from London to Karachi between 15 November 1926 and 8 January 1927. The remarkable feature of this flight was the aeroplane used, a tiny D.H.60 Moth lightplane. As

Bottom left: *Lt. Cdr. Richard E. Byrd, famed for his Pole flights. (US Navy)*

Bottom right: *Italian airship N.1. Norge, used by Amundsen to make the second flight over the North Pole in 1926.*

later paragraphs will relate, this was to be only the first of many epic long-distance flights using light aircraft.

Since the conception of the Orteig prize for the first non-stop flight between New York and Paris in 1919 (see page 92), many attempts had been made to win it. Some crews had died when their aircraft, overladen with fuel for the journey, failed to take off and burst into flames or just disappeared over the Atlantic. French fighter ace René Fonck narrowly escaped death by fire on 20 September 1926, although two of his three companions were not so lucky. Another French ace, Charles Nungesser, died in unknown circumstances with his companion after flying out to sea on 8 May 1927. But what was probably the greatest challenge of the time was bound to be conquered. It was, from 20–21 May 1927, but in the most difficult conditions imaginable.

Captain Charles Augustus Lindbergh, a young US Army Air Service reserve pilot, former barnstormer and mail pilot, had selected a small aircraft manufacturing concern to produce an aeroplane capable of flying the Atlantic without stopping, Ryan Airlines Inc. The outcome was the Ryan NYP (New York to Paris) monoplane named *Spirit of St Louis*, powered by a reliable Wright Whirlwind air-cooled radial engine. Because of its size and the huge amount of fuel that had to be carried, the NYP was a single-seater with direct forward vision blocked by a huge tank. One engine and one pilot; it was the most dangerous possible combination for a long flight.

Already tired from a sleepless night, Lindbergh set off in light rain from Roosevelt Field, his aircraft taking a long time to lift from the ground. Thirty-three hours, 30 minutes and 29.8 seconds later he landed at Le Bourget, Paris. It was the first solo non-stop Atlantic crossing by air. He became a world hero.

All at once a spate of light-plane flights filled the newspapers, many no doubt inspired by the young American's achievement. The South African Air Force pilot Lt. R.R. Bentley flew a Moth from London to South Africa during September 1927, Sqn. Ldr. 'Bert' Hinkler chose an Avro 581 Avian for his solo journey from Croydon to Darwin, Australia in February 1928. Lady Heath took an Avian III from South Africa to England between February and May 1928 to become the first woman to fly the route, and Lady Bailey made a return London–South Africa flight between March 1928 and January 1929 in a Moth. Over the period 5-24 May

1930, Britain's Amy Johnson piloted the D.H.60G Gipsy Moth biplane *Jason* on the first solo England-Australia flight by a woman, and in so doing became nearly as well-known as Lindbergh. Two years later, on 20 May 1932, American Amelia Earhart became the first woman to fly solo across the North Atlantic, taking a similar course to Alcock and Brown and landing more auspiciously in Londonderry, Northern Ireland. On 25 August that same year she made the first non-stop transcontinental flight across the USA by a woman. Both flights were made in a Lockheed Vega. The South Atlantic solo was the goal of New Zealand's Jean Batten,

Right: *Amelia Earhart, the first woman to fly solo across the Atlantic.*

Centre right: *Charles Augustus Lindbergh, the first person to fly the Atlantic solo and probably the most famous pilot in aviation history after the Wright brothers.*

Far right: *The unforgettable Wiley Post with his Lockheed Vega* Winnie Mae.

who accomplished this between 11 and 13 November 1936 in a Percival Gull (from Lympne, Kent, in England to Natal in Brazil). And these are only a few of the period's headline-making light-plane flights.

Meanwhile, larger aircraft had also been establishing 'firsts'. The Fokker F.VIIB-3m *Southern Cross*, flown by Captain Charles Kingford Smith and C.T.P. Ulm, and accompanied by two other crew members, made the first true trans-Pacific flight from 31 May to 9 June 1928, from California to Brisbane via Honolulu and Fiji. The same aircraft and crew later crossed the Tasman Sea from 10–11 September. RAF pilots used Fairey Long Range Monoplanes to make non-stop flights between England and India and England and South Africa during 24–26 April 1929 and 6–8 February 1933 respectively. One-eyed American Wiley Post, with Harold Gatty as navigator, flew the Lockheed Vega *Winnie Mae* on a record breaking staged round-the-world flight between 23 June and 1 July 1931, in just 8 days, 15 hours and 51 minutes. Actual flying time was approximately 106 hours. From 22–24 July 1933 Wiley Post accomplished the first solo round-the-world flight in the Vega. For Italy, new achievements over long distances included the first-ever formation flight across the South Atlantic in 1931, during which the 12 Sovoia-Marchetti twin-hull flying-boats were led by General Italo Balbo.

Chapter 8:
Helicopters

The first toy helicopters – whirling rotors spun into flight by the 'string-pull' method – appeared in the 12th century and were first illustrated in a Flemish manuscript of c.1325 and a painting of 1460. These had cruciform rotors and were undoubtedly derived in part from the sails of Persian horizontal windmills built from the 10th century, and the vertical tower windmills introduced in France and Britain in the 12th century as a result of the crusades. But between simple toys and the development of helicopters proper lay hidden technical problems that proved more difficult to solve than those that faced the pioneers of the aeroplane.

The methods of counteracting torque were discovered early and quite easily. The remedy lay in adopting twin rotors that turned in opposite directions to cancel each other's torque, or by using a small tail rotor. Even as we approach the 21st century both twin rotor and tail rotor systems remain in use, plus a new method that replaces the tail rotor with a stream of pressurized air vented from the tailboom. Helicopters whose rotors are driven round by blade-tip power supplies can be single rotor types not creating torque, though still having to deal with the phenomenon of unequal lift (see page 105).

Early pioneers
We owe the name *helicopter* to Leonardo da Vinci (see page 7). His design adopted a large corkscrew-type rotor covered with starched flaxen linen. But power was still a problem, and among several ideas was one for the pilot to wind a rope around the central rotor pylon, pull it to create a spinning effect, and continue the procedure throughout flight – a grand form of 'pull-string'.

Two and a half centuries later, in 1754, the Russian Mikhail Vasilyevich Lomonosov may have flown the first self-powered model helicopter in history. Not a great deal is known of this experiment and it is not universally accepted as fact, but those who give it credence suggest a clockwork-powered model with contra-rotating rotors. What is known is that Lomonosov (1711–65) was a man of great learning who founded the Moscow university, and whose researches into science included theories on electricity. Clearly, he had the background for such a breakthrough in aviation.

The other contenders for the honour of constructing the first self-powered model helicopter were the Frenchmen Launoy and Bienvenu who, on 28 April 1784, put on a demonstration at the Académie des Sciences in Paris. Their tiny model was ingeniously simple, comprising two twin-blade silk and wire rotors at the ends of a stick, contra-rotating as the string of a bowdrill (the stick passing through a hole in the centre of the bow) unwound from one end of the stick. Twelve years later, Sir George Cayley took simplicity still further by trimming eight feathers and pushing them into corks to form four-blade rotors. Cayley referred to the inclination in angle of the feathers as being 'like the sails of a windmill'.

Helicopter development continues
Of many experiments using model helicopters in the 19th century, a few stand out for their ingenuity. The Englishman, W.H. Phillips, used rotor-tip pressure jets to power a model that in 1842 flew many hundreds of metres; the ejected gas that turned the rotor came from the combustion of nitre, charcoal and gypsum. In France in 1863, Vicomte de Ponton d'Amécourt attempted to fly a very creditable model with a small steam engine driving two paddle-like contra-rotating rotors. Despite the inventive talent involved, the engine was just too heavy.

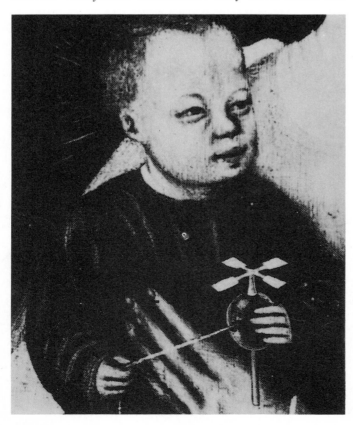

Right: *The earliest illustration of a helicopter model, France, c.1460.*

Far right: *A model of Da Vinci's helicopter design; its helical screw would have been powered by a clockwork motor.*

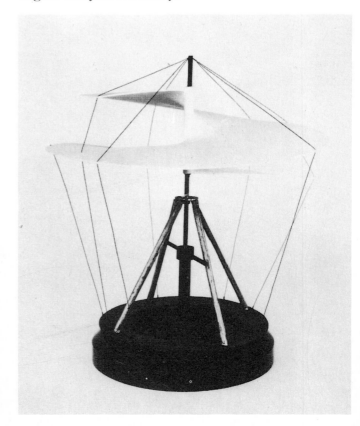

By the 1870s there seemed few realistic alternatives to steam power for a full-sized aircraft, and with this in mind many experiments with models sought the best use of steam. But the old power-to-weight ratio problem remained. In 1877 the Italian, Enrico Forlanini, built a model helicopter in which only the boiler was attached to the engine on the aircraft, the water having already been heated to the required temperature separately. This lightened the power plant sufficiently to allow the model to fly well, but without constant heating the water soon cooled, making flight duration short.

The helicopter progresses

A gamut of helicopter designs appeared in Europe and America in the first years of the 20th century, and they all had one thing in common: failure. Even the Wright brothers had contemplated helicopters, and Wilbur concluded in 1906 that it 'does with great labor only what a balloon does without labor . . . . The helicopter is much easier to design than the aeroplane but it is worthless when done.'

Then it happened. In 1907 Frenchmen Louis Breguet and Professor Richet completed their *Gyroplane No 1*, an ungainly contrivance featuring a cruciform open structure with an eight-blade rotor at each extremity. All four 8m (26 ft 3 in) rotors received power from a single reliable 50 hp Antoinette eight-cylinder petrol engine, the pilot sitting beneath at the centre of the machine. Weighing an impressive 577kg (1,270 lb), the *Gyroplane No 1* lifted from the ground at Douai on 29 September. Unfortunately, due to stability problems, four groundcrew had to steady the machine using long poles, which at one stroke disqualified it from the accolade of having been the first manned helicopter to fly in free flight. On a later occasion, the helicopter flew into a field of growing vegetables. Breguet's second helicopter, the *Gyroplane No 2*, was a more practical-looking machine, but was still a failure. After this Louis Breguet changed over to designing fixed-wing aeroplanes, used with great success before, during and after the First World War, before returning briefly and brilliantly to helicopters in the 1930s.

Less than two months after the first flight of *Gyroplane No 1*, another Frenchman achieved actual free flight in a man-carrying helicopter. Paul Cornu's tandem rotor machine was far more business-like, requiring only a 24 hp Antoinette engine to lift the 260kg (573 lb) machine and pilot off the ground to a

height of 0.3m (1 ft) for 20 seconds, at Lisieux on 13 November 1907. Interestingly, the Cornu helicopter had made its first free flight two days before the Breguet-Richet machine flew, but had only a sack of soot on board to represent the weight of a pilot.

Above: *Paul Cornu on board the world's first free-flying helicopter.*

Below: *The Cornu helicopter of 1907.*

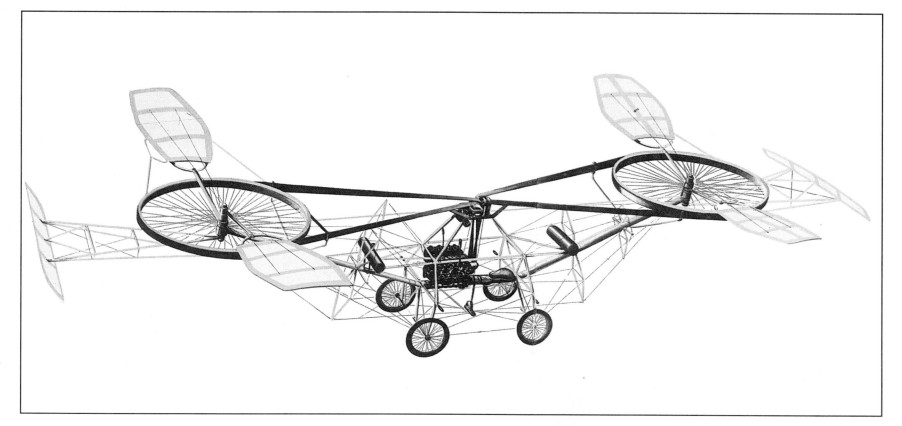

More height

Probably the most remarkable early helicopter experiments, and least remembered, were those of Oberstleutnant Stefan von Petroczy of the Austrian Army Balloon Corps and Dr. Ing. Theodor von Kármán, who attempted to produce a helicopter capable of tethered aerial observation during the First World War. Having experimented with models, von Petroczy first produced a full-size machine with a 190 hp electric motor, which proved capable of lifting three people before the motor burned out. His second and better machine was a fantastic achievement for the time, using a steel tube structure with three open booms, each boom carrying a 120 hp Le Rhône engine and 6m (19 ft 8 in) rotor. The observer and gunner were accommodated in a cylindrical 'cockpit' above the main structure, the helicopter (with rotors running) being winched out from and back to the ground. Incredibly, the helicopter was also designed to descend by parachute (automatically or by the action of the crew) should the engines fail or slow to a dangerously low rate of revolution. This helicopter managed 15 flights before being damaged, demonstrating an ability to stay up for over one hour at a time and remain stable in 17 knot winds. After this, in 1918, von Kármán conducted his own experiments with an electrically-powered helicopter designated PKZ-1.

Right: *Cierva C.4 Autogiro of 1923, the first practical rotorcraft in the history of flight.*

Helicopter technology defined

Conventional aeroplane-type surfaces, used on some early helicopters to vary the direction and speed of flight, did not address the problems of helicopter stability and control. This led to the development of cyclic pitch control or, in simple terms, the ability to adjust the pitch angle (about the lateral axis) of the blades during each 360 degree turn of the rotor. But first there remained the problem of unequal lift, which had not been apparent in the early days of helicopters with multi-rotors and poor performances. The invention of the single-rotor autogyro as a potentially highly practical rotorcraft by Spaniard Juan de la Cierva in the early 1920s, highlighted this problem before it was encountered by workable helicopters.

Unequal lift means that more lift is generated on one side of a turning rotor than the other when moving horizontally, thereby causing some early machines to flip over on their sides. This happened because the speed of the turning blades had to be added to the speed of the head-on airstream for the advancing blades during each rotation cycle, while the retreating blades had the airstream subtracted from the rotor's turning speed. This caused greater lift on one side of the rotor than the other, remembering that the amount of lift over a wing or rotor-blade is in proportion to the airflow over its surface.

To prevent unequal lift, Cierva hit upon the idea of not attaching the blades stiffly onto the rotor head but via flapping hinges. This system was first adopted successfully on his C.4 autogyro (or gyroplane – known to Cierva as Autogiro), which first flew on 9 January 1923 to become the very first practical rotorcraft. Flapping hinges allowed the blades themselves to move up and down slightly as they gained or lost lift during each rotation cycle. This usually prevented the machines flipping over. Flapping of blades remained an important aspect of rotorcraft technology even after the adoption of cyclic pitch (see below).

Cierva autogyros were not helicopters but hybrids marrying features of helicopters and aeroplanes. They had a conventional aeroplane fuselage with either short-span monoplane wings or no wings at all, and an unpowered rotor mounted above. A conventional aeroplane engine and propeller provided forward propulsion in the normal way, causing the rotor to turn of its own

accord until it was spinning sufficiently quickly to provide lift. Autogyros proved highly successful rotorcraft in the 1920s and 1930s before helicopters became practical. Various types joined air forces, and even proved capable of landing on a building during air mail demonstrations. Some were eventually armed: Soviet forces used armed autogyros against the invading Germans in 1941, and others went to sea with the Japanese as anti-submarine aircraft during the Pacific War.

In 1924, the Argentinian Marquis de Pateras Pescara

Above: *Cierva C.40 Rota II, one of a batch of five autogyros ordered by the British Air Ministry to Specification 2/36. The previous C.30A Rota I had gone into service with the RAF, the twelve machines delivered during 1934-5 equipping the School of Army Co-operation at Old Sarum.*

Left: *Kellet KD-1B autogyro, used on the world's first scheduled airmail service by a rotary-winged aircraft that began on 6 July 1939, operated for a short period by Eastern Air Lines.*

carried out the first successful demonstration of cyclic pitch control using his coaxial twin-rotor No 3 helicopter with a tilting rotor head, although a very basic form had put the flyable helicopter of the Dane, Jacob C.H. Ellehammer, into the history books back in 1912. On 18 April 1924 No 3 flew 736m (2,414 ft) at Issy-les-Moulineaux, France, a world record for helicopters. Cyclic pitch control meant that the lifting properties of the blades during each 360 degree turn were adjustable, in No 3's case by blade warping. No 3 also had collective pitch control (see below) for its coaxial rotors.

In modern terms cyclic pitch and its control solves both the problem of unequal lift and control of the direction of flight. The advancing blades automatically take a fine pitch angle when head-on into the airstream and the retreating blades take a greater angle to generate as much lift as possible from the reduced airstream, thereby equalizing lift on each side. By further adjusting the pitch angle of the blades for part of the rotation cycle, the whole rotor can be made to tilt for horizontal directional control. Pitch adjustment is also used to control vertical flight, by using collective pitch (via a collective stick – a collective-pitch lever) to simultaneously increase the pitch of all blades.

Another effect that had to be overcome was that advancing blades 'speed up', threatening distortion if anchored to the head in the horizontal plane. This too was overcome by using hinges, these drag hinges intended to allow marginal horizontal movement of the blades while accelerating. Dampers stopped excessive movement.

Pescara's ability to demonstrate neat little helicopters capable of successful control, and even autorotation should the engine fail, tended to overshadow the achievements of other contemporary helicopters. From 1920 to 1922 Frenchman Damblanc tested his *Alerion* coaxial helicopter that also had cyclic pitch control, though this aeroplane-based machine was less successful. Fellow Frenchman Etienne Oehmichen set the first 1 kilometre distance record for helicopters on 4 May 1924 in his No 2, but this was a highly impractical machine with four primitive main rotors and eight small control rotors all driven by a 180 hp Gnome engine.

In Britain, following some notable success with a primitive multi-rotor helicopter developed at the Leven Shipyard of William Denny Brothers and flown from 7 September 1912, secret experiments were conducted at the Royal Aircraft Establishment at Farnborough using a helicopter devised by Louis Brennan, inventor of the torpedo bearing his name. The Brennan machine had rotor-tip propellers driven by a centrally-mounted engine and flew seventy times in tethered and free form both inside a hangar and outside between 7 December 1921 and 2 October 1925, when it crashed due to control failure. The pilot was Robert Graham, and it was flown to heights of about 3m (10 feet) but was found to be inherently unstable.

In October 1930 the Italian d'Ascanio flew 1.078km (0.67 of a mile) in 8 minutes 45 seconds. His first helicopter had two large two-blade contra-rotating rotors, powered by a 90 hp Fiat A.50 engine. Such was its promise, the machine was purchased by the Italian Air Ministry. D'Ascanio continued his research, working on his third helicopter when the Second World War began. This was designed to have a single main rotor and a small anti-torque rotor.

By October 1933 the world endurance record for helicopters (FAI accredited) still stood at under ten minutes, set by the Belgian Nicolas Florine, and by the start of 1935 the FAI (Fédération Aéronautique Internationale) had not officially recognized for a world record any helicopter flight above a height of 60m (195 ft). Yet by then aeroplanes had flown to altitudes of 14,433m (47,352 ft), attained speeds of 709km/h (440 mph) and distances of 9,140km (5,657 miles). Perhaps the Wrights had been right – maybe the helicopter

wasn't worth a pile of beans!

Compared to the achievements of aeroplanes, helicopters were still hopelessly inefficient. Louis Breguet, by now a successful builder of aeroplanes, rose to the challenge. In 1931 he formed a syndicate with René Dorand to build a new helicopter, based around patented methods of stabilization.

The Breguet-Dorand *Gyroplane Laboratoire*, perhaps to be Louis Breguet's final stab at perfecting a helicopter, was a huge success in terms of flying ability and justified the vast effort involved in its development. Central to its design were the co-axial contra-rotating rotors, driven by a large 350 hp Hispano-Suiza 9Q engine. On 22 December 1935 this machine flew at just over 98km/h (60 mph), and in later tests attained an altitude of 158m (518 ft) and a distance of over 44km (27 miles). Trials and development continued until the outbreak of war in Europe, the aircraft finally falling victim to Allied bombs in 1943 while stored at Villacoublay.

In 1931 Heinrich Focke secured for the aircraft company Focke-Wulf a licence to construct Cierva autogyros. But aeroplanes remained its bread and

butter and in 1933 Focke, with aerobatic pilot Gerd Achgelis, founded Focke-Achgelis to concentrate on helicopters. This new company took over work on the Focke-Wulf Fw 61, a twin-rotor helicopter that had been enormously influenced by earlier autogyro manufacture. Two examples were constructed, the first making its maiden free flight on 26 June 1936. Powered by a 160 hp Siemens-Halske Sh 14A, it flew extremely well. Almost certainly as a result of the publicity received and the records the two machines set, the Fw 61 has been hailed by historians as the world's first successful helicopter, when more factually the Breguet-Dorand had already snatched this honour. Nevertheless, an Fw 61 flew for 1 hour 20 minutes in a closed circuit in June 1937 while piloted by Ewald Rohlfs, and during 1937–38 went on to attain a speed of 122km/h (76 mph), a straight line distance record of more than 230km (143 miles), and an altitude record of 3,427m (11,243 ft). Such a marvel was fully exploited by the Third Reich, and in February 1938 the famous German woman test pilot, Hanna Reitsch, demonstrated the helicopter's complete control by flying it inside the Berlin Deutschland-Halle.

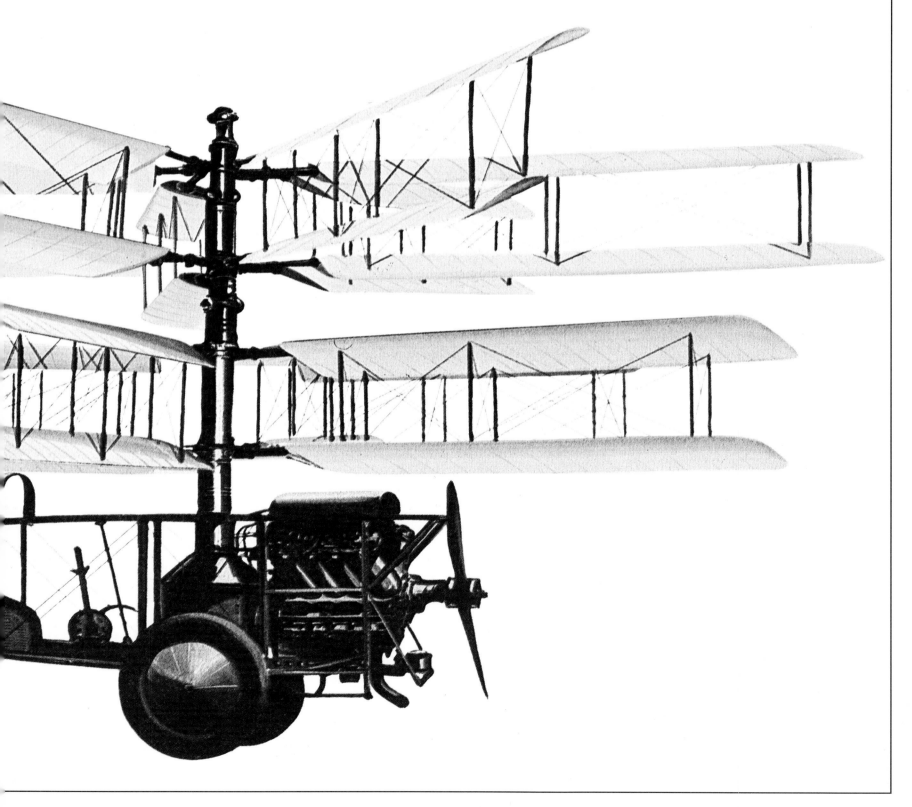

The one problem with the Fw 61 was that it had little or no working potential beyond research and sport flying. So, while the Fw 61 drew media attention, a new and much larger helicopter was designed as the Fa 266 Hornisse. Focke hadn't the slightest intention of dropping his successful twin-rotor layout and so scaled it up to marry the large fuselage needed to produce a six-seat commercial helicopter for the airline Luft-Hansa. This was the world's first purpose-designed transport helicopter but, by the time it was ready to make its first free flight in August 1940, the design had been taken over for military exploitation as the Fa 223 Drache.

Envisaged roles for the Fa 223 included transport itself, rescue, support, reconnaissance and anti-submarine warfare. As a transport it was capable of carrying a 1,280 kg (2,822 lb) load. Operational trials with the helicopter began in 1942 and all looked set for widescale production and service. But Allied bombing of factories prevented any worthwhile production, and instead of the 400 machines a month proposed, fewer than a dozen flew during the war.

Three Fa 223s were on hand with Luft-Transportstaffel 40 towards the end of the war in Europe, an operational unit which also flew a similar number of Flettner Fl 282 Kolibri helicopters. The Fl 282 had been developed from the non-production Fl 265, itself based on the fuselage and engine arrangement of the earlier single-rotor Fl 185 autogiro/helicopter. However, unlike the Fl 185, the later types were pure helicopters using side-by-side intermeshing rotors. A two-seater, the Fl 282 could attain 150km/h (93 mph) and fly up to 300km (186 miles) when only the pilot was on board. It appeared to have an outstanding

future as a ship-borne anti-submarine and spotter helicopter as well as for land-based roles. Very limited operational service began in 1943, used in part on board ship to spot for German convoys in the Aegean and Mediterranean. But again Allied bombing made mass production impossible and few of the thousands anticipated were built.

Although the Fa 223 and Fl 282 were the principal German helicopters of the war, other rotary-wing machines appeared. For example, Focke Achgelis produced a single-seat gyro kite designated Fa 330 Bachstelze, intended to be towed by submarines for over-the-horizon spotting. In an entirely different programme, compressed air and fuel, fed through hollow rotor blades and burnt at blade-tip combustion chambers, was the principle behind Friedrich von Doblhoff's full-size jet-driven helicopters of 1942–45, built for experimental use in Austria by WNF. These were the first of their kind in the world.

One rotor is sufficient

Before the USA became committed to the Second World War, helicopter experimentation in that country took much the same course as it had in pre-war Europe, although with less success. Designs came and went and autogyros ruled the rotary-wing scene. But for Igor Sikorsky, who had left his native Russia for America, his huge achievements with landplanes and flying-boats had not blunted a passion for his first love, the helicopter. Sikorsky had taken out patents to protect his helicopter innovations in 1931, believing in the single main rotor/small vertical anti-torque rotor layout. Of course, Sikorsky had not been the first to see the benefits, and it should be recorded that as early as 1874 Achenbach had suggested much the same.

Sikorsky's aircraft manufacturing company was then a division of United Technologies, and it was from this management that he had to seek permission in 1938 to begin serious development of a helicopter. The result-

Below: *Flettner Fl 282 Kolibri, one of the two types of German helicopter to become operational during the Second World War but in extremely small number due to Allied bombing of factories. The Fl 282 could attain 150km/h (93 mph) and fly 300km (186 miles) with the pilot only on board.*

At the USAAF's behest, Sikorsky had begun work in 1941 on a two-seater for experimental military use, and this XR-4 first took to the air on 14 January 1942. That May it was flown in short stages from Sikorsky's Stratford works to Dayton, Ohio, where military evaluation was to take place. This in itself was an epic journey of 1,225km (760 miles), and it was made without incident. That same year a further 30 R-4 type helicopters were ordered for operational evaluation as YR-4As and Bs, of which ten went to the US Navy and the RAF, as HNS-1s and Hoverfly Is respectively (their first ever helicopters), followed by other orders. The helicopter as we know it today had arrived.

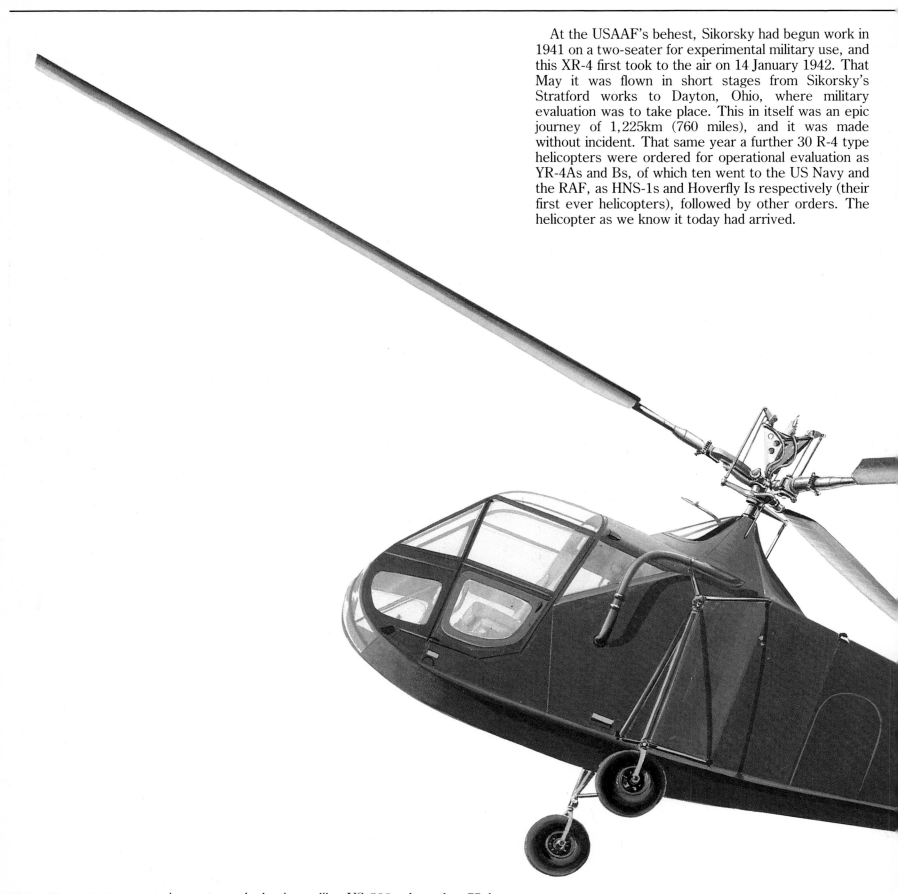

Right: *Sikorsky R-4B, the first helicopter to be built in considerable number on an assembly line and the first helicopter operated by the US and British services.*

ing extremely business-like VS-300 adopted a 75 hp Lycoming engine and had none of the huge rotor or undercarriage outriggers associated with the earlier Breguet-Dorand and Fw 61 helicopters. Tethered trials began on 14 September 1939, with Igor as pilot. The cyclic control system was found wanting, and in a retrograde step the VS-300 was modified to include a new tail structure incorporating short outriggers with small horizontal rotors for longitudinal and lateral control. The single main rotor and small vertical tail rotor remained, but the former was now only intended for lift. In this form the VS-300 made its first free flight on 13 May 1940 and was entirely successful. In April 1941 it became the first helicopter to take off from water, using flotation bags, and in May smashed the Fw 61's endurance record.

During the course of 1941 further modifications to the VS-300 gradually saw the re-adoption of the plain single main rotor/single small vertical tail rotor layout, with full cyclic pitch control and more engine power.

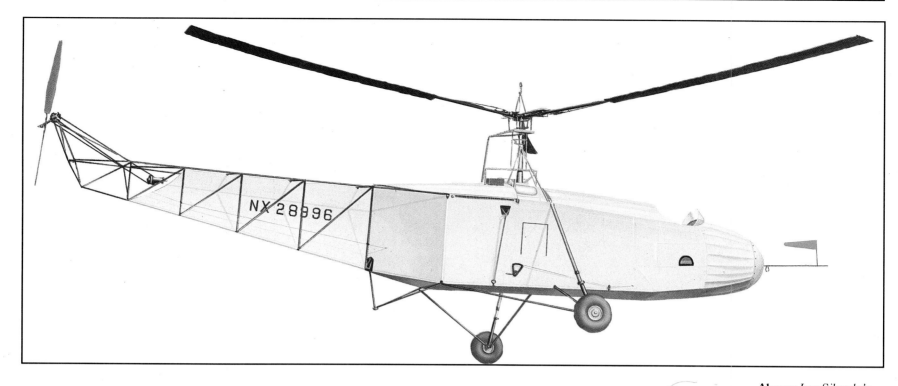

Above: *Igor Sikorsky's first successful helicopter, the VS-300 underwent several changes in shape during its four year development. Here, the helicopter is shown in its 1943 definitive form as the VS-300A.*

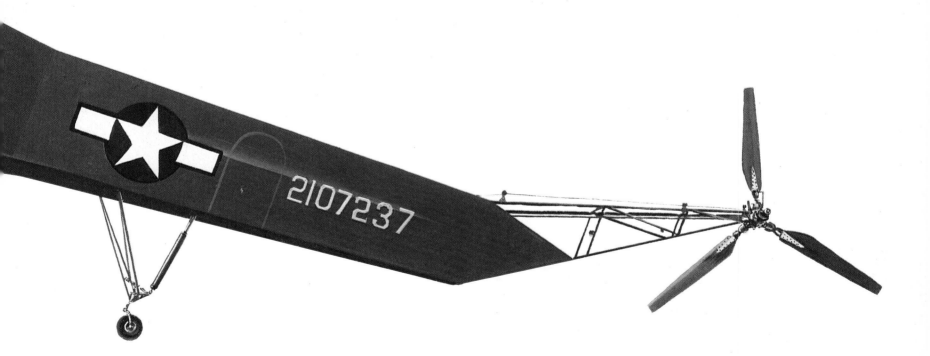

Chapter 9:
Military Aviation
between the Wars

At the beginning of November 1918, just days before the Armistice, the Royal Air Force had reached the peak of its size. But by the close of 1919 a massive transformation had taken place. Only 12 operational squadrons survived the axe for immediate post-war operations, plus a naval first-line strength of one full squadron for spotter-reconnaissance duties, half a squadron of torpedo-bombers, just one Flight of fighters and two Flights operating flying-boats and seaplanes. The RAF had, at a stroke, almost ceased to exist as a fighting force.

Of the RAF's 12 front-line squadrons, only two were kept in Britain. The remainder were deployed in India, the Middle East and in Germany. The wartime D.H.9A light bomber and Bristol F.2B two-seat fighter became general-purpose aircraft, active almost immediately to police Iraq, Aden and the North-West Frontier of India. In this new role they became highly successful. The British government, anxious to cut military expenditure to the bone, quickly seized on this success and in 1922 made the RAF entirely responsible for the internal security of Iraq, superseding the large army presence. Here was control of security without an army of occupation. Fortunately, from early 1920 the RAF had expanded again, providing the means to carry out the difficult and often hazardous task. In October 1922 the RAF began its exclusive 'air control' operations in Iraq, using four squadrons of D.H.9As, one of F.2Bs, one of Snipe single-seat fighters, plus two newly formed squadrons deploying Vickers Vernons, the world's first purpose-designed troop transports. Air Control kept the RAF alive in the early years after the Armistice, and eventually forced the purchase of new warplanes.

The naval side of British air operations also expanded in the early 1920s, but at a slower rate due to its sea-borne role. In 1922 and 1923 the Royal Navy received its first two post-war aircraft carriers, and accordingly by the start of 1924 the number of Flights had risen to 13. Later that year the naval air component of the RAF became known as the Fleet Air Arm (FAA), although not resuming independence from the RAF until 1939. Further expansion was slow, but two more carriers were taken in during 1928 and, with *Furious* and *Argus*, the Royal Navy had six carriers until 1938, when *Ark Royal* was added. Amazingly, the slow speed of aircraft in the 1920s allowed the FAA to operate without aircraft arresting gear on deck (except for a system of longitudinal wires on *Argus* until 1926), but a cross-wire system was introduced in the early 1930s. Meanwhile, an FAA Blackburn Dart torpedo-bomber had made the first-ever night landing on a carrier (*Furious*), on 1 July 1926.

Below: Popularly known as the 'Brisfit', the Bristol F2B fighter, along with the DH9A, enjoyed an extended operational life well beyond World War I, both being used very effectively to police Britain's then extensive interests within Africa, Asia and the Middle East.

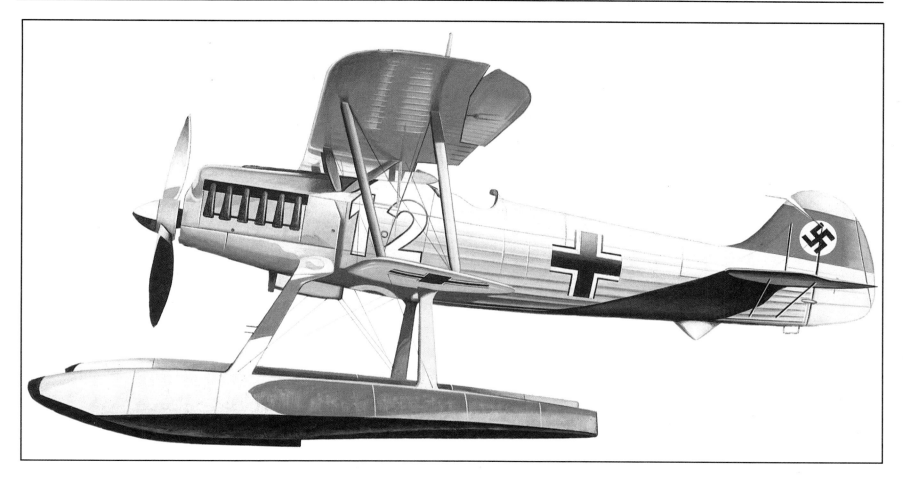

Japan's air force benefited from post-war French assistance, while the navy received British help. Indeed, the first aircraft to operate from Japan's initial aircraft carrier (the *Hosho*) in 1923 had been designed by an Englishman, and on the occasion of its first ship flights that February the Mitsubishi 1MF1 was actually crewed by a British pilot.

Another country to receive its first proper aircraft carrier at this time was the USA; a Vought VE-7SF fighter became the first aeroplane to fly from the USS *Langley* on 17 October 1922. In November and December 1927 the US Navy commissioned two new carriers, the *Saratoga* and *Lexington*. In 1927 France also acquired its own first carrier, the *Béarn*.

France, Italy and the Soviet Union had also begun the era of peace with greatly reduced air strengths. But Italy quickly passed into high gear, with the founding on 23 March 1923 of the new Regia Aeronautica by Benito Mussolini. Trouble with its African colonies kept Italian aircraft busy throughout the inter-war period. Typical of Italian colonial aircraft was the triple-engined Caproni Ca 133 that entered service in 1935, in time to help in the one-sided air war against the badly-armed tribesmen of Abyssinia (Ethiopia). Indeed, a Ca 133 made the

first photographic reconnaissance over Addis Ababa, on 6 March 1936. Resistance collapsed that May.

Abyssinia was only one war of many to breach the 'peace' of 1919–39. For the Soviet Union, fighting against Poland opened and closed the inter-war period. And Japan waged war against China almost continuously through the last decade of peace, starting with an attack on 18 September 1931. But of these and other conflicts to engage aircraft, the Spanish Civil War that began on 18 July 1936 became the greatest, threatening to spill over into a world-engulfing crisis.

Just two days after 17 Spanish military garrisons at home and in Morocco went into revolt against the elected Republican government, 20 German Junkers Ju 52/3mg3e bomber-transporters arrived at Seville to start an airlift of Nationalist forces from Morocco to support the rebellion. These were escorted by six Heinkel He 51 fighters. No fewer than 7,350 troops plus artillery were airlifted to Spain in about six weeks, and two more operations of this kind were undertaken in August. But just how was it that Germany, which according to the Treaty of Versailles should not have had an air force at all, could carry out the first mass airlift in history?

Above: *The handsome Heinkel He 51 was the mainstay of Germany's newly emergent fighter forces by the time they were first publicly revealed in 1935. Depicted here is the float-equipped He 51B variant primarily operated by units of the German Navy.*

Below: USS *Langley, the first US Navy aircraft carrier, had been converted from the collier* Jupiter. *The twin funnels could be lowered during deck landings. It was sunk by the Japanese in 1942.*

The Luftwaffe reforms

Almost from the signing of the Versailles Treaty, Germany had managed to flout many of its conditions regarding aircraft construction, either by agitation of the Allies to seek open change or surreptitious aeroplane construction abroad. Back-door means were sought to create the foundations of renewed military aviation. In 1921, the German Defence Ministry established a small air section, under civil guise. At the end of 1923 the Ministry concluded an agreement with the Soviet Union, who established a training camp for German air and ground crews at Lipezk, near Moscow. Meanwhile, to get around the manufacturing ban, some German companies set up production facilities abroad.

Junkers in 1923 opened a factory at Fili, again near Moscow, where it began by producing H-21 parasol-wing reconnaissance fighters, ostensibly for Soviet use. This production facility remained in business until 1927. Junkers had also built a factory at Limhamn in Sweden in 1923.

Dornier favoured Italy and Altenrhein in Switzerland, and it was from the latter that came the Do F, the final aircraft in a batch of so-called freight transports. From the Do F, first flown on 7 May 1932, Dornier developed its Do 11. A bold decision was made to produce it in Germany, under the guise of the same freighter role but actually intended to become a twin-engined bomber for the secretly reforming Luftwaffe. To hide their real purpose, while also giving aircrews flight experience, the first Do 11s went to the State Railways. From the Do 11 was derived the Do 13 and 23.

By the late 1920s Germany had already become the world's most air-minded nation. Its aircraft were, by any standard, at the forefront. In 1929 First World War air ace Hermann Göring was elected to the Reichstag and immediately pressed for the re-establishment of the Luftwaffe. German aircraft manufacturers were, of course, in a good position to put this into effect. As well as Dornier and Junkers, others had built up experience, including Ernst Heinkel, who during the 1920s had his designs built under licence in Sweden. He had also designed military products to contract for both Japan and the Soviet Union, including fighters.

In 1932 German President von Hindenburg offered Adolf Hitler the Chancellorship of Germany. Hitler refused unless granted full powers. On 30 January 1933 these powers were acceded and Hitler took office.

Göring became Reichskommissar for air, then air minister. The clandestine Luftwaffe was soon forming.

From the single-engined Ju 52 of 1930, Junkers developed the triple-engined Ju 52/3m, and in 1933 'Iron Annies' were converted into bomber-transports for the still secret Luftwaffe's auxiliary bomber force. They stayed on in service as bombers throughout the remainder of the 1930s alongside newer types such as the He 111 and Ju 86. Meanwhile, Arado had produced a prototype biplane fighter in Germany by 1930 as the Ar 64. From it was developed the Ar 65 of 1931 and this, with the Heinkel He 51, entered production in 1933, with examples of the former being delivered the same year.

On 27 May 1933 Japan withdrew from the League of Nations. On 14 October Germany did the same, marking the demise of talks on disarmament. Ten days later Winston Churchill made a speech in the British House of Commons, warning that Germany was rapidly becoming the world's most heavily armed nation. Few others in Britain or abroad, it seemed, wanted to know or risk a confrontation by insisting that the terms of the Versailles Treaty were obeyed.

On 26 January 1934 Germany concluded a ten-year non-aggression pact with Poland. That July, in the face of clear German military expansion, the British government attempted to gain Parliamentary support for an additional eight RAF squadrons a year for five years, but was defeated by the Labour and Liberal parties.

Signalled by these indecisions, on 9 March 1935 Germany announced to the world the existence of its reborn Luftwaffe. One week later, blaming other nations for not disarming, Germany repudiated the military clauses of the Versailles Treaty and announced a huge rearmament programme. Hurriedly, as a message of warning to Germany, on 2 May France and the Soviet Union signed an alliance agreement. The Soviets also formed an alliance with Czechoslovakia on 16 May. To this, Germany reacted by calling it a move to give the Soviet air force advanced bases from which to attack. Six days later the first moves were made by Britain to increase the size of the RAF after all.

Air structures

Up to the mid-1930s, the basic configuration of warplanes had changed little since the First World War. Of course, performance had risen greatly through

Right: Dornier Do 23G bomber, powered by two BMW VIU engines and capable of 260km/h (162 mph). Bombload was 1,000kg (2,200 lb). At the time of their manufacture the reborn Luftwaffe had not been announced, requiring the use of civil registrations to hide their real purpose.

Far right: Production of the Soviet Tupolev TB-3 metal heavy bomber lasted from 1931 to 1938, covering 818 aircraft. These represented the world's most potent bombing force, operating against the Japanese in 1938-9, Finland and finally the invading Germans. Here a TB-3 is being used for paratroop dropping.

streamlining and the use of much more powerful engines, but on the whole fighters and bombers were still mostly wood or metal biplanes with fabric covering, the majority having open cockpits and fixed landing gears, and the standard fighter armament remained twin machine-guns.

There were exceptions, including the Italian and German bomber-transport monoplanes already mentioned. Elsewhere, the Soviet Union had put big Tupolev all-metal cantilever monoplane bombers into service since 1929, and in the early 1930s TB-1s and TB-3s certainly represented the world's most potent heavy bombing force.

Across the border, the Polish air force had already deployed gull-wing PZL P-7s in 1932, making it the first in the world to have nothing but all-metal monoplane fighters in front-line use. But these were lightly armed, fairly slow and had both open cockpits and fixed undercarriages. From 1934 improved P-11s went into service, each with four guns. Much faster, they were the leaders of their time. But technology soon overtook them, and Poland was to pay a heavy price for not updating its P-7s and P-11s prior to the Second World War.

Above: *Heinkel He 51A, 84 of which were supplied to the Luftwaffe. The 135 He 51B fighters and He 51C ground attack fighters sent to Spain were soon outmatched by contemporary Soviet I-15s, although on their very first day of operations He 51s destroyed two Republican aircraft. Power was provided by a 750hp BMW VI engine.*

Out with the old

1935 was the year that marked the true entrance of modern warplanes into the world arena, albeit in prototype forms – cantilever monoplanes with enclosed accommodation and retractable undercarriages, more heavily armed and in most cases constructed of metal. They included the German Junkers Ju 87 dive-bomber and Messerschmitt Bf 109 fighter, the French Morane-Saulnier MS.406 fighter, US B-17 Flying Fortress bomber, and British Hurricane fighter.

Warplanes that first took to the air in 1936 included the graceful British Spitfire fighter, Whitley and Wellington bombers, German Messerschmitt Bf 110 strategic fighter and Junkers Ju 88 bomber, and Japan's Nakajima Ki-27 fighter.

So, by the end of 1936, many of the major combat planes to be used in the coming world war had flown as prototypes. The biplane, on the whole, was about to be relegated to the past, although never to be forgotten is the Fleet Air Arm's Fairey Swordfish torpedo-bomber that, despite its antiquated appearance, open cockpits, fixed undercarriage and 222km/h (138 mph) top speed, did not even enter service until 1936. And even later than the Swordfish was Italy's Fiat CR 42 Falco biplane, a traditional twin-gun fighter that first flew in 1939 and went on to serve throughout Italy's war.

Further and higher

In-flight refuelling, cabin pressurization and radar came into prominence in the late 1930s, and yet all stemmed from research conducted during or just after the First World War.

Britain's Squadron Commander John Porte, RNAS, the experienced pilot who had been expected to attempt a transatlantic air crossing in the Curtiss *America* in 1914, conducted the first serious flight refuelling experiments in 1917. The outcome of these trials is largely unreported and history usually jumps to 1923 for the next stepping stone. On 27 June that year Americans Captain Lowell Smith and Lt. John Richter gave the first fully successful demonstration of in-flight refuelling while crewing a D.H.4B over Rockwell Field in San Diego. Exactly two months later they began an endurance flight that lasted 37 hours 15 minutes 44 seconds, during which their aircraft was refuelled in the air on 15 separate occasions by another D.H.4B. Practical application of in-flight refuelling, however, had to wait until August 1939, when Imperial Airways (with the help of the British company, Flight Refuelling Ltd, that perfected a system) began operation of two Short S.23 C-class flying-boats on a transatlantic mail service that used air refuelling. Only 16 crossings were possible before the war in Europe ended the service.

Britain also devised another fascinating method of stretching range, so bold in its conception that it is hard to believe that Imperial Airways actually put it into service. This was the Short-Mayo Composite devised

Below: Fiat CR 42 fighter biplanes, which remained operational throughout Italy's participation in the Second World War.

Bottom: Fleet Air Arm Fairey Swordfish I torpedo-bombers, reconnaissance and spotter biplanes.

Left: *The US-built DH-4B version of the British D.H.4 Liberty Plane proved an ideal platform for the first USAAS in-flight refuelling experiments, the close proximity of the two cockpits allowing easy co-operation between the crew members.*

Below: *The Short-Mayo Composite, with the seaplane* Mercury *attached above the* Maia *flying-boat. The first take-off in coupled form was made on 20 January 1938, with the first test separation following on 6 February.*

Below: *German wartime Mistel composite, with a Focke-Wulf Fw 190 fighter above an unmanned Junkers Ju 88 packed with explosives.*

by Major R.H. Mayo. It saw a modified Short C-class flying-boat carry above its fuselage a smaller seaplane. Understanding that a great deal of fuel is used during take off, especially when carrying a heavy payload, the idea was for the seaplane (with engines running) to be carried into the air, from where it would separate and continue on its long journey. The first trial separation was made on 6 February 1938 and on 21 July the seaplane *Mercury* left *Maia* to carry newspapers and photographs non-stop to Montreal. Other flights were made, including one to the Orange River in South Africa from 6–8 October, a distance of 9,652km (5,997.5 miles), which remains in 1990 the official world distance record for seaplanes. But plans to further develop the concept were thwarted by war.

But warfare has its own requirements, and during the Second World War air launching of one aircraft from another did take place. The most dramatic example, perhaps, was a reverse of the Short-Mayo Composite, devised by Germany to use a small Bf 109 or Fw 190 fighter to guide and then release a large Junkers Ju 88 converted into a pilotless flying bomb, in the famous Mistel Composite operations. The hollow-charge warhead of each Ju 88 contained an impressive 1,725kg (3,802 lb) of high-explosive. Intended to be used mainly against shipping, the first Mistel operation was mounted on the night of 24-25 June 1944, striking Allied vessels in the Seine Bay.

Even before Smith and Richter began in-flight refuelling trials, another D.H.4 had been used for the first pressurized cabin experiments, conducted at Wright Field from 8 June 1921. But the ingestion period for this innovation was also protracted, and it was not until the end of 1938 that the first pressurized airliner flew as the Boeing Stratoliner. Some use of pressurization did take place during the next world war (most importantly by the Boeing B-29 Superfortress bomber), but pressurization only came into its own after the war.

A further American innovation of the early 1920s which came to fruition at the end of the next decade was radar, although it has to be remembered that the German Christen Hülsmeyer had patented a very basic design for a radar set as early as 1904. In September 1922, technicians at the Anacostia Naval Aircraft Radio Laboratory, USA, managed to generate the first radar signatures. A moratorium followed as the science of electronics had to advance sufficiently to allow further progress with radar. In June 1936 a workable but experimental radar was built in Britain under a team led by Robert Watson-Watt. With this an aircraft flying 27.5km (17 miles) away was detected – a major breakthrough. Work now gathered pace, and by July the range had more than doubled. It was trebled by September. With war in Europe looking increasingly likely, Britain established the Chain Home radar network of ground radar stations to help in its defence, with receiver and transmitter aerials suspended between groups of girder towers hundreds of feet high and able to detect at a range of 193km (120 miles) and at heights above 4,570m (15,000 ft). A low system followed. As events proved, the chain was vital to air victory during the Battle of Britain.

Left: *Artist's impression of a Boeing Stratocruiser, the type of airliner remembered historically as the first to adopt cabin pressurization.*

World War – 1937?

It would not be unreasonable to say that the Second World War began in 1937. On 7 July, following a night clash of Chinese and Japanese troops at Lukouchiao, close to Peiping, Japan launched a full-scale invasion. It was another nail in the coffin of peace, coming so soon after the German *Legion Condor*, backing the Nationalists in Spain, had bombed Guernica, seat of Spain's Basque government, on 26 April. This raid was much worse than the intensive air bombardment of Madrid on 6 November 1936, warning of things to come.

Hitler hoped that by supporting the Nationalists during the Spanish Civil War he would secure a new source of raw materials and help to establish another fascist state in Europe. It was also an opportunity to

Below: *German Messerschmitt Bf 109E-3 fighter-bombers operated by the so-called volunteer Condor Legion in Spain towards the end of the Civil War, carrying the distinctive Spanish Nationalist identification cross on the tail. (MBB)*

flex Germany's military muscle, test new aeroplanes and give German aircrews 'hands-on' experience of modern air warfare. The first German combat aircraft were not as good as those supplied to the Nationalists by Italy, but the late arrival in Spain of new Bf 109 fighters, Ju 87 dive-bombers, and He 111, Ju 86 and Do 17 bombers provided the Nationalists with their best aircraft of the Civil War.

Republican forces were supported internationally. The Soviet Union sent 1,409 of the 1,947 aeroplanes received from abroad, joining perhaps 300 Spanish machines. Initially, Soviet Polikarpov fighters and Tupolev SB-2 bombers had been at least a match for Nationalist machines, but the new German warplanes turned the table. In March 1939 the Civil War ended in victory for the Nationalists. Hitler was now more convinced than ever that his Luftwaffe could outperform the Soviet air force and any others that got in the way of his ambitions.

Meanwhile, in July 1938 heavy fighting broke out between Soviet and Japanese forces along the borders of Korea, Manchuria and Siberia, lasting almost a month and flaring up again later. That September Germany enforced narrow air corridors for foreign airliners flying over its territory, with the intention of masking the military activity that was taking place. But now a crisis was developing between Germany and Czechoslovakia, so serious that the British Prime Minister, Neville Chamberlain, flew to Munich in the hope of mediating. On the 23 September Imperial Airways began an evacuation of British citizens from Prague. The next day Czechoslovakia mobilized its forces. With the crisis peaking and threatening world war, on 29 July Britain and France agreed to allow Germany to annex the Sudetenland, home of three million Germans. Chamberlain returned to Britain, declaring 'peace in our time'.

Below: *The Polikarpov I-15 fighter entered Soviet service in 1935 and became one of the most important aircraft supporting the Republicans during the Spanish Civil War.*

Chapter 10: New Enemies and Old Friends

The Munich conference of 1938 had demonstrated the reluctance of the League of Nations to confront Germany's posturing, and there was nothing Britain and France could do at that time but accede to Hitler's ambitions, hoping the occupation of the Sudeteland would put an end to them. Little did they know that the occupation of Austria and the Sudetenland went only part of the way to fulfilling Hitler's secret *Lebensraum* plan of November 1937 for increased German 'living space'. The rest of Czechoslovakia plus Poland and the Soviet Union remained to be taken.

Far from helping to calm political tension, appeasement merely encouraged Hitler to press on with claims towards Czechoslovakia. The European situation was becoming desperate. Hand in hand with diplomacy, a signal was needed to warn Hitler off other expeditions. On 31 March 1939 France and Britain guaranteed aid to Greece, Poland and Romania in the event of outside aggression.

The countdown to war started in August 1939. On the 22nd, Germany and the Soviet Union signed a startling ten-year non-aggression pact in Moscow, which included secret clauses for the partition of Poland. Simultaneously, Hitler issued final orders for the invasion of Poland. British efforts to find a peaceful solution fell on uncompromising German ears. But Poland, expecting an invasion only from Germany, was confident in its mobilization. Its air force had 680 front-line machines, of which 129 were P-7 and P-11 fighters. On 31 August Britain too mobilized.

Blitzkrieg

In the very early hours of 1 September 1939 a sinister-looking cranked-wing Junkers Ju 87B of Stuka-geschwader I dived towards Poland's Dirschau railway bridge at Tczew, its engine screaming. It was the opening gambit of Germany's lightning war.

On 2 September ten RAF squadrons of Fairey Battle light bombers left for France and on the 3rd Britain and France declared war on Germany. The same day an RAF Blenheim IV crossed into German airspace to photograph naval units leaving Wilhelmshaven, and that night Whitley III bombers dropped propaganda leaflets on Bremen, Hamburg and in the Ruhr, hoping to rouse the populace against war. Over the coming days RAF Hurricanes, Blenheims and Lysanders flew to France. Meanwhile, on the 4th, Blenheim IVs of the RAF's 110 Squadron dropped the first British bombs of the war, striking the German Fleet in the Schillig Roads.

In accordance with its pact with Germany, on 17 September Soviet forces invaded Poland from the east. Poland's forces fought on. But the inevitable end came on 5 October. Poland was divided. On 30 November the Soviet Union turned towards Finland.

In Poland, Germany had shown the world that, despite fine words, it had scant regard for the distinction between military and civilian targets, and that given a weak opposition the Luftwaffe would ruthlessly apply the doctrines of total war.

The fight against the Allies began at a much slower

pace, leading some to wonder if there really was a proper war being fought and whether, even now, peace could be resurrected. It was the period of the so-called Phoney War. A Fairey Battle of No 88 Squadron of the RAF's Advanced Air Striking Force in France claimed the first British victory over a German aircraft, bringing down a Bf 109E on 20 September. On the 26th an FAA carrier-based Blackburn Skua forced down one of three German Dornier Do 18 flying-boats.

German aircraft raided the Allies, and the Allies struck Germany, each passing day gradually bringing more action. On 18 November German aircraft first dropped magnetic mines in British coastal waters, causing serious shipping losses. These were Germany's first secret weapons. Fortunately, one mine dropped on the 20th was recovered intact, giving the scientists a chance to find a countermeasure. Vickers Wellington bombers modified to carry 14.6m (48 ft) de-gaussing hoops to explode the mines was one answer, these coming into use in January 1940. By then the RAF had stopped most daylight bomber missions over Germany, since half the force of 24 Wellingtons sent out to make a reconnaissance of the Wilhelmshaven/Schillig Roads area on 18 December had been shot down.

Then, in April 1940, the Phoney War came to an abrupt end and matters turned very real. On the 9th Denmark fell without a fight. German intentions turned simultaneously towards Norway, but here there would be no easy capitulation.

On 10 May Germany invaded Belgium and the Netherlands. Faced by the small but committed joint air forces of Holland and Belgium, supported by French and available British aircraft plus anti-aircraft fire, now the Luftwaffe received its first real punishment. Again using its Blitzkrieg (lightning war) method of invasion, with fast-moving ground forces backed by airborne troops, heavy air cover and bombing of the enemy, Germany committed huge resources to battle. But by the end of that first day the Luftwaffe had lost a massive

304 aircraft destroyed and 51 damaged. The main casualties had been Junkers Ju 52/3m transports (157 lost) and He 111 bombers (72 lost or damaged). It was the heaviest German loss of any day in the entire war, but it still had the numbers to press on to victory. On 28 May British troops began evacuating from Dunkirk, RAF Fighter Command offering limited air cover. The evacuation was completed by 4 June.

On 5 June Germany regrouped its forces for the Battle of France. Five days later Italy declared war on the Allies and began its invasion of Southern France, and the following day bombed Malta. The RAF responded immediately by bombing the Fiat factories at Turin. On the 14th Paris fell and within four days the last flyable RAF aircraft based in France returned to Britain. On the 21st Hitler received French officials for the capitulation, meeting in the same railway carriage in the Compiegne Forest that had been used for Germany's surrender of 1918. The 25th marked the official end to Franco-German hostilities.

Above: *Vickers Wellington bomber converted to D.W.I form to carry a degaussing hoop to explode German magnetic mines.*

Facing page: *In 1938 the Bristol Blenheim IV entered production as a three-seat light bomber for the RAF, superseding the Blenheim I that had a much blunter nose.*

Below: *'Iron Allies', Junkers Ju 52/3ms, provided the Luftwaffe with its standard transport for the period 1933-45, and its initial bomber force.*

The battle to save Europe

Only Britain now stood in the way of Germany's European ambitions. Its fighting ranks were swelled by small numbers of Free French, Belgians, Poles and Czechs, plus the first Empire forces which rallied to One King – One Flag. The RAF could muster about 50 squadrons of Hurricane, Spitfire, Defiant, Blenheim and Gladiator fighters – some squadrons crewed by Czechs, Poles, New Zealanders, South Africans, Australians and Canadians – against which the Luftwaffe could range close to 3,000 fighters and bombers. If the Luftwaffe had learned anything from its invasion of the Low Countries it was that Blitzkrieg required the attacker to start with an overwhelming advantage in the air, and to use surprise.

From early in the war Britain had desperately sought material help from the USA, which had declared its neutrality at the outbreak of war and imposed an arms export embargo. But in early November 1939, the US government had enough popular support to allow sales to the Allies on a cash and carry basis, exacting a heavy price. It was not until March 1941 that President Roosevelt authorized Lend-Lease, allowing vital materials to be sent without requiring immediate payment.

Meanwhile, since 10 July 1940 the Luftwaffe had begun more frequent attacks on British shipping and naval bases and ports. They were strongly opposed by the RAF, a confrontation that marked the start of the Battle of Britain. Germany knew that if it was to press a mainly sea-borne invasion of Britain without catastrophic losses, the Royal Navy and RAF had to be neutralized. The early raids on naval targets forced the Admiralty to evacuate many of its warships from the Channel, making convoy protection around the south

Below: *The best remembered British fighter of the Second World War was undoubtedly the Supermarine Spitfire.*

Bottom: *The Boulton Paul Defiant was a new fighter of 1937 appearance with a 'sting' in its tail. Enemy aircraft tempted to attack from the side or rear were met with a hail of bullets from the four 0.303 in Browning guns in the dorsal turret. No other guns were fitted. Often mistaken by the Luftwaffe to be a Hurricane, the Defiant was reasonably successful at first. From August 1940 it was, however, proving vulnerable and assigned night fighter duties carrying A.I. radar. In this it proved outstandingly successful over the coming months. These Defiants belong to No 264 Squadron, RAF, based at Kirton-in-Lindsey.*

coast almost impossible. Now only the RAF stood before invasion. From 8 August the attacks on Britain gained in strength, hit and run raids by single or small groups of warplanes giving way to large formations of bombers escorted by many fighters. The order was to destroy the RAF to prevent air opposition during Operation Sea Lion, the invasion itself. On the 11th the first major attack was mounted, with He 111 and Ju 88 bombers striking Weymouth and Portland. On the 12th a huge force of 63 bombers raided the radar stations at Ventnor and also struck Portsmouth. But this was just the beginning.

It seemed Britain could not withstand such a weight of opposition, but it had two important advantages. In contrast to its earlier campaigns, the Luftwaffe had to fly across open sea to press attacks and then return to the continent. This not only stretched mission distances

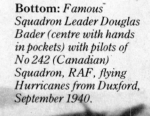

Above: *During the Battle of Britain, RAF fighter pilots had German bombers as their main targets, leaving many strewn over the English countryside. One of the worse hit German bombers was the Heinkel He 111, unable to evade or outgun the fighters and with too little armour protection.*

Bottom: *Famous Squadron Leader Douglas Bader (centre with hands in pockets) with pilots of No 242 (Canadian) Squadron, RAF, flying Hurricanes from Duxford, September 1940.*

but, because of Britain's radar network, the element of surprise had gone. Britain had 21 Chain Home radar stations looking out into the sky for the enemy, supplemented by 25 Chain Home Low stations with rotating aerials that could detect low-flying enemy aircraft at 80 km (50 miles) range. These radar stations multiplied the operational capability of RAF fighters, which could be scrambled against an incoming enemy whose direction and strength were known. Germany had also made the mistake of relying exclusively on twin-engined bombers, so that on long missions warload had to be measured against fuel requirements.

The ease with which the Luftwaffe had won its continental victories also worked in Britain's favour. Göring launched the same types of aircraft against Britain as he had against continental targets, and to Hurricanes and Spitfires the Ju 87 was simple prey. The evidence of this soon lay burning on the meadows of England. The Do 17 bomber was little better. The

Below: *Luftwaffe Major von Burlow, flying the Messerschmitt Bf 109 with Jagdgeschwader (Fighter Wing) 1.*

much vaunted Bf 110 bomber escort, unable to outgun or outmanoeuvre the single-seaters, provided another large target for RAF cannon. Before long Luftwaffe single-seaters were having to cosset the escorts intended to protect the bombers. But the Bf 109 proved excellent, and the high speed of the Ju 88 helped it survive as RAF fighters streaked through the escorts to reach the bombers; Luftwaffe fighter pilots had been given little training in bomber escort tactics.

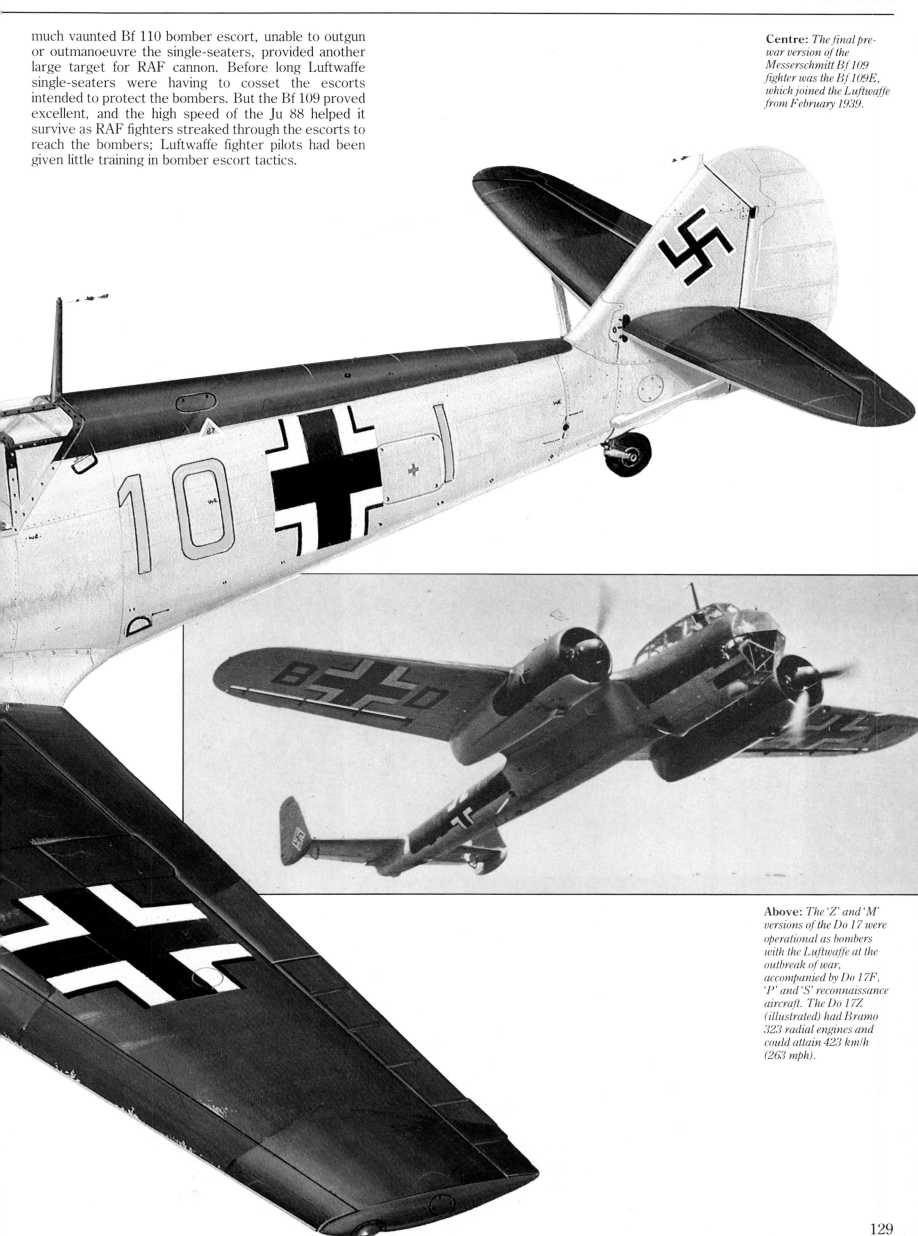

Centre: *The final pre-war version of the Messerschmitt Bf 109 fighter was the Bf 109E, which joined the Luftwaffe from February 1939.*

Above: *The 'Z' and 'M' versions of the Do 17 were operational as bombers with the Luftwaffe at the outbreak of war, accompanied by Do 17F, 'P' and 'S' reconnaissance aircraft. The Do 17Z (illustrated) had Bramo 323 radial engines and could attain 423 km/h (263 mph).*

Right: *Frustrated at not breaking the RAF, nor destroying its bases or radar chain, the Luftwaffe turned on British towns and cities but met a defiant civilian population.*

Believing a single massive blow would now cripple the RAF once and for all, on 15 August 1940 Göring despatched armadas of warplanes from Belgium, Denmark, France and Holland. Throughout the day radar operators desperately plotted new enemy formations, scrambling fighters time and time again and hardly allowing groundcrew breath to rearm and refuel. Airfields were struck and sometimes aeroplanes burned on the ground, but RAF operations continued, pilots returning to base exhausted, their machines sometimes in shreds. Still the enemy came, and again the crews climbed into the tiny cockpits to meet them. With darkness the skies fell silent. Not a single air base needed for the defence of the realm had been entirely destroyed, and only 28 RAF fighters had been lost. The enemy returned minus 75 machines. The RAF had won the day, but not yet the battle. Day after day the bombers returned, sure that Britain's resistance was breaking. In truth RAF Fighter Command was at full stretch. German frustration was vented during the night of 24–25 August, with the first raid on central London. Bomber Command retaliated by striking at Berlin the following night with 43 bombers.

August turned to September and still the RAF held ground, though it was now dangerously short of airworthy machines and their crews were exhausted. Although his own crews were suffering the strain of repeated long missions, Göring still had the numbers to achieve his goal. Lacking proper intelligence, he also became convinced that Fighter Command had virtually ceased to exist as a worthy opposition, so much so that a formation of He 111s was despatched from Bordeaux to bomb English coastal towns without fighter escort. Only 14 returned, ten so badly damaged that they were unfit for service. On 5 September 68 bombers made the

Below: *Engine fitters, armourers and electricians work on a Hurricane I to bring it back to combat readiness.*

London docks their target and 70 others went for Croydon. Fourteen RAF fighter squadrons scrambled with success. This was enough. Now, in a classic error of judgement, instead of pressing on, Göring switched his attention to London, which on the 7th took its first very heavy raid by night. For the coming week the Luftwaffe's main target remained London at night, but Göring had yet to learn that civilians could be as defiant as the fighters had been. When daylight missions resumed on the 15th, the rested Fighter Command threw everything at the enemy; the Luftwaffe lost 56 aircraft. Just two days later Hitler was forced to issue the order to postpone the invasion. From October daylight attacks became less frequent.

The radio war

Over the winter of 1940–41 German efforts turned once again to mass raids on cities and strategic targets by night. Since 13 August the Luftwaffe had sometimes used a secret weapon to achieve pinpoint accuracy, with bomber formations guided to their targets by specially-equipped 'leaders' carrying instruments to pick up radio direction-finding beams code-named *Knickebein,* transmitted from German-held territory. Beams were used on the night of 14–15 November 1940, when nearly 450 Luftwaffe bombers attacked Coventry. The damage was very extensive indeed. To counter *Knickebein,* British scientists evolved Bromide jammers. A second beam system, the *X-Gerät,* was introduced and proved harder to counter. But solutions were found, and a raid on the Rolls-Royce engine factory on the night of 8–9 May 1941 was diverted to the countryside by a beam bending technique. A new type of warfare had begun, a radio war requiring countermeasures.

Left: *Blitz damage to Coventry Cathedral and surrounding homes from the Luftwaffe raid of 14-15 November 1940, the 449 attackers using secret radio beams to pinpoint their target.*

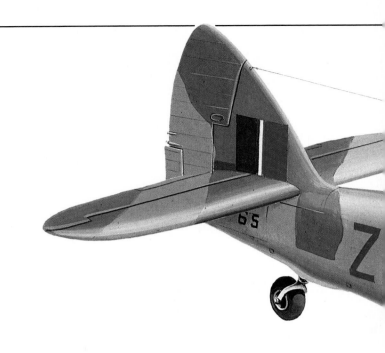

Below: *Messerschmitt Bf 110G-4b/R3 night fighter of 1943 onwards, equipped with Lichtenstein SN-2 radar and carrying two MK 108 cannon in a pack attached beneath the fuselage. One important aspect of SN-2 radar was that it could not be jammed by RAF 'window' countermeasures.*

Airborne Interception

In a separate field of radio technology, airborne radar had been fitted to specialized Blenheim IF night fighters at the beginning of the war, and one of these made the first successful radar interception, on the night of 2–3 July 1940. Blenheim night fighters were in operation throughout the Luftwaffe blitz of 1940–41. German Messerschmitt B 110 night fighters received Lichtenstein airborne interception radar in late 1941, making their operational debut with the equipment in 1942. The invention of the magnetron in 1940 gave the possibility of much higher frequencies, leading to great strides forward in airborne interception technology during the latter part of the war. RAF Coastal Command also became an important operator of airborne radar, used to search out sea targets. Air-to-surface radar was used successfully on 30 November 1941, when a Coastal Command Whitley VII sank the German submarine *U-206* in the Bay of Biscay.

New Fronts

During the late spring of 1941 the Blitz on Britain began to wither. Already the Luftwaffe had turned its main attention elsewhere. In April Greece (previously attacked by Italy) and Yugoslavia had been invaded, followed on 20 May by Crete. In Operation Mercury, the Luftwaffe used 493 Ju 52/3ms and 230 gliders to carry assault forces to the island of Crete. The assault comprised 10,000 parachutists, 5,000 troops landed by Junkers, and 750 in the gliders, plus equipment. Several thousand more troops came by sea. It was a stunning and successful use of air power, but the operation cost so many aircraft lost and troops killed that it cast a shadow over any further mass use of paratroops by Germany.

Above: *The British development of centrimetric wavelength airborne interception (AI) radars, such as seen on this AI VII-equipped Bristol Beaufighter, were not only more electronically efficient than their German counterparts, their compact antenna, housed within a thimble radome, appreciably reduced airframe drag compared with German-style externally-mounted systems.*

133

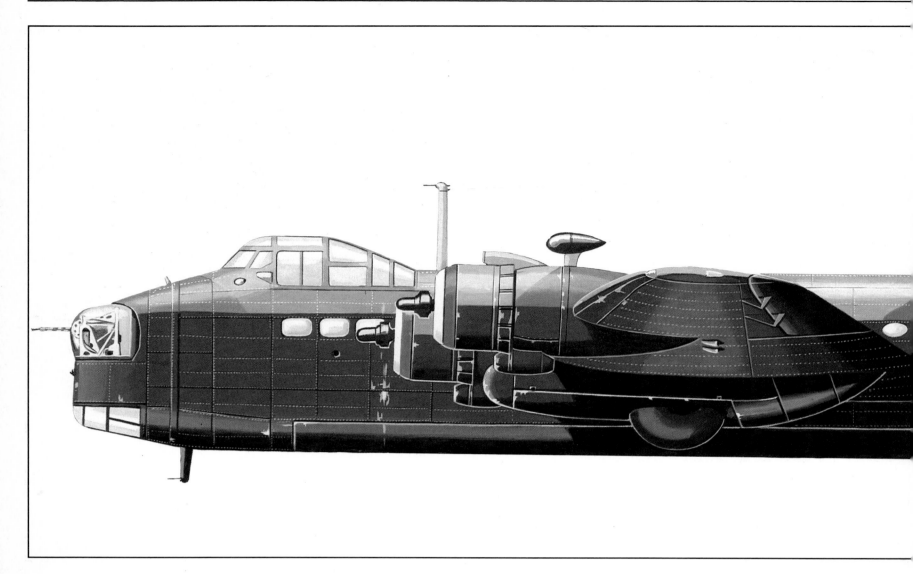

Above: *First flown on 14 May 1939, the Short Stirling became the RAF's first four-engined heavy bomber monoplane, delivered from August 1940.*

British bomber raids on targets in occupied Europe and Germany continued, helped since February 1941 by delivery of new four-engined Short Stirlings. Then, on 22 June Germany sealed its own fate. That day it began a massive surprise invasion of the Soviet Union. The initial air onslaught was unbelievably one-sided, with the Soviet air force losing 1,811 aircraft for only 35 German by nightfall, no fewer than 1,489 of which had been caught on the ground. Further battles would be lost before the Soviets recovered and produced the new MiG, Lavochkin and Yakovlev fighters and Ilyushin Il-2 ground attack two-seaters needed to stop the invaders. In the meantime, the Soviets received outside aid, initially from Britain which flew Hurricane fighters to Vaenga that September, and later from America through Lend-Lease.

Partly to draw fighters away from the Eastern Front to help the Soviets, and also because of a growing belief that strategic bombing could end the war by bringing the foe to a standstill, the RAF stepped up its raids on Germany. Most missions were by night.

But without the help of moonlight, RAF bomber crews often found it difficult to find their targets, and German defences caused considerable losses. Fillips came in March 1942, first with the operational debut of much better Avro Lancaster four-engined heavy bombers and then with the appearance of the new H2S blind bombing radar system on a Handley Page Halifax. However, H2S was not to be put properly to the test until July 1943, with a major attack on Hamburg.

Far right: *A four-engined development of the less successful twin-engined Avro Manchester, the Lancasters became the greatest of all RAF bombers of the Second World War.*

Right: *A Hawker Hurricane flies in the cold of a Soviet winter.*

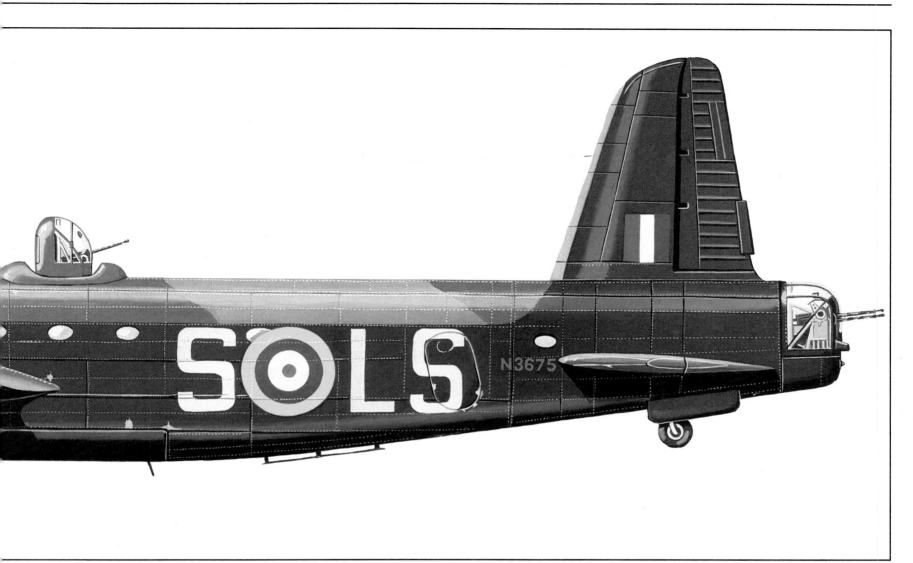

At the end of May 1942 the RAF took an incredible gamble and pushed all its front-line bombers, plus any others that could fly, into a 1,000-bomber raid on Cologne. Over half the 1,046 force comprised Vickers Wellingtons. As predicted, losses were relatively small but the result of the raid was devastating. It was only the first. To further help accurate bombing, the RAF established a Pathfinder force to mark the target prior to the arrival of massed groups, beginning operations on the night of 16–17 August 1942. The 17th also marked the beginning of US Army Air Force bomber raids from Britain, by B-17E Flying Fortresses of the 97th Bombardment Group of the Eighth Air Force. With the Americans best equipped for daylight raids and the British well experienced and equipped for night attacks, the Allies started a round-the-clock bombing campaign.

Losses, especially to the US bombers on daylight raids, remained substantial and, occasionally, crippling. Solutions were sought. One came by air dropping 'Window', vast numbers of metal foil strips that confused the enemy radar. Another was the deployment from 1944 of fully-fledged long-range escort fighters of North American P-51 Mustang and Republic P-47 Thunderbolt types.

Of course, other attacks by day and night continued in concert with the heavy raids, one of the most famous being the celebrated daylight breaching of the Mohne and Eder dams by Lancasters of 617 Squadron, using special 'bouncing' mines devised by Barnes Wallis and dropped from a low altitude on 17 May 1943.

All in all, Allied bombing stopped a number of new German weapons ever reaching operational units in

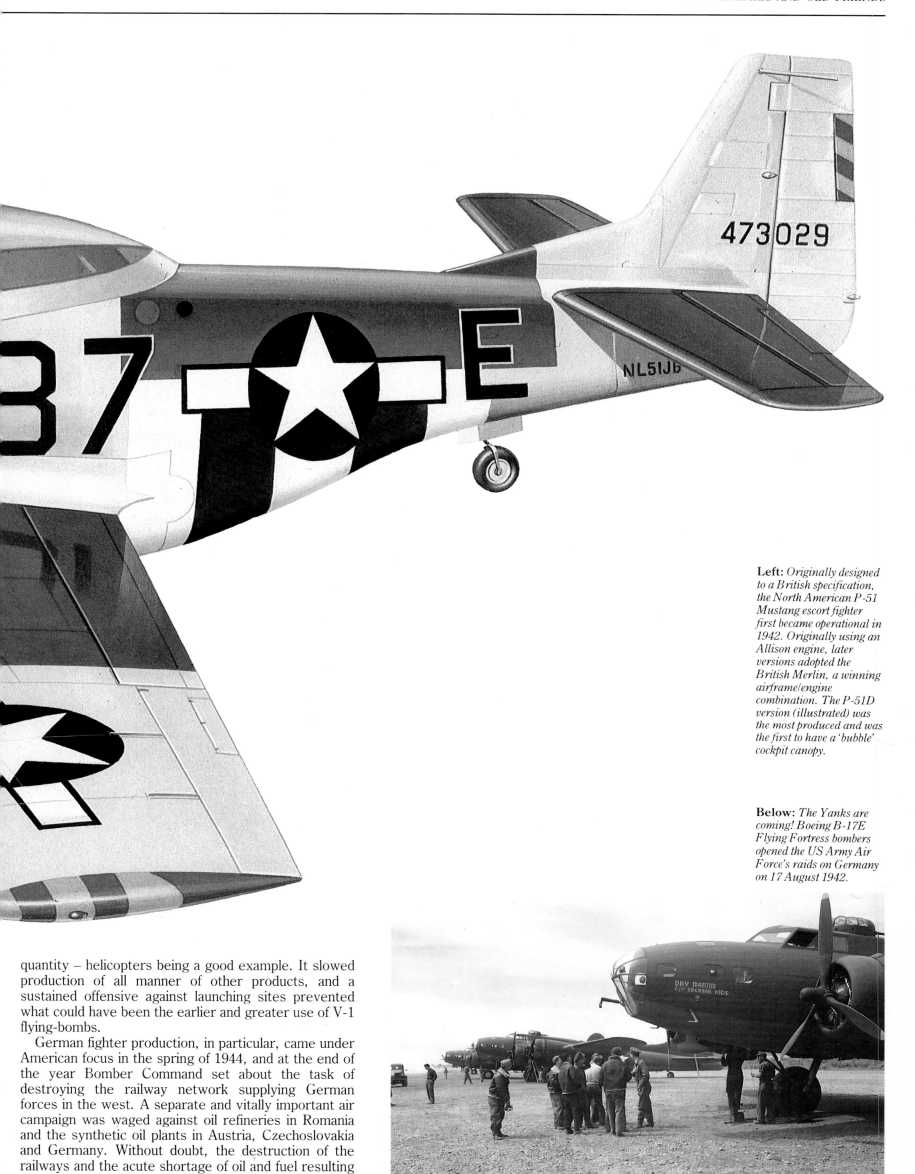

Left: *Originally designed to a British specification, the North American P-51 Mustang escort fighter first became operational in 1942. Originally using an Allison engine, later versions adopted the British Merlin, a winning airframe/engine combination. The P-51D version (illustrated) was the most produced and was the first to have a 'bubble' cockpit canopy.*

Below: *The Yanks are coming! Boeing B-17E Flying Fortress bombers opened the US Army Air Force's raids on Germany on 17 August 1942.*

quantity – helicopters being a good example. It slowed production of all manner of other products, and a sustained offensive against launching sites prevented what could have been the earlier and greater use of V-1 flying-bombs.

German fighter production, in particular, came under American focus in the spring of 1944, and at the end of the year Bomber Command set about the task of destroying the railway network supplying German forces in the west. A separate and vitally important air campaign was waged against oil refineries in Romania and the synthetic oil plants in Austria, Czechoslovakia and Germany. Without doubt, the destruction of the railways and the acute shortage of oil and fuel resulting from these campaigns were decisive factors in Germany's final defeat.

Masters of the unusual

The massive Allied raids on Berlin and other German cities in the latter part of the war became controversial. So terrible was the destruction wrought on Berlin from constant attacks that it almost ceased to exist. No fewer than 326 factories engaged on war work were destroyed or damaged between November 1943 and February 1944 alone. Of the other cities Dresden is particularly remembered. The Allied raids of 13–15 February 1945 during dry weather created an unexpected fire storm which ravaged the city; tens of thousands died.

The constant drone of Allied bomber formations overhead forced the Germans quite early on to expend much effort devising emergency point defence fighters. For this cause first came the tiny rocket-powered Messerschmitt Me 163 Komet, a 960 km/h (597 mph)

interceptor armed with two 30 mm cannon and capable of only minutes in the air while under full power. The only Komet combat unit formed was KG 400 in May-June 1944, with three Staffels at Brandis. USAAF Flying Fortresses were its first prey, on 16 August, but none were brought down on this occasion. Indeed, it is believed that Komets only ever shot down nine Allied aircraft, little enough for such a long and costly programme.

Another rocket-powered interceptor was the far less successful vertically-launched and expendable Bachem Ba 349 Natter. Armament was two dozen 73mm rockets packed into the nose. Fortunately for the crews, none were ever flown in combat.

The Heinkel He 162 Salamander was a somewhat more conventional emergency jet fighter designed to use non-strategic materials and to be constructed by

Below: Messerschmitt Me 163B Komet, whose initial rate of climb of 3,600m (11,800 ft) per minute quickly increased at height to 10,200m (33,460 ft) per minute but endurance was only about eight minutes on full rocket power. This, combined with a 960km/h (567 mph) top speed and the explosive nature of the rocket fuel, put great strain on the pilots.

semi-skilled labour in underground factories. It was a horror to fly because of its back-pack turbojet, and only a few reached the operational stage out of thousands planned. As an achievement though, the Salamander was probably unrivalled. Just 69 days elapsed between contract and first flight on 6 December 1944. But even while the Salamander was being constructed, in November 1944 the German RLM (Air Ministry) called for new fighters to be designed of even more simple form.

Remarkable as these achievements were, they had almost no impact on the war and certainly failed to stem the bombers. Indeed, many of Germany's late projects only came to fruition after the war as the Americans, British, Soviets and French took specimens of German technology back home to research and copy. Of greater importance to the Germans were other advanced technology weapons, devised at an earlier period when development time was no unaffordable luxury. These included air-launched missiles, strategic rockets and, of course, the Messerschmitt Me 262 twin-jet fighter and Arado Ar 234 Blitz twin-jet reconnaissance-bomber.

The quality of German research into missiles is one aspect of the Second World War that is often overlooked. In addition to a little-used anti-tank missile and the Rheinbote multi-stage artillery missile (hundreds were launched against Antwerp in November 1944), two air-launched missiles were deployed. The most important of these was the simple Ruhrstahl/Kramer Fritz-X, a radio-controlled bomb deployed operationally on the Dornier Do 217K-2s of III/KG 100 from August 1943. The unit's first success came on 9 September, when it sank the battleship *Roma* and damaged another vessel in a fleet of 23 Italian battleships, cruisers and destroyers being surrendered to the Allies. *Roma* was the first major warship ever to be sunk by an air-launched missile. Operational use of the rocket-powered and radio-controlled Henschel Hs 293 also started in August 1943, launched over the Atlantic and the Mediterranean from Do 217s, Heinkel He 177A-5s and even from that long-time shipping menace, the Focke-Wulf Fw 200 Condor.

Below: *German Henschel Hs 293 radio-controlled wire-link missile, using the warhead of a SC 500 bomb and a Walter 109-507B short-burn rocket motor to boost the missile's speed after launch. First used on 25 August 1943, on the 27th Do 217E-5s of II/KG 100 sank the British corvette HMS Egret in the Bay of Biscay.*

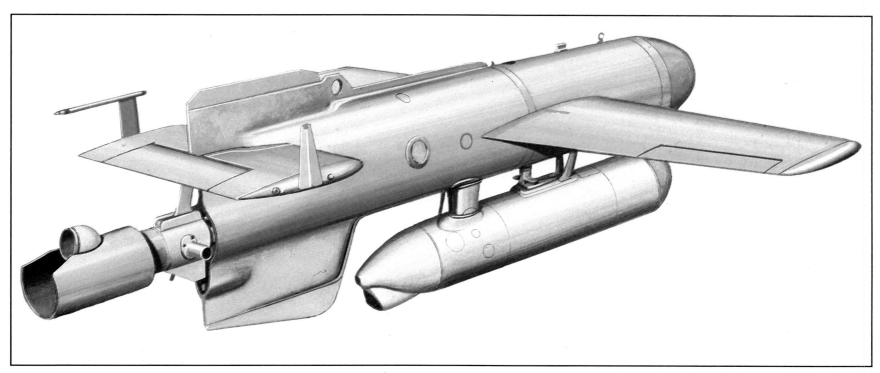

Operation Overlord

On 6 June 1944 the Allies launched their D-Day Normandy landings, code-named Operation Overlord, to liberate Europe. Preceded by huge airdrops, it became the greatest amphibious assault in the history of warfare. The massive use of air power included large numbers of troops and equipment carried by gliders towed by modified bombers and transports.

Between 6 and 7 June a stunning 13,000 Allied sorties were flown, partly to establish protective air cover over hundreds of square miles as men and supplies poured in. It was a venture of unprecedented co-operation between the fighting services, and close work between the air and ground forces enabled the Allies to break through substantial opposition and on towards the Rhine. Here the ground attack fighters really came into their element. Aircraft like the RAF's Hawker Typhoon made great formation sweeps at very low level against armoured columns and anything else they could find, cannon blasting, bombs exploding and rocket projectiles spraying from the wings. The Typhoon, one of the few small single-seat fighters capable of carrying two 1,000 lb bombs, was the master of this tactic. On 7 August Typhoons used rockets to knock out no fewer than 135 tanks in one day.

But the Allies were, even now, to suffer new enemy

Top: *A Fiesler Fi 103 (FZG-76), better known as a V-1 flying bomb, dives towards Piccadilly in central London, its Argus As 014 pulse-jet engine cut out. This was the first photograph taken of a V-1 in operation.*

weapons so crippling in their destructive power that the Germans still hoped to avoid outright defeat. On 13 June German forces began launching FZG-76 flying-bombs against Britain, the so-called V-1 revenge weapon. Powered by an Argus pulse-jet, each V-1 carried auto-pilot, range-setting and other equipment for their pilotless mission. Britons came to know the sound of V-1s passing overhead; the silence as the engine cut out and the missile dived to ground; and the explosion of its 850 kg (1,874 lb) warhead, increased by any fuel left on board. Fortunately, V-1 launches against Britain ended quickly, on 4 September, although other European targets had come under their sights.

The break was short-lived. On the 5th a highly sophisticated A-4 (V-2 revenge weapon) ballistic rocket fell on Paris, launched by a training battery. A few days later two were fired against England by a fully-fledged mobile artillery battery, taking victims. Range was from about 320km (199 miles). Britain continued to face V-2 attack until 27 March 1945. But for Allied bombing, the V-2 menace would have been much worse; one method of Allied attack saw unmanned Flying Fortress bombers diving into three permanent launching sites, at Siracourt, Watten and Wizernes, destroying them before any rockets could be launched and forcing the Germans to use mobile batteries.

Top: *Allied paratroops board transport aircraft in preparation for Operation Overlord, the invasion of Europe. Allied aircraft carried stripes to identify them during the massive air and sea operations.*

Left: *Conceived as an interceptor, the British Hawker Typhoon was subsequently developed into probably the finest ground attack aircraft of the Second World War.*

Vision of the future

On 27 August 1939, just days before the Second World War began, Heinkel had first flown its experimental He 178. This was the world's first aeroplane to fly on turbojet power alone. As leader of this technology in Germany, Heinkel went on to produce the first twin-jet aeroplane, the He 280 fighter, which first flew on 2 April 1941. But this was rejected for service. Instead, the Luftwaffe eventually took in the Messerschmitt Me 262 twin-jet, which first flew over a year later on 18 July 1942. Operational service began at Juvincourt on 10 July 1944, with just a handful of machines.

Hitler was convinced that the jet was best employed as a fighter-bomber in Me 262A-2 Sturmvogel form, and soon after fighter production had begun the assembly lines had to be altered to construct fighter-bombers. However, before long he put priority back on to fighters, and in particular the jets, resulting in Me 262A-1 Schwalbes coming off the lines in quantity. But now time was running out. Of more than 1,400 Me 262s built, only a small fraction were flown in combat.

Jets had the advantage of high speed at all altitudes, but they did not have it all their own way. Me 262 fighter pilots found attacking at high speed difficult to master and often slowed down, making them vulnerable. On 28 August American airmen of the 78th Fighter Group, Eighth Air Force, shot down their first jet. More than 100 Me 262s would be lost on missions or in accidents. But, until fuel shortages curtailed operations, the jets managed to exact considerable losses on the Allies. In a relatively short period, no fewer than 12 Luftwaffe Me 262 pilots became aces, with Obersleutnant Heinz Bar gaining 16 victories.

Britain too had developed turbojet engines with the pioneering pre-war efforts of Frank Whittle. His W/U centrifugal compressor engine built for Power Jets by the British Thomson-Houston Company at Rugby was

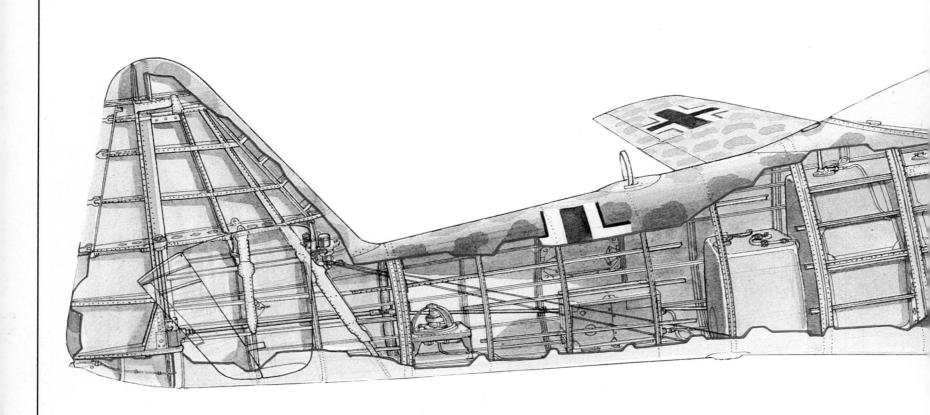

the first gas turbine engine in the world to be designed for aircraft use, and was started up for the first time on 12 April 1937. To Air Ministry contract, a new engine was produced as the W1, and this was fitted to the experimental Gloster E. 28/39, which made its first official flight at Cranwell on 15 May 1941. Gloster became responsible for producing the RAF's first jet fighter, the Meteor I with two Rolls-Royce W2B/23 Welland I turbojets, which served with 616 Squadron from July 1944, paralleling the Me 262. The Squadron's first missions were to stop V-1 flying-bombs, its initial success coming on 4 August.

It is thought that on no occasion did RAF and German jets meet in combat. The first American jet, the Bell P-59 Airacomet, had first flown on 1 October 1942 but production aircraft were not deployed operationally, and Lockheed P-80 Shooting Stars (prototype first flown on 8 January 1944) were too late for war service. Meanwhile, Germany had already fielded an operational jet reconnaissance-bomber as the Arado Ar 234 Blitz, its first mission from Juvincourt taking place on 20 July 1944. An Ar 234B also made Germany's last wartime sortie over Britain, on 10 April 1945, for reconnaissance purposes; the last Luftwaffe air attack by piloted aeroplanes had previously been recorded on the night of 20–21 March. On 7 May the war in Europe ended.

Far left, top: *Heinkel He 178, the first aircraft to fly on the power of a turbojet engine only, on 27 August 1939. The Heinkel HeS 3b turbojet was designed by Dr Pabst von Ohain, and had been flight tested earlier on an He 118.*

Left: *Gloster E.28/39 was the first British jet aircraft to fly, officially on 15 May 1941 in the hands of P.E.G. Sayer at RAF Cranwell.*

Far left, centre: *Luftwaffe Messerschmitt Me 262A-2a Sturmvogel, abandoned to the Allies. Note the underfuselage pylon for a 1,000kg bomb.*

Below: *Cut-away drawing of a Messerschmitt Me 262 jet fighter, which became operational in July 1944.*

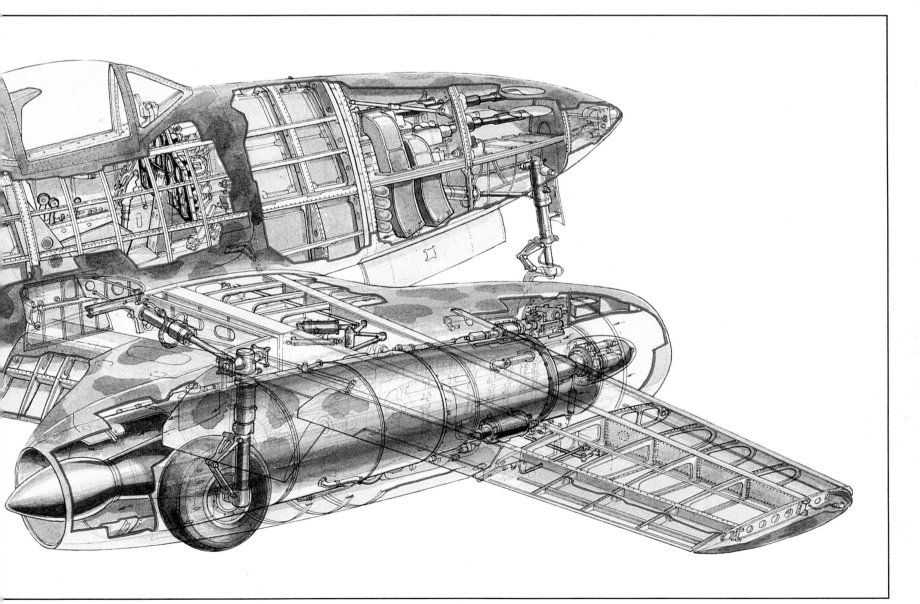

The Pacific

American aircraft received by Britain from 1940 were widely used by the RAF and Commonwealth air forces on several fronts, particularly in the African and Mediterranean theatres. The Curtiss Tomahawk, for example, became a common sight flying low-level missions over the Western Desert while in action against Rommel's armoured forces. Later Curtiss Kittyhawks were also among American types operated by Australian and New Zealand squadrons in the Pacific, and it was the outbreak of fighting in this region that had first brought the USA into the Second World War.

On the quiet Sunday morning of 7 December 1941 the Imperial Japanese Navy launched a surprise attack from six aircraft carriers on the US naval base at Pearl Harbor, Hawaii, guided to their targets by the radios playing music all over the island. The 350 Aichi D3A1 dive-bombers, Nakajima B5N2 bombers and Mitsubishi A6M2 Zero fighters dropped bombs and torpedoes and strafed, destroying naval and Army aircraft on the ground and battleships in the harbour. The damage was immense. The attackers left victorious. But all was not lost for the US Navy: the big US Navy aircraft carriers were elsewhere at the time, and the Japanese failed to hit the fuel and oil complex, the repair yards, the harbour's power system or the five submarines in their pens. These omissions would cost them dearly.

The next day Japanese aircraft raided RAF bases in Malaya and Singapore, preparing for an invasion of northern Malaya. The USA declared war on Japan. On 10 December USAAF Flying Fortress bombers began the first American air offensive of the war, striking at Japanese shipping. But Japanese victories against the Allies quickly mounted.

A propaganda raid on Tokyo and other cities was all that could be managed immediately against the Japanese homeland, and on 18 April 1942 16 North American B-25 Mitchell bombers flew a one-way mission against these targets from the aircraft carrier USS *Hornet*, with those aircraft which survived landing in friendly China. In charge of the raid was Lt. Col. James Doolittle. Although the damage caused was slight, it showed that Japan could be reached by a determined enemy. It also undoubtedly made Japan resigned to occupy part of the Aleutian Islands, to form a barrier to the US continent. This occupation formed part of its Midway strategy (see below).

Control of the sea was vital to Japan, as its forces occupied and fought in areas spread all over the Pacific. It had built up an impressive modern navy with a strong air element which, contrary to Allied opinion, was a match for existing Western types. This was again demonstrated on 4–8 May in what became known as the Battle of the Coral Sea, the first naval battle in history fought between opposing fleets continually out of sight of each other. The use of air power made this possible.

The Japanese intended to land forces at Port Moresby in New Guinea, with aircraft carriers offering substantial air cover. Using good intelligence work, the US Navy understood the threat and sent forces that included the carriers *Lexington* and *Yorktown* to intercept. Initially the US Douglas Devastator and Dauntless bombers and Grumman Wildcat fighters from *Yorktown* engaged transports and other vessels at Tulagi Harbor. *Yorktown* then joined the other carrier and headed out towards the main invasion fleet, which had been strengthened by the carriers *Zuikaku* and *Shokaku* of the strike force. Realizing the US threat, the invasion fleet turned away. But it was too late. On 7 May US Navy aircraft struck and sank the carrier *Shoko*. The next day wave after wave of opposing warplanes from the two fleets struck and counter struck, leaving the *Yorktown* badly damaged. *Lexington* had also been hit and had to be abandoned, finally sunk by torpedoes from a US destroyer. *Shokaku* was damaged, and other ships took strikes. The 69 US Navy aircraft lost in the battle included many that went down with *Lexington*, while the Japanese had lost 43 aircraft in sorties and others were pushed overboard from *Zuikaku* to make room for *Shokaku*'s pilots who could not land on their carrier.

The Battle of the Coral Sea was seen as an American victory for two reasons: it stopped the invasion and was the first major setback to the Japanese. The Japanese then turned their attention towards the island of Midway. The huge Japanese fleets assigned to the campaign included seven aircraft carriers, four to attack Midway Island itself. Again knowing the threat, the Americans began to assemble all they could, with the fighting capability of the carriers *Enterprise* and *Hornet* boosted by the repaired *Yorktown*. US Army Air Force as well as Navy and Marine Corps aircraft based on Midway were also available for battle.

Japanese operations began with a diversionary attack on the Aleutian Islands on 3 June 1942. Then on the 4th formations of Japanese aircraft flew against Midway. Defending land-based Wildcat and Brewster Buffalo fighters were outgunned and retaliatory attacks by US land bombers were again unsuccessful.

Sure of victory, and without the US Navy yet offering a major sea threat, bombers on board *Akagi* and *Kaga* were ordered to have their torpedoes replaced by bombs to strike again at Midway itself. But then came reports of approaching US warships. Suddenly torpedoes were needed and removal of the bombs started. While this took place, Japan's aircraft from the first wave were returning and needed to be recovered. Precious minutes ticked by. By the time rearming with torpedoes was underway again US Navy carrier aircraft were upon them.

Despite extremely valiant efforts to penetrate to the Japanese vessels, the first low-level attacks by US Devastators ended in almost entire annihilation. But the dive-bombing Dauntlesses that followed were more successful and within minutes *Akagi*, *Kaga* and *Soryu* had been hit and destroyed. By the afternoon *Hiryu* too had been sunk; but *Yorktown* was lost in the process. Other vessels too were struck on both sides.

The Battle of Midway was a conclusive American victory and marked the turning point of the Pacific War. But the Japanese still had other carriers left. Importantly, Japan had lost 258 aircraft and many experienced

Above: *18 April 1942, US Army Air Force B-25 Mitchell bombers test their engines, with firefighters standing by, prior to leaving USS* Hornet *to strike at the heart of the Japanese empire. (US Air Force)*

Facing page, top: *Tomahawk fighters, the RAF's version of the Curtiss P-40 Warhawk.*

Facing page, bottom: *The aftermath of the Japanese raid on Pearl Harbor on 7 December 1941, the USS* West Virginia *and* Tennessee *in ruins.*

Left: *Douglas SBD Dauntless bombers on board USS* Yorktown *shortly before the Battle of the Coral Sea. (US Navy)*

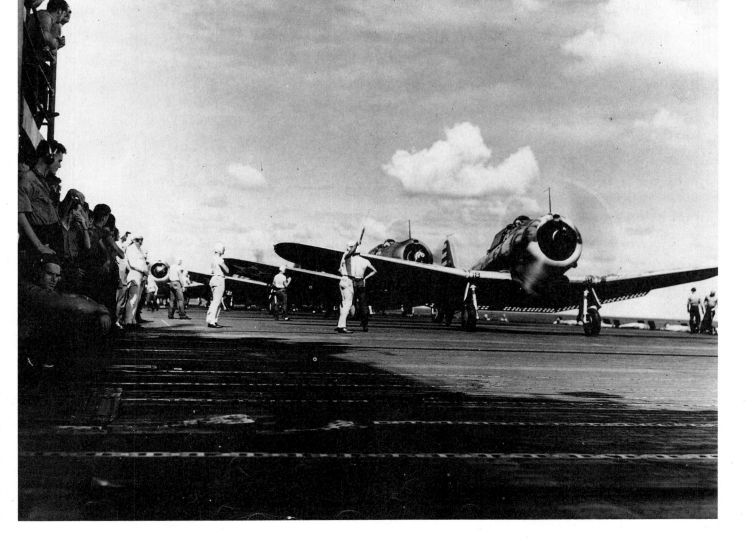

Above: *Consolidated B-24 Liberator on Eniwetok in the Marshall Islands prepares to fly a sortie over Truk, April 1944. (US Air Force)*

Facing page, top: *Boeing B-29 Superfortress bombers were initially flown against Japan from bases in China and India (as seen).*

Facing page, bottom: *Dr Nagai, medical instructor and X-ray specialist at the Nagasaki Hospital, a victim of radiation from the first atomic bomb dropped over Japan.*

Below: *First two Curtiss C-46 Commando transports to land at Aslito (Saipan), 24 June 1944.*

crews. The US was down by just 100 carrier planes and 40 more from land, and could rely on substantial replenishment.

The war in the Pacific was particularly hard fought, but Japan had relied on gaining its objectives before America could fully mobilize its vast resources. Now Allied victory was certain. Allied operations to recapture islands invariably involved air cover from carriers, allowing land bases to be established for the use of bombers and fighters. From these the Consolidated B-24 Liberator's excellent range made it a particularly useful weapon.

The ascendancy of Allied air power over the Japanese was crucial. When Burma was lost to the Japanese, the Allies had used transports like the Curtiss C-46 Commando to carry supplies over the 'hump' between India and China. During 1944 hundreds of thousands of tons of air-dropped supplies kept Allied troops going, while in early 1945 an entire army was air-lifted over the Japanese lines and kept supplied by air.

Boeing's latest bomber (and the heaviest warplane of the war), the pressurized B-29 Superfortress, became

available in 1944. It was decided to devote it exclusively to the Pacific Theatre, and there against Japan itself. First flying from China, B-29s of the USAAF's 20th Bomber Command opened Superfortress operations on 15 June 1944, the same day that aircraft carriers helped US forces land on Saipan in the Mariana Islands.

By October the situation for Japan was so desperate that it began *kamikaze* attacks on Allied shipping, diving bomb-laden manned aircraft into the vessels on suicide missions. The Battle for Leyte Gulf witnessed the start of these attacks, the escort carrier USS *St Lo* becoming the first victim. Initially, existing warplanes were adopted for this purpose, but from March 1945 the specialized rocket-powered and air-launched Yokosuka MXY7 Ohka became operational. *Kamikaze* missions continued until the very end of the war, the last on 15 August bringing the total number of sorties to 2,257. It is popularly believed that it was impossible to return from a *kamikaze* mission, but this was not so. About 936 attacks were abandoned, but none by Ohkas, which could not be relanded.

Old world – new world

In 1945, the first summer of European peace for five years began, but still Japan fought on. Since June incendiary attacks on all major Japanese cities had been launched by the USAAF, but still the foe remained entrenched. By the third week in July Japanese forces in Burma had been utterly destroyed by Allied Spitfires and Mustangs as they crossed the Sittang river, and still Japan would not surrender. On 1 August a huge armada of 851 B-29s struck Japan.

With no surrender in sight, and with the possibility of Allied losses running into millions if Japan had to be invaded, authorization was given by the US President to use the atomic bomb. On Monday 6 August 1945 the B-29 *Enola Gay* headed towards Hiroshima, followed by two other B-29s assigned photographic and scientific roles. At 8.15 a.m. the bomb *Little Boy* was dropped. The atomic age had begun.

With still no message of capitulation, on 9 August the B-29 *Bock's Car* dropped the *Fat Man* plutonium bomb on Nagasaki, the back-up target for the second atomic mission. Then, with no other atomic bombs available, conventional bombing resumed. On the 14th 754 B-29s escorted by 169 fighters raided. It was the final bombing mission by the Twentieth Air Force. Two Mitsubishi G4M bomber-transports carried a Japanese delegation to Ie Shima and on 2 September surrender documents were signed on board the warship USS *Missouri* anchored in Tokyo Bay. The Second World War was over.

Chapter 11:
A Fresh Beginning

The end of the Second World War was nothing like the end of the First. Because of the new division of Europe, the emergence of the USA and USSR as the world's superpowers, the invention of the atomic bomb and the obvious superiority of jets over piston-engined warplanes, aeroplane production did not suffer the same immediate cut-backs.

Commercial aviation wasted little time in getting back to business. On 31 May 1945, little more than three weeks after VE-day, British Overseas Airways Corporation (BOAC) and its Australian counterpart, Qantas, began a joint weekly service between Hurn, in England, and Sydney. Just over a month after the Japanese surrender in August, Swissair resumed services to the UK. In October, Qantas made its first post-war flight to Singapore, Sabena of Belgium and Air France re-opened their routes to London, and American Overseas Airlines inaugurated post-war transatlantic routes.

Swords and ploughshares

These and many other early post-war services were flown with a curious assortment of pre-war, wartime and improvised transports. Within Europe, many of them were flown by the defeated Luftwaffe's standard transport, the Junkers Ju 52/3m, large numbers of which had become available as spoils of war. Indeed, so useful were they that France built 400 additional examples after the war. Even more numerous was the Junkers' Allied counterpart, the Douglas DC-3, also built in huge wartime numbers (as C-47s or Dakotas)

and now no longer needed in this capacity. The Lancastrian, used by BOAC for its early long-distance services, was little more than a demilitarized Lancaster bomber with seats for a mere nine passengers, but it had the range to cross the Atlantic and enough speed to cut the England–Australia travelling time to three days. In 1946, a 13-passenger Mk III version enabled British South American Airways to begin operating to Buenos Aires and other destinations across the South Atlantic.

New generation

Valuable though such early operations were in re-establishing airline networks, more cost-effective aircraft of more modern design were clearly needed, especially on the longer routes and on those shorter ones with the heaviest traffic.

It was soon evident that the great money-spinning route was the North Atlantic – and here the United States had a clear advantage. While Britain and the rest of Europe had much lost ground to make up, the USA had ended the war with two four-engined long-range aircraft virtually tailor-made for transatlantic services: the Douglas DC-4 (the type with which AOA had re-opened North Atlantic services in October 1945) and the Lockheed Constellation. Both were, in fact, pre-war designs, even though their first flights were not made until 1942 and 1943 respectively and their first incarnation had been as military transports. The DC-4 could carry 44–86 passengers, while seating in the 'Connie', which entered service with Pan American in February 1946, ranged from 44–81.

Far right: *Military and commercially operated Lockheed Constellations in post-war use.*

Below: *Handley Page Halton, a civil transport conversion of the Halifax bomber accommodating ten passengers.*

Comfort

The Constellation, however, had two great advantages over the DC-4: it was about 160km/h (100 mph) faster, and it had a pressurized passenger cabin. This latter amenity, nowadays taken for granted, had first been introduced on an earlier four-engined US transport, the Boeing 307 Stratoliner, which had seen brief pre-war commercial service with Pan American and TWA before being acquired, still with their airline crews, for military transport duties in 1942.

Passenger comfort, especially on long flights, was clearly an important factor in the battle for customers. Douglas's response to the Constellation was the DC-6, essentially a pressurized development of the DC-4; it entered service in April 1946. Meanwhile, from mid-1949 this had ceased to be a two-horse US race, for Boeing had entered the lists with its 55–100 passenger Stratocruiser. Following Stratoliner precedent, this too was based on a bomber – the B-29 Superfortress – but with a new 'double bubble' pressurized fuselage providing a spacious two-deck interior with a highly popular lounge and cocktail bar on the lower deck. Although built in relatively small numbers, it served with BOAC and four major US airlines, its standards of passenger comfort hardly being bettered until the large-scale introduction of jet transports in 1958.

Swan song

This group of airliners, all landplanes, represented the peak of development in piston-engined air transport and had already – sadly, to many minds – seen off the flying-boat as an effective competitor. The pre-war golden era of flying-boat air travel never returned after the war was over, despite several valiant attempts to keep it alive. BOAC, which under its pre-war title of Imperial Airways had had such a spectacular success on the empire routes with the superb Short 'C' class, had only just acquired flying-boats with true transatlantic range – Boeing 314 'Clippers' – a few months before the outbreak of war. But thanks to the war itself and the post-war boom in air transport, the world was now endowed with many miles of concrete runways, had no shortage of good land-based aircraft to use them, and was no longer interested in this once-popular means of travel.

The gas turbine revolution

Revolution is by no means too strong a word to describe the impact of the gas turbine upon aviation. Only just beginning to get into its stride in military aircraft in the closing stages of the Second World War, its development proceeded apace in the late 1940s and early 1950s. Its most immediate advantage was seen as enabling the speed, and therefore the combat superiority, of military aircraft to be increased by an order of magnitude hitherto impossible.

Breaking the barrier

When the Second World War broke out, the world absolute air speed record, set by Flugkapitän Fritz Wendel of Germany in the experimental piston engined Messerschmitt Me 209 V1, stood at 755.138km/h (469.22 mph). Record attempts, suspended during the war, were resumed in 1945, the first new (and first jet) record for speed being set on 7 November at Herne Bay, England, by Gp. Capt. H.J. Wilson in a re-engined Gloster Meteor 3. His speed of 975.875km/h (606.379 mph) represented an increase of nearly 30 per cent

Below: *The pressurized and air-conditioned 'double bubble' Boeing Stratocruiser, a highly luxurious post-war airliner with an upper deck passenger compartment and lower deck lounge, connected by a circular stairway.*

over the pre-war figure. This record lasted less than a year before being beaten by another Meteor, and then alternately by British and US aircraft over the next few years.

As speeds increased, designers and test pilots began to encounter the effects of compressibility upon their airframes created by the build-up of shock waves as the aircraft approached the speed of sound – the so-called 'sound barrier'. For a time this barrier seemed impassable, and several good aeroplanes and valuable test pilots were lost in the attempt, but eventually the technological problem was met and overcome. The barrier was, in fact, broken first by an aircraft ineligible for speed record attempts (because it was air-launched) and powered by a rocket motor rather than a jet engine. This was the American Bell X-1, in which Capt. Charles 'Chuck' Yeager, on 14 October 1947, successfully

achieved a speed of 1,078km/h (670 mph) in level flight, equivalent to 1.015 times the speed of sound (or Mach 1.015).

In this and subsequent flights the X-1 series of research aircraft confirmed not only that Mach 1 *could* be exceeded but that, more importantly, beyond it there were no further purely aerodynamic barriers to ever-higher speeds through the air. The first supersonic world air speed record (1,215.298km/h; 755.15 mph) duly followed on 29 October 1953, set by Lt. Col. F.K. Everest, USAF, in a YF-100A Super Sabre fighter. Two and a half years later, the then-standing record was surpassed by the largest margin ever recorded – an amazing 38 per cent – when test pilot Peter Twiss outpaced the sun by flying Britain's Fairey Delta 2 at 1,822.00km/h (1,132.136 mph), making this also the first record to exceed 1,609km/h (1,000 mph).

Above: *Largest of all flying boats was the Hughes H4 Hercules, designed originally for wartime military service but officially abandoned and completed post-war at a personal cost to Howard Hughes of a reported $22 million. It made just one flight of about 1.6km (1 mile) at Los Angeles Harbor on 2 November 1947.*

Left: *First of three Bell X-1 research aircraft, used by Captain Charles 'Chuck' Yeager to make the first flight through the so-called 'sound barrier'.*

Military jets

Korea provided the backdrop for the first post-Second World War hostilities and the world's first military encounters between jets. The war began on 25 June 1950, when Communist forces from the North invaded South Korea. Two days later the United Nations Security Council called upon its members to assist the South. A USAF North American F-82G Twin Mustang claimed the first aircraft shot down, a Yak-9, but both were piston-engined. On 3 July US Navy Grumman F9F-2 Panther jet fighters flew from USS *Valley Forge* to engage Northern forces. By then B-29s and B-26s had already begun bombing railway installations in the North and South. Then, on 8 November, a USAF F-80C Shooting Star of the 51st Interceptor Wing, piloted by Lt. Russel J. Brown Jr., shot down a Chinese MiG-15 over North Korea, marking the first ever victory between jets. The following day a US Navy Panther brought down a MiG-15. However, the MiG in general was a superior fighter and an equal only came with the North American F-86 Sabre. The air combats between MiG-15s and Sabres over Korea are legendary.

The RAF can claim to have deployed the first jet night fighter squadron, its No 25 having become operational at West Malling in July 1951 with de Havilland Vampire NF. Mk 10s. These followed a few Meteor NF. Mk 11 night fighter conversions that went to No 29 Squadron a few months before.

The Grumman Panther, mentioned earlier, had not actually been the first pure jet on US Navy carrier decks, this honour having already gone to the McDonnell Douglas FH-1 Phantom. The first major post-war innovation for aircraft carriers was the angled deck to allow simultaneous launch and recovery operations, used initially on USS *Antietam* that began trials in 1953.

Supersonic

USAF North American F-100 Super Sabres were the world's first fighters capable of sustained supersonic speed, the first prototype flying on 25 May 1953. The US Navy gained supersonic performance with deployment of the Grumman F-11F-1 Tiger several years later. The first MiG which had true supersonic capability was the MiG-19, it being a contemporary of the Super Sabre.

Below: *Seized Mikoyan-Gurevich MiG-15 jet fighter being made ready for an evaluation flight by US personnel in Korea. (US Air Force)*

Left: *USAF North American F-86 Sabres achieved greater results than MiG-15s in Korea mainly because of better pilot training, the MiG having possessed a better rate of climb and a tighter high-altitude turn rate.*

Below: *North American F-100D Super Sabre launching a Bullpup attack missile.*

Above: *Northrop F-89J Scorpion converted from an F-89D, fitted with the avionics needed to launch Hughes Falcon air-to-air missiles.*

Right: *The largest helicopter ever flown was the Soviet Mil Mi-12, known to NATO as Homer. With four 6,500shp Soloviev D-25VF turboshaft engines providing power, the total rotor tip to rotor tip width was 67m (219 ft 10 in).*

Below: *First test fired on 11 September 1953, the US Naval Weapons Center AIM-9 Sidewinder remains a popular short-range air-to-air missile in the 1990s.*

First post-war air-to-air missiles

Cannon had remained the most common air-to-air weapon during the Korean War, but things were about to change. From 1956 the USAF received examples of its first air-to-air guided missile, the Hughes GAR-1 Falcon, the development of which had started in 1947. GAR-1s with semi-active radar homing heads were deployed on some Northrop F-89 Scorpions, which since 1950 had been in service as the USAF's first all-weather jet interceptors. From the original version of Falcon came pursuit-course infra-red homing GAR-2/2As, produced in tens of thousands.

Since 1953 the simple short-range Sidewinder had been another air-to-air missile under test, and such was its later popularity that even today very advanced versions are built. The Soviet equivalent of the US Sidewinder was the K-13A *Atoll*, also being developed into advanced form. And with attempts in the 1950s to fit nuclear warheads to almost every type of major weapon, on 19 July 1957 a USAF F-89J Scorpion launched a live round of the first nuclear-tipped air-to-air missile, the AIR-2A Genie. Carrying a 1.5 kiloton warhead but unguided, Genie was designed to be fired automatically and detonated by the aircraft's fire control system.

Because of the success of these and other missiles, cannon began to disappear from new aircraft. It was a mistake. During the Vietnam War it quickly became apparent that cannon remained a vital close-in weapon. Guns were quickly reinstated, and today no fighter is produced without at least provision to fit cannon as well as missiles.

Maid of all work

Having established a place in military service, helicopters were set for a post-war boom. Several designers, including Kamov in the Soviet Union, took the old contra-rotating twin-rotor layout to new heights of efficiency, while most other new 'twins' adopted either the intermeshing rotors as favoured by the American Kaman company, or tandem rotors. The tandem layout first came off the production line in 1947 with the Piasecki HRP-1 'Flying Banana' for the US Navy, and continues today with the H-46 Sea Knights and H-47 Chinooks of the related Boeing Helicopters company. The old outrigger-type 'twin' quickly fell from favour, but it must be recalled that the largest helicopter ever built – the Soviet Mil Mi-12 prototype that first flew on 12 February 1969 – returned to this configuration in a much refined way.

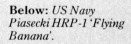

Below: *US Navy Piasecki HRP-1 'Flying Banana'.*

Above: *Bell H-13s (Model 47s) became known as* Korean Angels *for their outstanding work in transporting United Nations casualties in the front line to mobile army surgical hospitals (MASHs). (US Air Force)*

Right: *A US Marine Corps Sikorsky S-51 (military designated HO3S-1) leaves the battle line in Korea with a Corpsman injured while rescuing a colleague from a minefield, September 1951. (US Navy)*

The first helicopter to receive a Type Approval Certificate for commercial operation was the US Bell Model 47, on 8 March 1946, and 'NC-1H' was the first registration issued. The Model 47, most with the 'goldfish bowl' cockpit enclosure that typified the class, amazingly remained in production in the USA until 1974 and even longer through Italian construction. During its separate career in military service it helped establish the helicopter as an indispensable workhorse in the field. During the Korean War of the early 1950s, it has been estimated that Model 47s (known by the military as H-13s) alone carried 18,000 of the total of 23,000 United Nations casualties airlifted to field hospitals, earning the name 'Korean Angel' and helping to set a record for the lowest percentage of casualties to die of wounds in the whole history of warfare.

Meanwhile, even with acceptance of the R-4B into military service, the USAAF saw the need for improved models, and Sikorsky quickly responded with the R-5 (Sikorsky Model S-51). This was originally still a two-seater but with the crew in tandem in a well-glazed cabin and, despite weighing nearly twice as much as the R-4B, offered improved performance. It was flown as a prototype on 18 August 1943. The R-5 eventually went into military service and was the first of a long run of Sikorsky helicopters built under licence by Westland in the UK. The significance of the British connection is that Westland-built commercial S-51s, known as Dragonflies, inaugurated the first British airmail service by helicopter on 1 June 1948, the first ever regular night helicopter service on 17 October 1949 (by British European Airways), and BEA also established the first British night airmail service by helicopter that same day with an S-51. Meantime, Los Angeles Airways had begun the world's first scheduled helicopter service, using an S-51, on 1 October 1947, having already received a certificate for mail carrying on 22 May of that year. Later versions of the R-5 offered increased accommodation.

The next innovations in helicopter design concerned the engine arrangement. Once again America took the initiative. The Sikorsky S-55, first flown in November 1949, was the first production helicopter to have the engine in the nose in order to free maximum cabin area, while the first helicopter to fly with a turbine engine was a re-engined Kaman K-225 belonging to the US Navy, on 10 December 1951. A US Navy Kaman HTK-1 became the first with twin turboshafts.

Two Sikorsky S-55s became the first helicopters to make a staged east-west crossing of the North Atlantic, from 13–31 July 1952. Using similar helicopters, the Belgian airline Sabena opened the world's first international helicopter service on 1 September 1953, linking Brussels with Lille, Maastricht and Rotterdam.

Below: *Sabena Sikorsky S-55 at the Allee Verte heliport in Brussels. (Sabena)*

At war

Helicopters used during the Korean War had flown unarmed, and the same was true of British Commonwealth helicopters operating in Malaya. But the French, fighting a long and hard conflict in Algeria, soon realized the value of suppressive fire during battlefield operations as their helicopters came under increasing attack. Not long passed before machine-guns were joined by rockets and then wire-guided anti-armour missiles.

But it was the Vietnam War that put the helicopter into the front-line as a machine for dedicated attack. American involvement in a war between the communist North and Western-influenced South had followed French participation in the 1950s. US help began in a low-key manner, with the Piasecki helicopters of the 57th Transportation Light Helicopter Company arriving at Tan Son Knut in December 1961 to help train the South Vietnamese how to disembark from helicopters, before despatching 360 infantry on an actual mission on the 23rd of that month. In the following year 13 Bell UH-1A Iroquois helicopters belonging to the Utility Tactical Transport Helicopter Company operating in Vietnam were experimentally armed with guns and rockets as make-shift escorts, and other Iroquois models followed.

Then, in August 1964, President Johnson ordered US carrier-based aircraft to attack naval targets in North Vietnam in retaliation for North Vietnamese attempts to attack US destroyers. Limited actions between the powers soon broke out to full-scale fighting. On 7 December 1965, having anticipated a requirement by the US Army for a specialized attack helicopter for service in Vietnam, Bell first flew its new Model 209 HueyCobra. A tandem two-seater with a fuselage frontal width of only 0.965m (3 ft 2 in) to make it a hard target to hit from the ground, it was evaluated against armed versions of existing helicopters from Kaman and Sikorsky and then ordered into production as the AH-1G. Deliveries started in mid-1967. The purpose-designed gunship helicopter had arrived. The first HueyCobras were deployed by August and the impact was immediate.

In late 1968 Hughes Aircraft began producing the TOW (Tube-launched Optically-tracked Wire-guided) anti-armour missile for use from US Army vehicles. In 1972 evaluation of the missile for possible future deployment from helicopters started. However, although only eight HueyCobras were modified to be TOW-capable, it was decided that some of them should be despatched to Vietnam immediately, as intelligence indicated a pending Viet-Cong offensive. These went in April after their crews had fired only one TOW each in training. From Kontum they flew into action, claiming 39 armoured vehicles, trucks and howitzers by 27 June. In view of this decisive result, other HueyCobras were

Right: Bell Iroquois operating over Vietnam in July 1969.

Left: *The first major version of the Soviet Mil Mi-24 assault/attack helicopter to go into service was code named* Hind-A *by NATO. Unlike later versions of the Mi-24 which opted for tandem individual cockpits for the pilot and weapon operator, this had the crew of three accommodated together in a glazed cockpit. The large fuselage meant that eight troops could be carried in the rear cabin.*

assigned for modification and anti-armour became a standard role for attack helicopters. Today, specialized tandem-seat attack helicopters are built also in Italy, South Africa and the Soviet Union and operate with many nations. Soviet Mi-24 *Hinds* (used in Afghanistan) have since been joined by newer attack helicopters that may introduce designed-in air-to-air capability.

The final frontiers

Today there seems very little beyond the capability of helicopters. Back in 1967 (31 May–1 June) two US Sikorsky HH-3Es used flight refuelling to make the first non-stop transatlantic crossing by helicopters. In August 1970 two HH-3Cs flew non-stop over the Pacific. Proving the military was not alone in setting records, between 1 and 30 September 1982 Americans Ross Perot Jr. and Jay Coburn used a Bell Model 206L LongRanger II named *The Spirit of Texas* to make the first-ever staged round-the-world helicopter flight. But even while this was underway an Australian, Dick

Smith, had set off (on 5 August) in Bell JetRanger III *Australian Explorer* to attempt the first solo round-the-world helicopter flight, completing his mission on 22 July the following year.

In 1985 the Mil Mi-26 *Halo*, the world's largest operational helicopter, became a standard workhorse of the Soviet forces. Even this giant adopted a single main rotor/tail rotor layout; its 32m (105 ft) main rotor was the first with eight blades, and it is driven by two mighty 11,240 shp Lotarev turboshaft engines. It still features flapping and drag hinges and dampers. But helicopter development never stands still and some smaller helicopters, examples being the latest French Aérospatiale models, have exchanged the conventional hinges on each blade for a single balljoint requiring no maintenance. And on 19 March 1989 the prototype Bell-Boeing V-22 Osprey first flew, expected in production form to introduce tilt-rotor technology to operational squadrons of the US forces, the first anywhere in the world.

Right: *The Bell/Boeing V-22 Osprey on its first flight on 19 March 1989. The Osprey is intended to be the world's first operational tilt-rotor aircraft, combining the flight attributes of a speedy 24-troop transport aeroplane with the vertical flight capabilities of a helicopter. For vertical flight the two 6,150shp Allison T406-AD-400 turboshaft engines and their three-blade rotors tilt upwards. Uses include transport, assault, search and rescue and anti-submarine.*

The passenger revolution

It was realised at an early stage that the gas turbine engine offered more than just speed for speed's sake. In air transport terms, the first writing on the wall can be dated back to 1946, when Britain's Ministry of Supply placed orders for two prototypes each from Vickers and de Havilland, the latter powered by four 'pure' gas turbines (turbojets) and the former's four harnessed to drive conventional propellers (turboprops). As the Viscount and Comet, they made their first flights on 16 July 1948 and 27 July 1949 respectively, paving the way for a revolution in commercial air transport. When BEA borrowed the prototype Viscount in July 1950 to augment its summer peak services, passenger reaction to its speed, comfort and quietness was so emphatic that the airline promptly ordered 26 of a larger version, which entered regular service in April 1953. In several models, 444 Viscounts were eventually built, and not least of the type's achievements was its popularity in the US and Canadian markets: by 1956 there were more Viscounts flying in North America than in the whole of Europe – a most unaccustomed situation for a British aeroplane.

Meanwhile the de Havilland Comet, within six months of its first flight, was making demonstration flights at cruising speeds of around 724km/h (450 mph) – comparable to the maximum speeds of many Second World War fighters – and giving a foretaste of standards of air travel to come. On 2 May 1952 it entered service on BOAC's London–Johannesburg route, becoming the world's first jet airliner in regular commercial service. Soon it was flying on other BOAC routes and with such other national carriers as Air France and Canadian Pacific Airways; jet-powered air travel had arrived.

For nearly two years, during which those early Comets flew more than 30,000 revenue-earning hours, the world was their oyster. Then, in April 1954, the fifth in a series of tragic and unexplained crashes caused Comets everywhere to be grounded. The subsequent recovery of fragments from the Mediterranean sea-bed, the gigantic jigsaw puzzle of their re-assembly, and the discovery by Britain's Royal Aircraft Establishment at Farnborough of metal fatigue as the cause of the accidents, came to be recognized as one of the most remarkable pieces of detective work in aviation history. It was four years before the bigger, safer and much improved Comet 4 could be put into service with BOAC on 4 October 1958. On that date it scored another 'first' – the first fare-paying jet services across the North Atlantic – but by then the Comet was not alone.

Above: *The Vickers Viscount was the first turboprop-engined airliner to go into service and became remarkably successful with airlines on both sides of the Atlantic. Its development stemmed from a wartime Brabazon Committee recommendation for a turboprop-powered short/medium-range airliner, the Brabazon IIB, and in April 1945 Vickers began work on the prototype as the VC2, later becoming the Viscount.*

Left: *The prototype de Havilland Comet with its engines and wingtips still to be fitted.*

Enter Boeing – and others

By contrast with the early Comet 1 and 1A, the Comet 4 in its first two years of operation clocked up some 68,000 revenue hours – more than double its predecessors' total – but during those four lost years of 1954-58 de Havilland's competitors had not been standing still. The public had sampled jet travel, and wanted more; and US manufacturers were not going to see them disappointed. Boeing's commercial Model 707, already on the drawing board as the Model 367-80 tanker/transport for the US Air Force before tragedy struck the first Comets, made its first flight on 15 July 1954. (It was not, as is often stated, the first US jet transport to fly, having been preceded more than three years earlier by the experimental Chase XC-123A.) Air Force approval had to be given before, in the summer of 1955, the 707 could be offered as a commercial derivative, and initial market reaction may, in retrospect, seem surprising. For several months nobody wanted to be the first to buy the new jet: most major world airlines had only recently re-equipped with the newest versions of the piston-engined DC-7 and Super Constellation, and the last thing they wanted was to have to scrap them for even costlier replacements before they had earned their keep.

Then, in October 1955, Pan American – as so often in its past – gave the rest of the world a lead by ordering 20 examples of the 707 and 25 of the contemporary Douglas DC-8 jet, which was then still on the drawing board. Almost overnight, an international race developed, with hardly a major world airline wanting to be seen *not* buying jet airliners. The first 707s went into operation on Pan Am's New York–London route on 26 October 1958, only 22 days after the re-introduced Comet 4; DC-8 operations started less than a year later. With their greater capacity, speed and comfort, they introduced the era of the 'big jets' and transformed the way the world wanted to travel.

Above: *With Pan American's order for the Boeing Model 707, the era of the big jet airliner began. The Model 707-120 (illustrated) was the initial version, intended for US domestic routes but used to inaugurate transatlantic services by PanAm.*

Left: *Boeing's 707-121 as operated by PanAm on their initial trans-atlantic jetliner service in October 1958. Although beaten into service over this most prestigious of routes by BOAC's Comet 4, that had started flights a few days earlier, the 707 was soon to emerge as the victor in the far more important competition for orders.*

Faster with fewer

With jet travel now firmly established, there were two directions the next stages of development could take: to carry more passengers at the same speeds, or smaller numbers at significantly higher speeds.

First to enter the SST (supersonic transport) stakes were Britain and France. In November 1962 they signed a formal undertaking to develop what was to become the Aérospatiale/BAC Concorde. In mid-1965, at the Paris Air Show, the Soviet Union displayed a model of its proposed SST, the Tupolev Tu-144, and in January 1967 US President Lyndon Johnson gave approval to Boeing's proposed Model 2707-300, the outcome of a design competition launched by his predecessor, President Kennedy, in 1963. Both Western programmes became widely controversial, mainly over astronomical development costs and major en-

vironmental issues such as sonic 'bangs' and airport noise. As a result, the US programme was cancelled in March 1971 before it had really started. Untroubled by such considerations, the Tu-144 became the first SST to fly, on 31 December 1968, preceding Concorde (2 March 1969) by just over two months. Gestation periods of both types were long, and entry into passenger revenue service was not achieved until January 1976 (Concorde) and November 1977 (Tu-144). However, despite much redesign the Soviet SST proved an expensive failure, being withdrawn from service seven months later and never reinstated. Concorde continues in service, its popularity (with those who can afford its fares) undiminished in its 14th year of service. Aesthetically and technologically, it is a brilliant achievement, but high development costs and a production run of 16 aircraft is not a successful recipe.

Right: *The world's only successful SST (supersonic transport) has been the Anglo-French Concorde, which flies more hours supersonically than any military aircraft.*

Never mind the velocity, feel the width

By contrast, the philosophy of 'more passengers, same speed' has gone from strength to strength, bringing in its train a quantum jump in airliner sales and annual traffic figures. The traditional way of getting more passengers into the same aircraft had been to 'stretch' the fuselage with one or more 'plugs' in which additional seats could be installed. In 1966, however, Boeing broke the mould with its Model 747, the first of a new generation of 'wide-bodied' airliners in which the previously standard five- or six-abreast seating could be increased to eight, nine or more abreast. Quickly dubbed the 'Jumbo jet', the 747 flew for the first time on 9 February 1969 and instantly offered an increased seating capacity of at least 50 per cent when compared with existing standard-width types. Inevitably, others followed, one of the greatest successes coming from the European Airbus consortium.

Joining the fan club

Choice of engine, in the context of this new generation, meant more than just opting for existing turbojets from this or that manufacturer. Whereas in a turbojet all propulsive air passes through the engine core, a turbofan, as its name implies, has larger-diameter blades (the 'fan') in the first few compressor stages, the tips of which compress surplus air that is then ducted, or bypassed, round the core to be discharged at the rear, where it helps to slow down the speed of the exhaust gases without incurring any loss in engine power. Turbofan development began in the 1950s, and in the late 1960s Pratt & Whitney developed a large turbofan known as the JT9D, aimed specifically at the Boeing 747 and similar aircraft. At a stroke, such engines made possible significant reductions in both fuel consumption and engine noise – both highly attractive to airline operators – and today virtually all major subsonic big jets are turbofan powered.

Bypass ratio – the ratio between the total external mass of air accelerated by an aero-engine and the amount actually passing through the engine – is an important way of measuring propulsive efficiency. Turbojets, which bypass no air, have a zero ratio, while that of current large turbofans is usually about 5 or 6 to 1, and most modern turboprops have a BPR in the 70–100 range. This has led some manufacturers to aim for a middle-ground ratio figure with a new propeller plus turbine combination known variously as a propfan or unducted fan (UDF) engine. General Electric's GE36 UDF engine, which completed flight testing in March

1988, features a double row of contra-rotating, scimitar-shaped fan blades turning externally in the exhaust flow, and has a bypass ratio of 36. Flight trials of the 578-DX, a UHB (ultra-high bypass) propfan by Allison and Pratt & Whitney, began in April 1989. An engine of similar concept is under development in the USSR, and design studies for such engines have been made by Rolls-Royce in the UK. We may expect to see at least one such type powering new generations of commercial air transport in the 1990s.

Below: *A CFM 56 bypass engine used to power the Boeing 737 series.*

The change to jet bombers

It took only until 1947 for the first American and Soviet pure jet bombers to appear: the B-45 Tornado and the Ilyushin I1-22. Others quickly followed, intended as medium aircraft to supplement the first post-war heavy bombers that still used piston engines.

The first new American heavy bomber to go into post-war service with the newly formed Strategic Air Command (SAC) was the B-50, an improved and more powerful version of the B-29; the B-50 *Lucky Lady II* made the first-ever non-stop round-the-world flight during early 1949. The Tupolev Tu-4 was a Soviet copy of the B-29 and remained in use until the late 1950s. The peak of the piston-engined strategic bomber came with the deployment of the Convair B-36 by the USAF from 1947. The largest bomber of all time, it had a span of 70.1m (230 ft) and was powered by the unusual arrangement of six pusher engines. It was eventually retired from service in 1959, by which time the eight-turbojet-engined Boeing B-52 Stratofortress had taken over. And, to emphasize America's global capability, in January 1957 three B-52Bs made a non-stop round-the-world flight.

Supersonic strategic stand-off missiles began to replace previous weapons as primary armament on some B-52s in 1959 (AGM-28 Hound Dog), and a succession of newer weapons led to today's air-launched cruise missiles. However, it was Boeing's other jet bomber, the six-engined medium B-47 Stratojet that first deployed a US stand-off missile, when SAC received its first Bell GAM-63 Rascals in 1957. While the very last B-47s went out of service in 1969, the B-52 in G and H versions continues to be used in strategic, conventional and anti-shipping roles, supplemented by the new swing-wing Rockwell International B-1B. In the 1990s SAC will receive Northrop B-2A flying-wing strategic bombers, taking the stealth technology of the B-1B to much higher levels.

Above: *Strategic Air Command's latest operational bomber is the Rockwell International B-1B, far faster than the B-52 and offering up a radar signature one-hundredth the size because of its stealth technologies.*

Left: *The Northrop B-2A is the most expensive aircraft ever built, expected in 1990 to cost a staggering $530 million each. First flown as a prototype on 17 July 1989, full scale production of the 132 required by the USAF for strategic bombing may start in 1993, allowing initial service in the latter 1990s.*

Below: *The Vulcan strategic bomber entered service with the RAF in 1957 and remained its main nuclear strike carrier for almost 30 years.*

The Soviet equivalent of the B-47 was the later and better twin-jet Tupolev Tu-16, which remains in standard use alongside its heavy bomber contemporary, the turboprop-powered Tu-95/-142. But whereas the USA went straight to a Mach 2 delta-winged aircraft for its first supersonic bomber (the Convair B-58 Hustler, which became active in 1960 but was superseded by the swing-wing General Dynamics FB-111A), the Soviets aimed at a lower speed for the supersonic Tu-22. Mach 2 was introduced into Soviet bomber units with the swing-wing medium Tu-26, and a similar speed can be managed by its new large swing-wing strategic bomber known to NATO as *Blackjack*. Quite early on the Soviet air force became a great exponent of stand-off air-to-surface missiles, and remains in the forefront today.

The only other nation to construct a supersonic bomber was France. Its Mirage IV, designed to carry the nation's first nuclear weapon, entered service in the mid-1960s. France's main nuclear deterrents today, however, come from submarines and land-based missiles, though the modified IV-Ps have recently been issued with a new nuclear missile.

In Great Britain, the English Electric Canberra had entered service with the RAF in 1951 as a light jet bomber. In the mid-1950s, it was joined by three long-range medium bombers: the Vickers Valiant, Handley Page Victor and Avro Vulcan. These were best known under the collective name of V-bombers. Unlike the USA, USSR and to a degree France, Britain did not attempt to built up a triad system of nuclear weapons – air-launched, submarine-launched and land-based – but gave up its air nuclear stand-off missile when Polaris submarines came on stream, and has had little experi-ence of land-based ballistic missiles. It was a Canberra that on 21 February 1951 made the first non-stop and unrefuelled crossing of the North Atlantic by a jet – Lindbergh would have been proud! Today the RAF relies on small single- or two-seat fighter-bombers or attack aircraft of fighter size to carry its bombs; these tactical aircraft carry heavy loads at high speed but lack great range. Tactical fighter-bombers are also used by air forces maintaining conventional bombers.

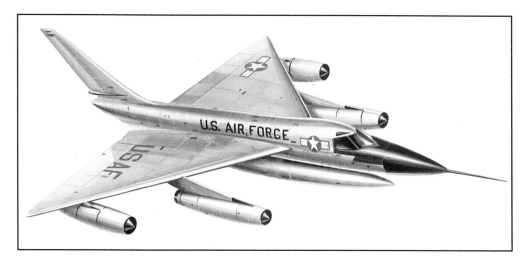

Top: *The USAF's first supersonic bomber was the Convair B-58 Hustler.*

Above: *The flight deck of the European Airbus A320.*

Electronics in the cockpit

No less remarkable than the revolutions in aircraft and aero-engine technology has been the post-war transformation within the cockpit. Even before 1945 the simple autopilot had grown into a fully powered control system able to govern mechanically the precise movement of an aeroplane's aerodynamic control surfaces. Airborne radars developed during the war have been adapted to enable a pilot to 'see' the weather many miles ahead and, if it threatened safety, to fly above or around it. In the past two or three decades electronics, cathode ray tubes (CRTs) and, above all, computers, have all made their appearance as ingredients of the modern flight deck, necessitating the coining of a special word, avionics (aviation electronics), to describe them. For increased safety, most modern airliners are fitted with some form of stall warning, collision avoidance or ground proximity warning system, and sometimes with all three. If the worst does happen, a cockpit voice recorder and/or a flight data recorder, designed to survive almost any kind of crash, can reveal the incidents leading up to the accident and help to avoid a repetition. Navigation systems now routinely include such equipment as ADF (automatic direction finding, showing instantly an aircraft's bearing in relation to any selected ground station) and instrument or automatic landing systems.

Computers, with their ability to store data until it is needed and then display it on command upon a CRT screen, have helped to make modern flight decks less cluttered with dozens of dials. Powered flight control systems are changing from the former mechanical systems of linkage to those in which actions are signalled by multiple electrical circuits ('fly by wire') with built-in fail-safe provisions. There is currently no better example of this new 'glass cockpit' approach than the European Airbus A320 which, in addition to a full suite of EFIS (electronic flight instrumentation system) equipment, has full 'fly by wire' controls and is flown by a two-man crew with only a small side-stick for each pilot instead of the more usual yoke-type control column. The aircraft's entire system is so designed that the A320 cannot be over-speeded, over-stressed or stalled, no matter what the pilots do.

The military pilot also has the added benefits of an electronic head up display (HUDs) that allows him to look ahead through a transparent plate that shows flight information, as well as night vision systems and radars capable of tracking and engaging multiple targets simultaneously.

Despite being technically the most sophisticated airliner ever built, Concorde has what may now be regarded as an old-fashioned instrument layout for the flight crew. Below, is the pilot and co-pilot's station.

No barrier for Harrier

Another revolution has been the deployment of aeroplanes capable of vertical or short take-off and landing (V/STOL). Many V/STOL aircraft were designed in the 1950s for experimental work or possible military deployment, but it was not until July 1969 that such an aeroplane went into service as the RAF's Hawker Siddeley (now BAe) Harrier. Itself developed from the experimental Hawker Siddeley P.1127 and Kestrel, the first of which began hovering trials in 1960 and performed transitions from vertical to horizontal flight from September 1961, the Harrier introduced operationally the concept of two pairs of rotatable (vectoring) nozzles on the fuselage sides to direct engine thrust vertically or horizontally to achieve the chosen direction of travel – even backwards.

The Harrier was developed as a close support aircraft, and in this it is a master. Needing no runway, it can hide itself among natural features, move up with ground forces, and land almost anywhere. Aircraft developed from the original Harrier have included the Sea Harrier, which has enabled small aircraft carriers to be built for fixed-wing warplanes. Sea Harriers are expected to undertake fighter, reconnaissance and strike roles, carrying nose radar for this purpose. During the Falklands conflict between Britain and Argentina in 1982, just 28 Sea Harriers flew 2,376 sorties, claiming 22 Argentine aircraft in air-to-air combat without loss, although a few were lost to accidents or ground fire.

Other Harrier/Sea Harrier users are the US Marine Corps, Spanish navy and Indian navy. The Soviet navy has its own V/STOL combat aircraft, the Yakovlev Yak-38 Forger. This combines a horizontal engine and one pair of vectoring nozzles with two almost vertically-mounted liftjets. An improved Soviet V/STOL is believed to be under development as the Yak-41.

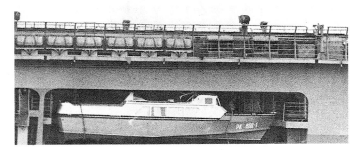

Above: *Hawker Siddeley Kestrel, prototype to the Harrier, in the three nation markings of the UK, USA and West Germany.*

Left: *The Soviet Navy introduced V/STOL warplanes to its fleet with the Yakovlev Yak-38 Forger.*

Below: *Sea Harriers on board HMS Ark Royal.*

Harrier GR.3s of No. 1 Squadron on deployment in Norway.

Chapter 12:
Into the Space Age

After the Second World War, many had assumed the missile would dominate post-war military tactics, so much so that manned bombers would become a thing of the past and manned interceptors sent to the scrap heap. Of course, this belief was not universal, and most military planners knew there was a place for bombers, interceptor-fighters, strategic and anti-aircraft missiles.

Many of the top German scientists of the war period were cajoled into helping evolve the missile programmes of other nations, none more so than those of the USSR and USA. The Soviets had captured the secret Peenemünde rocket research establishment during the final stages of the war and thus had at their disposal not only technical documents but actual rocket components. It was therefore easy for that nation to test launch its first ballistic missile on 30 October 1947 as a reconstructed V-2, fired from Kazakhstan. From the Soviet V-2 type came Pobeda with a 900km (559 mile) range, first launched in 1948 and put into mass production as the missile later known to NATO as the SS-3 *Shyster*. On 23 September 1949 the USSR exploded its first atomic bomb, and the possible combination of missile and warhead worried NATO (the Western Alliance of 12 nations founded in 1949) and the Americans in particular. *Shysters* were also used in dog-launching experiments from 1949–52.

Without question the USA was behind in surface-to-surface missile technology, and in 1951 could only deploy the Martin TM-61A Matador flying-bomb as a tactical weapon, based at home and in West Germany, South Korea and Taiwan. The Firestone Corporal then joined the US Army and the British Army. Although ballistic and with a kiloton warhead, it was again a tactical weapon with a range of up to 160km (100 miles).

The race is on

It was clear that the development of massive rockets for launching intercontinental ballistic missiles (ICBMs) could also provide the means of propelling man-made payloads, and eventually man himself, beyond the earth's atmosphere. The first targets, set for achievement during the International Geophysical Year of 1957-58, were to place artificial satellites in orbit around the earth.

The Soviet Union, widely believed to be running second in the so-called 'space race', staggered the world when, on 4 October 1957, it placed an 83.6kg (184 lb) satellite called Sputnik 1 in an elliptical orbit. This was followed a month later by Sputnik 2, carrying a live cargo in the form of space dog Laika.

Missile mania

The Soviet success with Sputnik horrified the US military. If the USSR could put a satellite into orbit, it could also put a bomb, was the argument. In 1955 the USAF had assumed responsibility for all US guided missiles with a range of over 322km (200 miles) and had instigated a crash programme to develop intermediate and intercontinental range ballistic missiles. So, in response to the Soviet missiles, it was not too long before the USAF began to deploy not only a winged non-ballistic missile with intercontinental range called the Northrop SM-62 Snark (which first became operational in 1959), but intermediate range ballistic missiles (IRBMs) that needed to be stationed in NATO nations if they were to reach their targets. The latter were Jupiter and Thor, and 60 Thors were based in Britain for a short period. Although the Thors were under RAF control, a dual-key system was devised in order to prevent the possibility of any British decision to launch without US approval. It was a Jupiter that provided the launch vehicle for the first American satellite to go into Earth orbit, the 1.5kg (3.25 lb) Explorer I, on 1 February 1958 after an initial launch failure the previous December.

However, development of a lightweight thermonuclear warhead by the USA allowed it to step into the intercontinental ballistic missile field, and in November 1958 a full-range test flight of the Atlas carrier missile took place. The later Atlas D became the first operational version.

The Soviets too had by then built bigger and better missiles. An improvement in the medium class was the 1,750km (1,100 mile) range SS-4 *Sandal,* deployed in

hundreds from 1959. SS-5 *Skean* followed two years later as an IRBM, regarded as the ultimate development of the V-2 type missile, carrying a megaton warhead. The same year came SS-7 *Saddler,* an ICBM with a five megaton warhead and then the SS-8 *Sasin* ICBM. But of all these early ballistic missiles, east and west, none was more formidable than the Soviet SS-9 *Scarp,* operational from 1965 and exhibited in a Moscow parade on 7 November 1967 to mark the 50th anniversary of the Revolution. This giant was developed to have three different types of warhead, the first a massive 25 megaton, the second three separate warheads of five megatons each, and the third a special fractional orbital bombardment system.

The first and only huge warhead put on a US missile was fitted to Titan, the last of America's first-generation ICBMs. But in comparison with *Scarp*'s, it was not that big, the US relying instead on accuracy to destroy a target. At the height of the Cold War, in 1961, the Soviets detonated the largest warhead ever, estimated at 62-90 megatons. The shock wave went round the Earth three times.

On the fringe of space

Meanwhile, the rivalry between the superpowers found a potentially less lethal means of expression in the race to put a man in space. A vital prelude to this venture was the air speeds and altitudes attained by the

remarkable North American X-15 jet. Designed in 1955 to explore flight at speeds up to Mach 7 and altitudes up to 80,470m (264,000 ft), the X-15 was air-launched from a specially modified B-52 bomber, making its first rocket-powered flight on 17 September 1959. Milestones of 3,219km/h (2,000 mph) and 4,828km/h (3,000 mph) were passed in August 1960 and April 1961, culminating on 3 October 1967 in a speed of 7,297km/h (4,534 mph), equivalent to Mach 6.72.

Less spectacular, perhaps, but equally important as a prelude to man's venture into space were the altitudes attained during the X-15's lengthy research programme. These reached their peak figure of 107,960m (354,200 ft) in August 1963, but flights near the edge of the atmosphere were so commonplace that six of the 12 pilots assigned to the X-15's nine-year test programme flew high enough above the earth to qualify for astronauts' wings.

Today's absolute air speed record – that is, the record established by a plane taking off from ground level – stands at 3,529.56km/h (2,193.17 mph): nearly double the remarkable figure established by Peter Twiss in his Fairey Delta 2 in 1956. The current record was set by the USAF Lockheed SR-71A strategic reconnaissance aircraft on 28 July 1976: the fact that this record has stood for more than 13 years suggests the limitations of conventional design. The SR-71A was recently withdrawn from service.

Above: *North American X-15 still attached under the wing of its B-52 motherplane.*

Beyond the Earth's atmosphere

Less than four years after launching Sputnik 1, the USSR achieved the even greater step of putting a man in space – Major Yuri Gagarin of the Soviet Air Force, who made a single 108-minute orbit of the Earth in the spacecraft Vostok 1 on 12 April 1961. America's first two space flights, both sub-orbital and lasting a little over 15 minutes each, were made by Alan Shepard in Mercury 3 and Virgil Grissom aboard Mercury 4 in May and July of 1961 respectively. In August, Soviet cosmonaut Gherman Titov, in Vostok 2, made a 17-orbit flight lasting just over 25 hours, and on 20 February 1962 John Glenn became the first US astronaut to go into orbit, when his Mercury 6 capsule made a three-orbit flight of almost five hours.

Subsequent manned flights by both nations gradually perfected re-entry and recovery techniques, docking with other spacecraft, extended periods in orbit, and EVAs (extra-vehicular activities, or 'space walks'), all with the moon in mind as the next objective. America's Project Apollo, inspired by an historic address to Congress by President Kennedy in May 1961, had as its target the landing of a man on the moon, and returning him safely to Earth, before the end of the 1960s. The USSR, despite its greater experience of manned spaceflight, opted for an entirely unmanned programme of lunar exploration. Both countries first sent unmanned craft to take close photographs of the moon, including its hidden side, and to land robots on its surface and return them with soil samples.

Then, on 21 July 1969, television viewers the world over saw Neil Armstrong and Edwin Aldrin step from the Apollo 11 lunar module *Eagle* and on to the moon's surface. Even more anxiously, they watched as the two astronauts blasted off for the return stage of their mission, docking successfully with the command module, and making a copybook return to earth.

While space exploration further afield has been left to unmanned interplanetary probes, manned spaceflight has followed the course of developing earth-related programmes in the form of space stations, to perform research impossible or impracticable within the atmosphere, and re-usable space vehicles. In the former category, many such missions have been conducted by the Soviet Salyut series of orbital laboratories (from 1971), the larger US Skylab (launched in 1973) and the European Spacelab. Soyuz 'space ferries' were used to transfer successive teams of cosmonauts and scientists to the Salyuts, and to bring home completed experiments and their personnel. In 1975, the USA and the Soviet Union combined their resources in a joint Apollo-Soyuz test project, a three-man Apollo spacecraft docking in July with a two-man Soyuz 225km (140 miles) above the Earth.

Since that time, in an effort to reduce the enormous cost of using huge expendable rockets for every launch, both nations have developed re-usable space 'shuttles' to carry personnel and payloads to and from orbit. America's first shuttle orbiter was *Columbia*, launched on 12 April 1981; the generally similar *Challenger* flew the first operational shuttle mission two years later. Each of these 'aerospaceplanes' blasts off from Earth with relatively small booster rockets, mounted on the back of a huge tank of propellant. The boosters are jettisoned on reaching escape velocity, and the tank is discarded just before the shuttle attains orbit. The spacecraft itself has a sustainer engine for orbital flight, plus a group of manoeuvre engines that can be used also as retro-rockets to position it for re-entry. Heat-protected as it descends through the atmosphere, it then glides down to an unpowered landing on a conventional runway.

A tragic interruption to the US shuttle programme occurred in January 1986, when *Challenger* blew up shortly after lift-off with the loss of all on board, but it was resumed successfully in 1989 after extensive redesign of both the orbiter vehicle and its launching system. The USSR's first space shuttle, named *Buran* (Snowstorm), was launched for the first time on 15 November 1988, and plans for even more sophisticated shuttle-type vehicles have been announced by France, Japan and the UK.

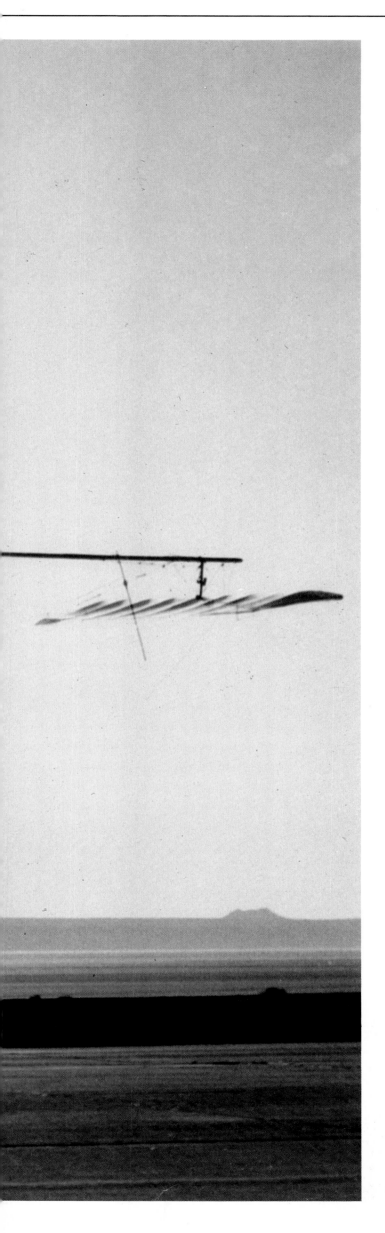

da Vinci would be pleased

Recent years, however, have also seen some remarkable air achievements that were the very antithesis of speed, altitude and power. Despite the technological wonders of the space age, the old dream of a man-powered aircraft remained stubbornly alive. Indeed, it was the existence of light, strong modern materials that made the dream at last a reality. The first of the Henry Kremer awards was a prize of £50,000 for the first 1 mile (1.6 km) figure-of-eight flight by a human-powered aircraft; it was won on 23 August 1977 by the *Gossamer Condor* pedal-power aircraft designed by an American team under the leadership of Dr. Paul MacCready. The pilot/power unit for this flight was racing cyclist Bryan Allen who completed the course in a time of 7 minutes 27.5 seconds.

The second, and by far the most challenging test of a man-powered aircraft, was covered by the Henry Kremer prize of £100,000 for the first man-powered flight across the English Channel. This was achieved by the MacCready *Gossamer Albatross*, again piloted and pedalled by Bryan Allen, which flew from Folkestone, Kent, to Cap Gris Nez, France, on 12 June 1979. The overall distance of 35.82 km (22.26 miles) was covered in a time of 2 hours 49 minutes, a remarkable personal achievement for Bryan Allen.

Just one more MacCready aircraft deserves mention for passage over the English Channel. On 7 July 1981, the *Solar Challenger* solar powered aircraft piloted by Steve Ptacek took off from Cormeilles-en-Vexin, France, and landed 262km (163 miles) away at Manston aerodrome, Kent, in a flight time of 5 hours 23 minutes.

Where – and what – next?

Already mentioned are propfans that may be the next major step forward in aero-engine technology. Plastics, long the prerogative of sailplane and light aircraft manufacturers, are being employed increasingly for advanced combat and commercial aircraft as new combinations of fibres appear that can be as strong as metals but much lighter. And designers are already looking into the 21st century with plans for a 'trans-atmospheric vehicle' able to cruise at Mach 5 to Mach 15 within the atmosphere and Mach 25 in orbit, fuelled by liquid hydrogen, taking off on rocket power with 'scramjets' (supersonic combustion ramjets) for the cruise mode – and yet able to use existing airport runways. As someone has already commented: 'We aren't quite ready yet to send granny to Australia in two hours in a rocket', but a sub-scale proof-of-concept testbed for such a craft, the X-30 National Aero-Space Plane, is being built by the US industry and will fly before the end of the 1990s. The third half-century of aerospace promises to be no less exciting and challenging than its two predecessors.

Left: *MacCready* Gossamer Albatross, *the first man-powered aircraft to fly the English Channel. Pilot and power plant was Bryan Allen.*

Above: Solar Challenger *on its flight across the English Channel.*

TABLE OF HISTORIC FLIGHTS

Below: *A pleasing in-flight study of a Piper PA-24 Comanche cruising above cloud.*

1937 *Hindenburg* destroyed by fire at Lakehurst, effectively ending commercial airship activity for almost fifty years
1939 Germany flies first jet-engined aircraft in the shape of the Heinkel He178
1940 RAF night fighter Blenheims make world's first successful radar-directed interceptions
1940 Igor Sikorsky makes first untethered flight in his VS-300 helicopter
1941 RAF Whitley bomber makes first radar-directed U-boat kill
1942 US enters the jet age with the first flight of Bell's XP-59 Airacomet
1943 Germans field world's first series production guided missiles
1944 Germans first launch V-1s, soon followed by V-2s, against London, England
1944 Germans employ rocket-powered Me163 Komet fighters against US B-17 formations
1945 US Army Air Force B-29s drop nuclear weapons on Hiroshima and Nagasaki speeding end of W.W.II
1947 Charles E. 'Chuck' Yeager exceeds Mach 1 in the rocket-powered Bell XS-1
1948 Britain flies the Vickers Viscount, destined to become the world's first turboprop airliner
1949 Britain takes the lead in developing jetliners with the first flight of the DH Comet
1950 World's first jet fighter combat, with Lt. Brown in his F-80C downing a MiG-15 over Korea
1952 DH Comet jetliner enters service on BOAC's London-Johannesburg route
1954 DH Comet grounded following five tragic fatal accidents

1955 A Fairey FD2, flown by Peter Twiss, becomes first aircraft to set a world airspeed record in excess of 1,000 mph
1955 Pan Am orders both Boeing's 707 and Douglas's rival DC-8 jetliners
1957 Soviets orbit Sputnik I, shortly followed by the dog-carrying Sputnik II
1958 US launches its first earth-orbiting satellite in the shape of Explorer I
1958 Britain's resurrected DH Comet just beats Pan Am's Boeing 707 into service, but loses the subsequent orderbook race
1959 US Air Force B-52s equip with Hound Dog long-ranged, supersonic nuclear-tipped missiles
1960 Strategic Air Command fields its Mach 2 Convair B-58 Hustler bomber
1961 Britain's Hawker P1127, Harrier prototype, makes first vertical to horizontal flight transition
1961 North American's X-15 research aircraft exceeds 3,000 mph
1961 Yuri Gagarin of the Soviet Air Force makes first earth-orbiting manned space flight
1962 John Glenn becomes first American to orbit the earth
1963 NASA's X-15 climbs to over 67 miles, not to be bettered until the first shuttle mission in 1981
1969 US astronauts Neil Armstrong and Edwin Aldrin set foot on the moon
1970 Pan Am launches the wide body jetliner era with the start of Boeing 747 services
1975 US and Soviets join forces in space with the docking of the 3-man Apollo and 2-man Soyuz
1977 America's *Gossamer Condor* wins Henry Kremer manpowered flight prize
1988 Airbus's A320 becomes first fly-by-wire airliner to enter service

Below: *SAAB 35 Draken.*